Twice-Born Hymns

J. Irving Erickson

Twice-Born Hymns

Twice-Born Hymns

J. Irving Erickson

cp
covenant press
3200 west foster avenue · chicago, illinois 60625 312·478-4676

Design, cover art, and layout by Mary M. Helfrich
Production assistants: Linda Youngman and Judy Youngman

Photos by Robert L. Nay, Ralph Varde,
and from the Covenant Archives and the COVENANT COMPANION.

Contents

Preface

Several years ago, when I was chaplain and director of the library at North Park Theological Seminary, many of the Friday chapel services centered around the hymns of the Church. In introducing each hymn some background information was given concerning the text, tune, author, composer, and translator. A number of students inquired about the sources of this material, and they were directed to various hymn studies and handbooks. But there was little information available in English concerning the hymns translated from Swedish, and I promised that some day I would attempt to prepare such a study. This book is the fulfillment of that promise.

Part I is a historical sketch, tracing the development of this hymnody from the Reformation in Sweden to *The Covenant Hymnal* (1973). It is not a comprehensive treatment listing every hymnist and hymnal, but an attempt to indicate the main streams. Some attention is given to Scandinavian sources other than the Swedish.

Part II is concerned with the texts and tunes of the hymns. The list is limited to 104—the songs translated from the Scandinavian appearing in *The Hymnal* (1950) and *The Covenant Hymnal* (1973). The unevenness in the information given is due primarily to the lack or abundance of source material available.

Part III includes biographies of the authors, revisers, translators, and composers. Here the unevenness of the treatment is due in part to the hymnological importance of the individual and in part to the information available. Non-Scandinavian composers are not treated in the biography section, but they may be identified in Part II in connection with the tunes.

I have made every attempt to be accurate, but errors will doubtless be found. My research has revealed differences in information relative to names, dates, places, and spelling. In some instances the resolution depended on the majority opinion of scholars; in others, on the writer's judgment.

To many individuals, some known only through correspondence and telephone conversations, I am indebted for the kind provision of otherwise unavailable data. Several names must be mentioned in this regard. Foremost among them is Dr. Oscar Lovgren, Sweden's greatest living hymnologist. Without his research, made available in many books, through personal correspondence, and during a visit to his home, this study would scarcely have been possible. Most sincere gratitude is expressed to Dr. Karl A. Olsson for his constant encouragement and his assistance in many problems of translation and Covenant history.

Genuine appreciation is expressed also to the Rev. Mandus Egge, recently retired executive director of the Commission on Worship of the American Lutheran Church; Mr. Jan-Erik Wikstrom, editor-in-chief of Swedish Covenant publications and director of Gummesson's Book Company in Stockholm; Dr. Eric G. Hawkinson, Covenant archivist; and the Rev. Joel Lundeen, Lutheran Church in America archivist.

A word of personal gratitude must be given to the Rev. James. R. Hawkinson, executive secretary of Covenant Publications, whose personal counsel and confidence have provided encouragement and motivation.

I wish to acknowledge my debt to scholars of the past and present who have shared their research and thought with others through their publications. The ones consulted are listed in the bibliography.

Finally, I wish to thank my wife, Myrtle, for her patience and constant reassurance, which in no small way furthered the project.

J. Irving Erickson
May, 1976

Twice-Born Hymns

ANDELIGA SÅNGER
med accompagnement
af
Pianoforte eller Guitarre,
dels componerade, dels samlade
samt
Fru
Jenny Lind-Goldschmidt
vördsammast tillegnade
af
OSCAR AHNFELT.

Stockholm.
Fosterlands Stiftelsens Förlags Expedition.

Title page from first edition of *Ahnfelt's Songs*, 1850.

Historical Sketch

In *By One Spirit* Karl Olsson characterizes the early Covenanters in this way: "The unifying experience of the Mission Friends was salvation. They were one in the Crucified. They gave the freest expression to this in their singing. The name *'läsare,'* by which Mission Friends were designated in Sweden, emphasized the importance of a devotional reading of the Bible and related literature; it would have been equally correct to call these people 'singers.' For nothing seems to have brought them closer to a union with Christ than the singing of their hymns. And in the hymns the constantly recurring theme is the friendship of Jesus in the vicissitudes of life and the final 'closing' with him when the mists have vanished."

Singing is important among Covenanters today as well, and this singing is enriched by lyrics and melodies written and composed by hymnists and musicians from the time of ancient Israel to the present—and representing faiths from Pentecostalism to Unitarianism. Gradually the hymnals of most groups have moved toward greater diversity and an inclusiveness of the whole Christian tradition. This has been true of the hymnals of the Evangelical Covenant Church as well, although material peculiar to that particular heritage has not been sacrificed. As far as I know, this cannot be said of any other American denomination which has its roots in Scandinavia. In the early days of the Scandinavian-American churches there was a body of hymnody quite common to all, but now it seems that the Covenant has become the custodian of this tradition. And it is with this tradition that we are concerned in this book.

The songs and hymns in question come from several sources, but there are two main streams. In *Images in Covenant Beginnings*, Eric Hawkinson describes them well: "The one psalmodic, rich in objective content and poetry, the other more subjective in content and having less poetic depth, set to the rhythms of folk music." An example of the former is the advent hymn written by Johann Wallin, translated by Ernst Olson, and set to a well-known German chorale tune:

Jerusalem, lift up thy voice!
Daughter of Zion, now rejoice!
Thy King is come, whose mighty hand
Henceforth shall reign o'er ev'ry land.

The Swedish Psalmbook

This type of hymn is well represented in the *Psalmbok*, the official hymnal of the State Church of Sweden. When the Reformation was introduced into Sweden by Olavus Petri, he gave the people in 1526 a little hymnbook which bore the name, *Swedish Hymns or Songs*. Although there is no known copy in existence, it is believed to have included five of Petri's lyrics and five translations from Luther's *Achtliederbuch* of 1524. This was followed by several later hymnbooks with more songs by Petri. Although none of them was accepted officially for use in the corporate worship of the church, Petri's influence on the hymnody of Sweden was considerable—in the 1937 edition of the *Psalmbok*, no less than nineteen hymns are credited to him as author or translator. He is represented in *The Covenant Hymnal* (1973) as the translator from German to Swedish of "Now hail we our redeemer." Petri's work was carried on by his brother, Laurentius, who published four editions of the first volume to bear the name, *Den Svenska Psalmboken*.

During the next century several editions of the hymnbook appeared. One revision was done in Uppsala in 1622 and came to be known as *The Old Uppsala Psalmbook*. Another revision came out in 1645 under the title, *Den Svenska Uppsala Psalmboken*. In 1691, Bishop Jesper Swedberg was commissioned to prepare a new hymnal. With a committee of gifted assistants, the task was completed in 1694. The book contained 482 hymns in Swedish and some in Latin. It met with violent attack because it was alleged to contain heresies of a "theological, anthropological, Christological, soteriological, and eschatological" nature. Although a new commission was chosen to revise it, the final product had been so influenced by Swedberg that it came to be called by his name. The *Psalmbok* of 1937 retained thirty-three of his original hymns or translations. Swedberg is represented in our hymnal by the prayer, "O Lord, give heed unto our plea."

"Swedberg's Psalmbook" remained the official hymnal of the Church of Sweden for 130 years. The new book, which appeared in 1819, was, for a large part, the work of one man, Johan Olof Wallin. He was a young gifted pastor-poet who later became the archbishop. Of the 500 hymns in "the Wallin Psalmbook," as it came to be known, no less than 342 were his revisions, translations, or original lyrics. There was no major revision of the book until 1937, and Wallin's name still was connected with a third of its contents. He is represented in our hymnal by five texts, one of which is the great Christmas song, "All hail to thee, O blessed morn." Other important contributors to the *Psalmbok* whose work appears in our hymnal are Jakob Arrhenius, Johan Åstrom, Frans Michael Franzén, Samuel Hedborn, and Laurentius Laurinus.

Many of the musical settings in the *Psalmbok* are German chorale tunes. Some are Swedish folk melodies, and some are original compositions of Swedish musicians. There are also a few tunes from the metrical psalm tradition.

The 1937 edition includes several settings of American and English origin. The hymnal was often criticized for its many dull and somber melodies, a great number of which were in the minor key.

Other Scandinavian Sources

While the other Scandinavian countries have contributed few hymns to our collections, they are deserving of mention here. The development of *Den Danske Salmebog* was largely the work of the great triumvirate of Danish hymnists: Thomas Kingo (1634-1703), Hans Adolph Brorson (1694-1764), and Nikolai F.S. Grundtvig (1783-1872). The 1953 edition of the Danish hymnal contains 96 hymns by Kingo, 107 by Brorson, and 173 by Grundtvig. Our hymnal includes one each by Kingo and Brorson and two by Grundtvig. Wilhelm Andreas Wexels, who was involved in the development of the hymnbook of the Norwegian church, has given us "O precious thought! some day the mist shall vanish," and his niece, Marie Wexelson, the delightful Christmas carol, "How glad I am each Christmas Eve." Significant in the growth of Norwegian hymnody were the musical settings of Ludvig Lindeman (1812-1887). Three of his tunes are included in our hymnal; one of them is used twice and another, three times.

In Finland there are two official hymnals, one Finnish and the other Swedish. Among the creators of the latter volume was Finland's national poet, Ludvig Runeberg. We still love to sing his hymn, "What joy there is in coming." Another song from Finland is "Lord, as a pilgrim," by Wilhelmi Malmivaara. Iceland's contribution is the majestic "How marvelous God's greatness," by Valdimar Briem (1848-1930).

It should be noted that some of these hymns from the other Scandinavian countries have come to us by way of Sweden and were included in the early Swedish collections in this country. Others were translated into English and appeared in Lutheran hymnals, especially Augustana's, and came to use in the Covenant through our last two hymnals.

The Moravians and Early Pietists

Of the hundred or so texts of Scandinavian or Scandinavian-American origin in *The Hymnal* (1950) and *The Covenant Hymnal* (1973), about 20 percent can be classed with the group we called "psalmodic." That means that the greater number of these heritage songs are of the more personal, subjective type. In all of the Scandinavian hymnals mentioned, however, the two streams often run close and at times even merge. Some of the hymnists were pietists or Herrnhuters, or they were influenced by these revival movements.

Their songs often reflect the warmth and spiritual appeal of religious renewal. The Swedish *Psalmbok* included several texts of the earlier pietists and Moravians, and in later editions, some of those from the nineteenth century.

The first pietistic collection, *Mose och Lamsens visor* (Songs of Moses and the Lamb), consisting of sixty-one songs, was published in 1717. This was largely the work of a pietistic hymn writer, Georg Lybecker, although the book appeared after his death. More songs were added in later editions, and in 1724 it was combined with *Evangeliska Läro och Böne-Psalmer* (Evangelical Teaching and Prayer Hymns). The songbook went through nineteen editions, the final one in 1868. In its development it took on some of the flavor of Herrnhutism, which came to Sweden about 1730. The Moravian hymnal, *Sions Sånger* (Songs of Zion), which was published in 1743, was even more popular and more frequently printed. Anders Carl Rutström was a state church pastor who was active in the Moravian movement. Because of his politics and religion (and perhaps more because of his personality), he was often maligned and he spent the last months of his life in prison. After his death his friends published, in 1778, a collection that included many of his songs. It was called *Sions Nya Sånger* (New Songs of Zion), but was often referred to as "Rutströms sånger." The songbook included "Chosen seed and Zion's children," one of the most popular lyrics of the "läsare" a century later. *Sions Nya Sånger* went through at least thirty-five editions, the final one published in 1923 as *Bibeltrogna Vänners Sångbok* (Bible-believing Friends Songbook).

The Revival of the Nineteenth Century

The central figure in the revival of the mid-nineteenth century was Carl Rosenius (1816-1868). He was the editor of *Pietisten*, a religious monthly that played a major role in the evangelical revival and the free church movement. Rosenius had no church, so his preaching was done in smaller gatherings called conventicles. Although the practice was in violation of the Conventicles Edict, this type of ministry was typical of the revival movement throughout the country.

The conventicle contributed to the development of a revival hymnody. Certain hymns from the *Psalmbok* were used, but the most popular were from *Sions Sånger* and *Sions Nya Sånger*, thus reinforcing the impact of Moravian piety upon the revival. Now new songs began to appear. Rosenius wrote several and published them in *Pietisten.* Lina Sandell, who was to become the foremost hymnist of Sweden in the second half of the century, began to write lyrics. It was the musical genius of Oscar Ahnfelt (1813-1880) that helped to spread many of the hymns of Rosenius, Sandell, and other pietists. After his conversion he assisted Rosenius in meetings, singing and accompanying himself on a ten-stringed guitar. With the financial help of Jenny Lind, who was herself a pietist, Ahnfelt published the first section of

Andeliga Sånger (Spiritual Songs) in 1850. This was followed by an additional eleven parts appearing at intervals until 1877. In the text volume there were 208 songs—many by Sandell and Rosenius. The music edition was very impressive with its arrangements for guitar and piano. About half of the settings were original compositions by Ahnfelt.

Rosenius and his friends had no interest in leaving the established church, and in order to further the revival and keep it in harmony with Lutheran faith and practice, they founded "Evangeliska Fosterlandsstiftelsen" (The Evangelical National Foundation) in 1856. Lina Sandell joined its editorial staff, and one of her first tasks was to assist in the production of a hymnal. The volume appeared in 1889 and was given the name *Sionstoner* (Melodies of Zion). No less than 126 of the 550 songs were the work of Sandell. The latest edition of this hymnal, 1972, has seventy-six of her original texts and five translations of English hymns.

Betty Ehrenborg-Posse was another important songwriter of this period. Her interest in Sunday school work led her to translate a number of English songs. In 1852, these appeared under the title, *Andeliga Sånger för Barn* (Spiritual Songs for Children). In two succeeding editions she included more translations as well as some of her own lyrics.

She was encouraged in this work by Gustaf Palmquist, a Baptist preacher, and his brother, Per, a printer. In 1859, they published *Pilgrims-Sånger*, a collection of 221 songs, 100 of which were translations of English hymns. There were also some new songs by Mrs. Posse, Lina Sandell, Carl Rosenius, and others. Three years later they added a supplement of eighty-eight numbers, half of which had been written or translated by Gustaf Palmquist. *Pilgrims-Sånger* became a popular hymnal and went through forty-three editions, totaling 400,000 copies.

Joel Blomqvist, a singing preacher and colporteur, wrote about 400 lyrics and composed almost as many melodies. He published several song collections: *Kanaan* (1867), *Pilgrimen* (1869), three editions of *Melodier till Sions Nya Sånger* (1873-1875), *Sabbatsklockan* (Sabbath Bells) in two parts (1877-1878), and *Fridstoner* (Songs of Peace) in three parts (1879-1882). Blomqvist was co-editor of *Hemlandstoner* (Homeland Melodies), a hymnal of 523 songs published in 1883. This collection was used in many free church circles, especially Svenska Missionsförbundet (The Swedish Mission Covenant).

Although the hymns of Fredrik Engelke (1848-1906) have not been included in our English hymnals, they were used quite extensively in many pietistic circles. Engelke was Herrnhutish in doctrine, and his songs dwell on the blood and wounds of Christ. They were published in six parts between 1871 and 1875 under the title, *Lofsånger och Andeliga Visor* (Hymns of Praise and Spiritual Songs). The collection included several translations of English and American hymns.

Other hymn writers who contributed to the song collections of the revival period were Nils Frykman (more will be said about him in connection with the Swedish-American writers); Anders Lindqvist, "God's name is a refuge to hide me"; Jonas Lundgren, "When toil is done, a Sabbath rest is waiting"; Anders Nilsson, "Christ the Lord is risen!"; Erik Nyström, "O Zion, acclaim your redeemer"; Anna Ölander, "If I gained the world"; and Otto Ottander, "Trust in the Savior." Among the composers were Fredrik Ekström, Carl Sjögren, and Wilhelm Söderberg.

The Swedish Free Churches

By the time the free churches had organized, each group had begun to develop its own collection of hymns. There were certain songs from the *Psalmbok* and the Moravian and pietistic hymnbooks that were common to all, but each organization had its particular slant. The Methodists were naturally partial to the hymns of the Wesleys and other Methodist writers in England and America. Many of the songs of A.M. Toplady, William Cowper, Fanny Crosby, Ira D. Sankey, and others had been translated into Swedish.

We have referred to the work of Betty Ehrenborg-Posse and the Palmquist brothers. Their *Pilgrims-Sånger*, with its many translations, several selections from the *Psalmbok*, and a good representation of the "läsare" songs, became the favorite of the Baptists. Publisher Per Palmquist commissioned Erik Nyström to edit a new collection, which was published in 1878 under the title, *Församlings-Sångbok* (Congregation's Songbook). Nyström, who earlier had produced a collection of translated Sankey songs (*Sånger till Lammets Lov*), included a great number of these in the new collection. It was given a cool reception, and an official Baptist hymnal, *Psalmisten*, appeared in 1880.

The Swedish Mission Covenant had its beginning in 1878. The constituent congregations and societies had used most of the hymnals mentioned above, especially Ahnfelt's *Andeliga Sånger*, Palmquist's *Pilgrims-Sånger*, Engelke's *Lovsånger och Andeliga Visor*, Nyström's *Sånger till Lammets Lof*, and the collections of Blomqvist. In 1884, Erik J. Ekman (1842-1915), later president of the Swedish Covenant, put out a collection of 358 hymns, entitled *Fridsbasunen* (The Trumpet of Peace). The volume included several songs by some of the younger Covenant writers like Carl Boberg and Selma Sundelius-Lagerström. All of the foregoing books, however, were the products of private publishers, and there was agitation for a "Svenska Missionsförbundets Sångbok."

Erik Nyström was appointed chief editor in 1892, and both text and music editions were ready in 1894. The task was not easy; Nyström could not legally use his earlier translations since they were the property of other publishers. Some of the original texts of writers like Sandell were not available either. This resulted in retranslating and revising texts. In spite of the difficulties, it was a praiseworthy and comprehensive hymnal of 703 numbers, representing many text traditions and musical styles. Seven years after publication there was talk of revision. The people wanted more of the "läsare" songs. A new edition was published in 1920, and again in 1951, when the name was changed to *Sånger och Psalmer.*

Many of the musical settings for the "läsare" songs were Swedish folk melodies whose composers are unknown. These derivative sources often were questioned, but this was justified by the idea that "the devil should not have all the good tunes." We have noted that Oscar Ahnfelt provided many tunes. Some were originals, and others were adaptations. A number of the melodies were of English and American origin. Amanda Waesterberg (1842-1918) is one of the few Swedish composers who have contributed more than one tune.

The Emigrant Church

It was only natural that the early Scandinavian churches in America should use the songbooks of their respective groups abroad. The Swedish Lutheran churches had the *Psalmbok,* and in 1893 the Augustana Synod made it their official hymnal. It had already been printed by the Swedish Lutheran Publication Society. But perhaps the first Swedish songbook published in this country was *Femtio Andeliga Sånger* (Fifty Spiritual Songs). Most of the songs were from Ahnfelt's *Andeliga Sånger.* The compilation was made in 1856 by T.N. Hasselquist, who became the first president of Augustana College. Not long after, *Salems Sånger* was put out by Eric Norelius, a pioneer pastor and historian.

Söndagsskolbok came out in several editions beginning in 1884. The edition of 1903 contained 238 Swedish hymns and 165 in English, of which twenty-nine were translations from Scandinavian. The *Psalmbok* was used in the morning worship services, but for vespers and other informal services the publication of *Hemlandssånger* (Songs of the Homeland) was authorized in 1892. This volume included 500 songs, one-fourth of them by Lina Sandell. Most of the "läsare" hymnists were well represented. In 1901, the first complete English Augustana hymnal was published. Of the 355 hymns, about 16 percent were translations from the Scandinavian—a few of them from the pietistic tradition. *The Hymnal and Order of Service* was published by the Augustana Synod in 1925. This volume of 663 hymns included seventy-three translations from the Swedish and fifteen from other Scandinavian sources.

The first Norwegian hymnbook to be published in the United States appeared in 1874. It contained a few originals and translations, but the greater part was from the hymnal of the church of Norway. The latter book, usually called "Landstad's Hymnal," became the basis for a joint publication of the

United Lutheran Norwegian Church and the Hauge Synod in 1893. To it were added ninety-six songs, only one of which had been translated from English sources. An English hymnal, published at Decorah, Iowa, in connection with the Missouri Synod, was primarily German in background.

In 1898 the United Norwegian Church brought out *The Church and Sunday School Hymnal,* but only two of the 316 hymns were translations from Norwegian or Danish. An important volume appeared in 1913 under the title, *The Lutheran Hymnary.* Of its 618 numbers, 262 were translations from Danish and Norwegian sources. This became the official hymnal of the Evangelical Lutheran Church when it was formed in 1917 through the merger of three cooperating bodies. The Danish Lutherans in America produced no notable hymnals in the Danish language, and it was not until 1927 that an adequate English hymnal was provided—the *Hymnal for Church and Home.*

The Swedish Baptists followed the tradition set by the Palmquists by publishing *Pilgrims-Sånger.* This book was published in Chicago by the Engberg and Holmberg Printing Company. Several other hymnals were put out by private concerns. Among them were *Nya Pilgrims Sånger, Fridsbasunen,* and *Valda Hymner* (Selected Hymns). Many of the hymns in these collections were translations of the Moody-Sankey type gospel songs. *Valda Hymner* was in two parts. The first was based on a translation of *Select Gems,* a hymnal put out by the American Baptist Publication Society. The second part was a mixture of songs translated from English and American sources plus a good number taken from hymnals used in Sweden.

The first official hymnal of the Swedish Baptists in the United States was *Nya Psalmisten,* which came into use in 1903. This fine volume of 675 numbers included a good many translations, but the songs of Sandell, Ahnfelt, Frykman, Blomqvist, Skoog, and other pietists were there as well. There were also a few selections from the *Psalmbok.* In 1925, the Swedish Baptists published their first English songbook, *The New Hymnal.*

One of the earliest hymnals of the Swedish Methodists in America was *Andeliga Sånger for Böne-, Klass-, och Förlängda Möten* (Spiritual Songs for Prayer, Class, and Protracted Meetings). The compilation was made in 1859 by Victor Witting, who had translated a number of Wesley hymns. In 1860 the Methodist Book Concern published *Psalmer och Sånger,* with J. Bredberg as chief editor. This book of 720 songs was used for twenty-four years. A revision appeared in 1884 under the title, *Metodist Episkopal-Kyrkans Swenska Psalmbok.*

The most important of the Swedish Methodist hymnals was published in 1904. The title was virtually the same as that of its predecessor and included about half of the same hymns. This was a fine, balanced collection, making use of chorales, translations of standard English and American hymns (especially those of Charles Wesley), some of the "läsare" songs, and a few from the gospel song tradition. Smaller collections for special groups and meetings were published from time to time. Among them were *Basunklangen, Segersånger, Herdestämman, Jubelsånger, Valda Sånger,* and *Evangeliska Sånger.*

The Evangelical Covenant Church of America

One of the earliest collections used by the Mission Friends was *Samlingssånger*. This was published by the Mission Synod in 1876 and was based on the *Psalmbok, Ahnfelts Sånger,* and *Pilgrims-Sånger.* There was also a collection of the translations of Sankey's songs. In 1882, a four-part harmony version of *Ahnfelts Sånger* was put out by a Chicago publisher. The first moderately adequate hymnal was *Evangelii Basun,* a joint project of E. August Skogsbergh, then pastor of the Tabernacle Church in Chicago, and his music director, A.L. Skoog. The first part appeared in 1880, and a second in 1883. The two sections were combined in 1894 to form a single volume of 563 songs, plus a section of fifty choral arrangements. The book borrowed heavily from the usual Swedish sources, but it also had a number of original texts and tunes by the two editors.

Several other collections were available during the later years of the century. J.A. Hultman published *Cymbalen I* in 1885 and *Cymbalen II* three years later. The complete volume contained 200 songs, a number of which were original texts and musical settings by Hultman. The rest were mainly from the *Psalmbok* and the pietistic collections.

In 1890, A.L. Skoog published *Lilla Basunen* (The Little Trumpet), designated "for Sunday school and home." Nearly one-fourth of the material was the original work of Skoog. In 1896, Skoog and Hultman collaborated in the publication of *Jubelklangen* (The Sound of Jubilation), a volume containing 245 hymns. More than a third of the songs, both texts and tunes, were originals by the compilers.

At the turn of the century P. Benson published *Hemlands-Klockan* (Bells of the Homeland), a hymnal of 425 songs, three of which were in English. The foreword stated that the "songs are a selection of the best available in Swedish, as well as a great number of altogether new hymns by both Swedish and American writers." The book included several texts and melodies by Nicholas L. Ridderhof, the musical editor of the volume. Guitar chords were indicated with the settings.

John J. Daniels, a Covenant pastor in Minneapolis, published *Sions Glädjebud* (Zion's Joyous Message) in 1904. The foreword stated that he tried "to include only the most unfaded of our old hymns and songs . . . and the best of the new songs." There were 262 numbers, sixty-two of which were designated choir and solo songs. Guitar chords were provided for many of the settings.

A popular Sunday school hymnal in the churches of the Eastern Missionary Association was *Svenska Söndagsskolans Sångbok.* The Eastern Sunday School Association had purchased the rights to N.J. Russell's *Nya Sånger för Söndagsskolan,* a great part of which was the original work of Russell. The new volume was a reprinting of Russell's book with the addition of more than 200 songs, many of which were by Sandell, Frykman, Hultman, and Skoog.

The best and most popular of the independently published hymnals was *Sionsharpan.* It was produced in 1890 by the Mission Friend's Publishing Company, and for at least twenty years was the most used hymnal in Covenant churches. Included among the members of the editorial committee were David Nyvall, Fridolf Risberg, and Nils Frykman. The *Psalmbok* was well represented in the hymns, as were the songbooks of the "läsare." More of Joel Blomqvist's works were included than in any other hymnal produced in America. Other writers whose names appeared often were Frykman, Sandell, Wallin, and Crosby. Some of the main composers were Blomqvist, Ahnfelt, Frykman, Söderberg, Bliss, Doane, Bradbury, and McGranahan, the last four being American gospel song writers. There were a good number of translated American songs and a few from English sources. A second edition of *Sionsharpan* appeared in 1908 with an additional seventy-five hymns, making a total of 700. Among the new songs were several by A.L. Skoog and two by J.A. Hultman. None of the latter's work had been included in the original edition.

The first official hymnal of the Covenant was *Sions Basun* (Zion's Trumpet), published in 1908. In his master's thesis, *A Study of the Hymnody of the Evangelical Covenant Church of America,* Norman Johnson characterized it as "a worthy hymnal in every respect, having been early enough to avoid much of the romanticism and secularization of the twentieth century." Besides 704 Swedish hymns, there were twenty-seven in English. The editorial board consisted of the triumvirate of Swedish-American hymn writers: Nils Frykman, Andrew L. Skoog, and Johannes A. Hultman, along with pastors John J. Daniels, Albert M. Johanson, Fred M. Johnson, and A.G. Sporrong. All committee members made some original contributions to the book. Frykman had 120 texts and nineteen melodies; Skoog, seventeen texts and forty-one tunes; and Hultman, five texts and seventeen musical settings. Johanson contributed eight lyrics, and the remainder, one or two each.

In some respects *Sions Basun* was similar to *Sionsharpan;* they had more than 300 hymns in common, and both included texts and tunes by most of the same authors and composers. The *Psalmbok* was well represented in both hymnals. Except for the fact that *Sions Basun* had such a great number of Frykman texts, it had a better-balanced representation of the various pietistic writers and translations from American and English sources.

The increasing need for English songs resulted in the publication of *De Ungas Sångbok* in 1914. It included favorites from *Sions Basun* and other Swedish hymnals along with several of British and American origin. The title declared it a songbook for young people, but out of a total of 264 hymns, there were only forty-two English texts. Consequently, its usefulness was short-lived, and within a few years it was decided that an all-English songbook should be prepared.

This volume of 223 numbers, called *Mission Hymns*, was put out in 1921. It contained a good selection of standard American and English hymns and gospel songs and thirty translations from the Swedish, nine of which had been done by Skoog. Also included were four of his original texts in English along with his tunes. Many of the other translations had appeared earlier in the Augustana *Hymnal*, 1901. *Mission Hymns* was received enthusiastically by the churches even though it was rather inadequate. It, too, had a short life, and in 1929 the Covenant Annual Meeting recommended the preparation of a new hymnal.

The result was *The Covenant Hymnal* of 1931, commonly referred to as "the brown hymnal." The editorial board consisted of Carl A. Hognander, A. Samuel Wallgren, Raymond Helsing, Albert Wilson, Arthur Goranson, George Hultgren, Oscar Green, and Frank Earnest. There were 476 hymns in the collection, thirty-six of which were translations from Swedish. Twenty-one new tunes and eleven new texts were contributed by younger American Covenanters. The greater part of the collection was made up of standard hymns and gospel songs secured from Hope Publishing Company. The book was well received and attracted commendation from many quarters.

By the mid-forties "the brown hymnal" was no longer thought adequate, and in 1944 a hymnal commission was appointed. This group, with Oscar Olson as chairman, consisted of Carl Philip Anderson, Bert E. Carlson, A. Milton Freedholm, Ebba H. Goranson, E. Gustav Johnson, Nils W. Lund, Leslie R. Ostberg, A. Eldon Palmquist, Carl N. Peterson, and Elmer G. Westlund, with Marjorie M. Nelson as secretary. *The Hymnal* (1950) was a great success—not least because of the many new translations, twenty-two of them by E. Gustav Johnson. Of the 600 hymns, eighty-two were translated from Swedish, three from Danish, and two from Norwegian. In *By One Spirit* Karl Olsson wrote that *The Hymnal* "in every respect was a vast improvement over its predecessors. Not only did it have a wider selection of the great hymns of the church; it also provided a rich flora of the hymns of the denominational fathers in excellent English translation. The works of Ahnfelt, Rosenius, Sandell, Frykman, Skoog, and Hultman could now be sung by the younger generation, and the distant past was linked to the present by a visible musical tradition."

Then came the 1950s and 1960s with their discoveries, movements, and rebellions that upset the status quo in all quarters. The new generation was concerned with space flights, civil rights, racial equality, ecumenicity, the new morality, women's lib, folk music, and rock music. Many of the hymns of the nineteenth and early twentieth centuries were hardly relevant to the new issues, and most denominations began to prepare new hymnals.

The Covenant authorized the appointment of a hymnal commission in 1967. The members were Carl Philip Anderson, James P. Davies, A. Royce Eckhardt, J. Irving Erickson (chairman), Eric G. Hawkinson, James R. Hawkinson, Norman E. Johnson, Bryan J.H. Leech, Marjorie M. Nelson (secretary), Harry P. Opel, and Glen V. Wiberg. As a result of their work, *The Covenant Hymnal* was completed in 1973. About two-thirds of the titles in the former hymnal were retained with some minor revisions of certain texts and musical settings, or, in some cases, with different tunes. The new material consisted of some traditional and recent great hymns representing diverse traditons, some contemporary items, and a few more translations of Scandinavian texts, including one each from the Finnish and Icelandic. Six of the new translations from the Swedish were done by Karl A. Olsson. Nineteen of the hymns of Covenant heritage that had appeared in *The Hymnal* (1950) were not included in the new hymnal, leaving a net total of seventy-three.

Conclusion

The Evangelical Covenant Church of America has grown from a small emigrant church to a denomination with full stature in the world community, and the trends in its worship, theology, education, and mission have been matched by its music and hymnody. Each succeeding hymnal has drawn from wider sources, but has never found any deeper wells than those of its own heritage. In many ways we and our hymnody have become sophisticated and our standards have been raised, but we have not become spoiled. Proof of this can be seen in the wide acceptance and acclaim of the text that comes out of Moravian pietism in Sweden in the late eighteenth century and set to a lilting folk melody of unknown origin. The translation is by Karl Olsson.

O let your soul now be filled with gladness,
Your heart redeemed, rejoice indeed!
O may the thought banish all your sadness
That in his blood you have been freed,
That God's unfailing love is yours,
That you the only Son were given,
That by his death he has opened heaven,
That you are ransomed as you are.

If you seem empty of any feeling,
Rejoice—you are his ransomed bride!
If those you cherish seem not to love you,

And dark assails from ev'ry side,
Still yours the promise, come what may,
In loss and triumph, in laughter, crying,
In want and riches, in living, dying,
That you are purchased as you are.

It is a good ev'ry good transcending
That Christ has died for you and me!
It is a gladness that has no ending
Therein God's wondrous love to see!
Praise be to you, O spotless Lamb,
Who through the desert my soul are leading
To that fair city of joy exceeding,
For which you bought me as I am.

147. EN DAG I SÄNDER

Capotasto på 2dr bandet.
gitarr
sång
piano
Blott en dag ett ö-gonblick i sän-der; O, vad tröst, e-vad som kommer
på! Allt ju vi - lar i min Faders hän-der, Skulle jag som barn, väl ängslas
då ! Han som bär för mig ett fadershjär-ta, O, han gi - ver ju åt varje
dag Hult dess lil - la del av fröjd och smärta, Så av mö - da som be - hag.

Swedish arrangement of "Day by Day and with Each Passing Moment," from *Ahnfelts Sånger*.

Texts and Tunes

A Quivering Chord Is Broken

Using the metaphor of a broken musical chord, Anna Ölander describes the death of a Christian. The chord is restored in heaven where it vibrates continually in praise to God. The text first appeared in Sweden in a collection of poems called *Vingeslag* in 1912. Its first use as a song was in J.A. Hultman's *Solskensstrålar*, which was published in Worcester, Massachusetts, in 1917. "Det brister en sträng härnere" was translated by E. Gustav Johnson and included in *The Hymnal* (1950).

DET BRISTER EN STRÄNG was composed for the text by J.A. Hultman.

During the big strike in Stockholm in 1909, Mr. Hultman was asked to sing in one of the State churches of that city. He sang to a full audience that had paid admission. A rather rough-looking man who appeared to be under the influence of liquor suddenly arose and with deep emotion said: "Pastor Hultman, will you please sing again the song, 'Det brister en sträng'?" The request and the singing made a profound impression upon the listeners. After the concert a pastor conveyed the gratitude of the clergy and expressed the belief that if Hultman sang more often for them, there would be much less restlessness and strain.

On one occasion Hultman was stranded in a small town in the western United States without a place to stay. He accepted the invitation of a tavern keeper to stay at his home. During the evening he learned that the man recently had lost a daughter whom he loved dearly. His host played a phonograph record which had brought him much comfort, and Hultman heard himself sing: "Det brister en sträng härnere." In telling the story he added: "Who knows but that even in his heart there was a broken string that some day may vibrate again?"

HEAVEN AND HOMELAND

511 A Quivering Chord Is Broken

Det brister en sträng

8.7.8.7.8.7.

ANNA ÖLANDER (1861-1939)
Trans. by E. GUSTAV JOHNSON, 1932

J. A. HULTMAN (1861-1942)

Confidently

1. A quiv-er-ing chord is bro-ken, When some-one is called be-yond;
2. A quiv-er-ing chord is bro-ken, When God takes a soul a-way,
3. A quiv-er-ing chord is bro-ken, Up yon-der it is re-stored,

A chord that is filled with long-ing, For heav'n and the saints' sweet bond.
To join the great, white-clad num-bers, In man-sions of peace to stay.
And all thro' the bliss-ful re-gions, It vi-brates to praise the Lord.

31 Again a Day Has from Us Gone

Nun danket all' und bringet Ehr (Störl)
C.M.

JOHANN F. HERTZOG, 1670
Trans. by GERHARD W. PALMGREN, 1947

JOHANN GEORG CHRISTIAN STÖRL, 1710

Devoutly, with movement

1. A - gain a day has from us gone, Gone ev - er from our sight;
2. But Thou re - main-est, God of grace, For - ev - er - more the same;
3. Safe in Thy keep-ing let me rest, When day-light fades a - way;
4. And if death's sol-emn call I hear, While in my sleep I lie;

Once more, its dai - ly la-bors done, Come peace and rest of night.
Thou all our nights and all our days Didst num-ber ere they came.
With joy-ful praise Thy name be blest When morning breaks o'er-head.
What com-fort, Lord, that Thou art near; In Thee I live and die. A-men.

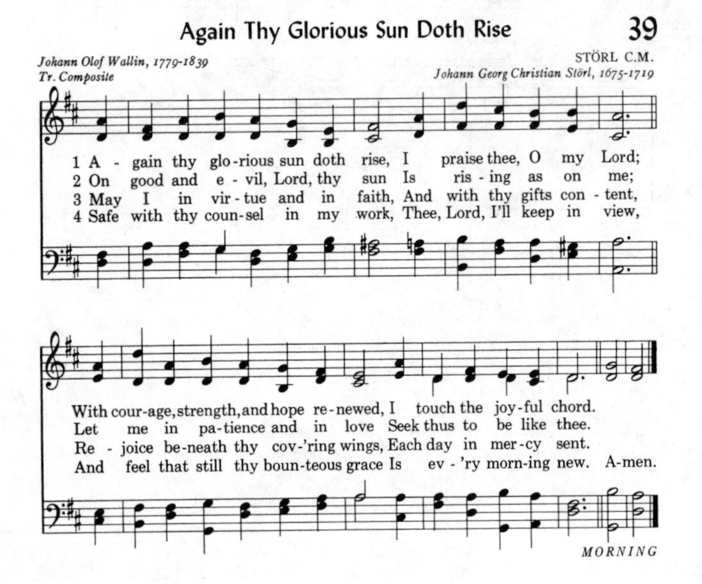
Again Thy Glorious Sun Doth Rise
39
Johann Olof Wallin, 1779-1839
Tr. Composite
STÖRL C.M.
Johann Georg Christian Störl, 1675-1719
1 A - gain thy glo-rious sun doth rise, I praise thee, O my Lord;
2 On good and e - vil, Lord, thy sun Is ris - ing as on me;
3 May I in vir - tue and in faith, And with thy gifts con - tent,
4 Safe with thy coun-sel in my work, Thee, Lord, I'll keep in view,
With cour-age, strength, and hope re - newed, I touch the joy-ful chord.
Let me in pa-tience and in love Seek thus to be like thee.
Re - joice be-neath thy cov-'ring wings, Each day in mer-cy sent.
And feel that still thy boun-teous grace Is ev - 'ry morn-ing new. A-men.
MORNING

Again a Day Has from Us Gone

Johann Friedrich Herzog probably wrote the text, "Nun sich der tag geendet hat," when he was a law student at Wittenberg. It appeared under the title, "Andakt om aftonen" (Evening Prayer). The first stanza appeared in *Neue Arien* published by Adam Krieger in Dresden in 1667. Here it was set to Krieger's tune. Evidently Herzog took this stanza and added several more. The text was reworked by C.F. Neander and was included in the third edition of his *Geistliche Lieder* in 1779. It was from this version that Johan Wallin translated the text into Swedish. "Så går en dag än från vår tid" appeared in the Swedish *Psalmbok* and other Swedish hymnals. It was included in both *Sionsharpan* and *Sions Basun* and was translated by Gerhard Palmgren for *The Hymnal* (1950).

The tune, STÖRL, appeared first in Johann Georg Christian Störl's *Neubezogenes Davidischen Harpfen- und Psalter-Spiel* in 1710 and is assumed to have been composed by him. Störl was a composer of choral music and for some time was the leading organist in Stuttgart. The tune is most generally used as a setting for "Again Thy Glorious Sun Doth Rise," but in this country has also been used with the evening text.

Again Thy Glorious Sun Doth Rise

"Din klara sol går åter opp" is one of Johan Wallin's most widely sung hymns. In Sweden it was especially popular in schools and camps. No doubt the pleasant and easily learned melody, with which it always has been associated, has helped its popularity. It first appeared in 1814 in a collection called *Proposal for Improved Church Songs*, one of the many trial volumes that preceded the actual *Psalmbok* of 1819. The translation is a composite work.

For a note on the tune, STÖRL, see "Again a Day Has from Us Gone."

Johann Forsèn, a gifted preacher and singer, spent several weeks at the close of his life in a Stockholm hospital. He shared a room with two younger men who were ill-humored and often troublesome. One beautiful morning as the sun shone into the room, Forsèn asked if he might sing a song. No one answered, and he accepted the silence as consent. He sat on the edge of his bed and sang in a beautiful clear voice: "Again thy glorious sun doth rise, / I praise thee, O my Lord. . . ." The other patients listened quietly. It was like a worship service in church. Everyone received something to think about and had a beautiful memory of a sunny morning.

All Hail to Thee, O Blessed Morn

"Var hälsad sköna morgonstund" is the most loved and best known of Wallin's hymns. It has been associated so long with our celebrations of Christmas that one could not imagine a Julotta service without it. It came in the eleventh-hour work on the *Psalmbok* as a request from Archbishop Lindblom, who wanted a Christmas text set to Nicolai's chorale. Frans Michael Franzén had tried, but his work was rejected. Samuel Hedborn's contribution was accepted, but the text was better suited to Epiphany. Wallin was successful, although he wrote when he was ill and depressed. No doubt he is expressing his own mood when he makes reference to "our sorrows" and "our cup of woe." Ernst W. Olson translated the text for use in the Augustana *Hymnal*, 1901. This is the version which has been included in all Covenant English hymnals beginning with *Mission Hymns*, 1921.

WIE SCHÖN LEUCHTET gets its name from "O Morning Star. . . ." It was with this text that the tune was first published in the appendix to Philip Nicolai's *Freuden-Spiegel*, a volume of meditations written during the Black Plague, which had devastated his city. The tune is sometimes called the "Queen of Chorales." The present form is taken from Bach's *Cantata I*, composed in 1740. Nicolai was a Lutheran pastor in Germany.

124 All Hail to Thee, O Blessed Morn!
Johann Olof Wallin, 1779-1839
Tr. Ernst W. Olson, 1870-1958
WIE SCHÖN LEUCHTET 8.8.7.8.8.7.4.8.4.8.
Philipp Nicolai, 1556-1608
1 All hail to thee, O bless-ed morn! To ti-dings long by proph-ets borne
2 'Tis God's own im-age and with-al The son of man, that mor-tals all
3 Like oth-er men, he tears will shed, Our sor-rows share, and be our aid,
4 He comes, for our re-demp-tion sent, And by his glo-ry heav'n is rent
Hast thou ful-fill-ment giv-en; O sa-cred and im-mor-tal day,
May find in him a broth-er; He comes with peace and love to bide
Thru his e-ter-nal pow-er; The Lord's good will un-to us show,
To close up-on us nev-er; Our bless-ed Shep-herd he would be,
When un-to earth, in glo-rious ray, De-scends the grace of heav-en!
On earth, the err-ing race to guide, And help, as could no oth-er:
And min-gle in our cup of woe The drops of mer-cy's show-er:
Whom we may fol-low faith-ful-ly And be with him for-ev-er:
Sing-ing, ring-ing, Sounds are blend-ing, Prais-es send-ing
Rath-er gath-er Clos-er, fond-er, Sheep that wan-der,
Dy-ing, buy-ing Thru his pas-sion Our sal-va-tion,
High-er, nigh-er, Glo-ry wing-ing, Prais-es sing-ing
Un-to heav-en For the Sav-ior to us giv-en.
Feed and fold them, Than let e-vil pow-ers hold them.
And to mor-tals O-pen-ing the heav'n-ly por-tals.
To the Fa-ther And his Son, our Lord and broth-er.

Var hälsad, sköna morgonstund,
Som av profeters helga mun
Är oss bebådad vorden!
Du stora dag, du sälla dag,
På vilken himlens välbehag
Ännu besöker jorden!
Unga sjunga Med de gamla,
Sig församla Jordens böner
Kring den störste av dess söner.

BIRTH

Words from *The Lutheran Service Book and Hymnal*, by permission of the Commission on the Liturgy and Hymnal.
Other harmonizations may be found at Nos. 157 and 263

320 All That Our Savior Hath Spoken

Löftena kunna ej svika
8. 6. 8. 6. with refrain

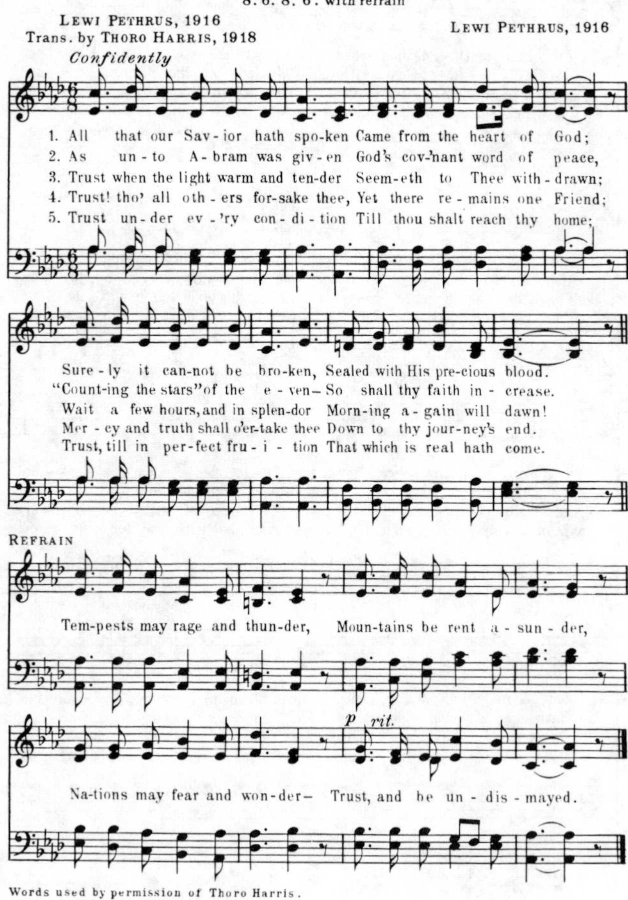
LEWI PETHRUS, 1916
Trans. by THORO HARRIS, 1918
LEWI PETHRUS, 1916
Confidently
1. All that our Sav-ior hath spo-ken Came from the heart of God;
2. As un-to A-bram was giv-en God's cov-'nant word of peace,
3. Trust when the light warm and ten-der Seem-eth to Thee with-drawn;
4. Trust! tho' all oth-ers for-sake thee, Yet there re-mains one Friend;
5. Trust un-der ev-'ry con-di-tion Till thou shalt reach thy home;
Sure-ly it can-not be bro-ken, Sealed with His pre-cious blood.
"Count-ing the stars" of the e-ven- So shall thy faith in-crease.
Wait a few hours, and in splen-dor Morn-ing a-gain will dawn!
Mer-cy and truth shall o'er-take thee Down to thy jour-ney's end.
Trust, till in per-fect fru-i-tion That which is real hath come.
REFRAIN
Tem-pests may rage and thun-der, Moun-tains be rent a-sun-der,
p rit.
Na-tions may fear and won-der- Trust, and be un-dis-mayed.
Words used by permission of Thoro Harris.
Music used by permission of Lewi Pethrus.

All That Our Savior Hath Spoken

"Löftena kunna ej svika" has been the most popular song written by Lewi Pethrus. In 1913, his wife became gravely ill, and the doctor recommended immediate surgery. The couple believed that God could heal and they prayed for healing, but there seemed to be no answer. They began to consider recalling the physician. It was a dark period for Pethrus. Many times he had preached that faith in God would bring healing. Should he now turn to man for help? They both decided to trust in continued prayer and were joined by the entire congregation. Pethrus related that at home he and a friend "sank to our knees and commended the whole matter to God, and we experienced a wonderful peace in the Lord." In a few hours there was a change for the better, and soon she was well again.

It was during this time that he wrote the first two verses of the song. The remaining stanzas came some time later when his church and the Pentecost revival came under attack by the press. The newspapers urged the police to close the church, and in the words of Pethrus, "painted us in the most terrifying colors." To add to his grief, he saw excesses in the revival which he could not approve. The complete hymn appeared first in *Brudgummens Röst* (The Voice of the Bridegroom) in June, 1915. It was translated by Thoro Harris in 1918 and included in Nathaniel Carlson's *Songs of Trust and Triumph* No. 1, 1929. *The Hymnal* (1950) omitted stanza four.

The tune, LÖFTENA KUNNA EJ SVIKA, had been composed earlier by Pethrus, but he had no text for it.

Are You Dismayed, Lonely, Afraid

Selma Lagerstöm early came in contact with the revival in Sweden and was drawn to the "läsare." She often visited an influential godly woman, Britta Persson, in Storfället, Fryksände. It is said that it was in connection with one of these visits that she wrote this text about God's faithfulness, "Är du i nöd, har du ej stöd." The poem first appeared in *Psalmisten* in 1880, and with this tune in *Pilgrimstoner* in 1886. It was included in both *Sionsharpan* and *Sions Basun* and was translated by E.G. Johnson for *The Hymnal* (1950).

The source of the tune, GUDS TROFASTHET, is unknown. Evidently it is an old Swedish folk song.

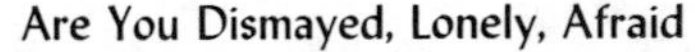
83 Are You Dismayed, Lonely, Afraid

Selma S. Lagerström, 1859-1927
Tr. E. Gustav Johnson, 1893-
GUDS TROFASTHET 4.4.7.D.
Swedish Folk Melody
1 Are you dis - mayed, Lone - ly, a - fraid,
2 Mer - cy and love, Gifts from a - bove,
3 Friends may de - ceive, Cause you to grieve,
4 Al - ways his grace You may em - brace,
5 Cour - age and might, Guid - ance and light,
6 Praise now his name! Hear him pro - claim,

Think - ing your-self for - sak - en? God is your stay,
Come in a - bun-dant mea - sure. Great things and small
God is your con - so - la - tion! Faith - ful and true
He is your con - stant bless - ing. When you are tried,
God will in mer - cy ren - der. In ev - 'ry pain,
"I will for - sake you nev - er!" Un - to the end

Trust him and pray; New hope he will a - wak - en.
God gives to all, Gra - cious - ly in his pleas - ure.
He is to you, Com - fort in trib - u - la - tion.
Flee to his side, Need for his help con - fess - ing.
Con - flict and strain, He is your true de - fend - er.
On him de - pend, He is the same for - ev - er!

GOD'S LOVE AND FATHERHOOD

502 As Pilgrims in This World

Vi bo ej här

11. 10. 11. 10.

O. A. OTTANDER, 1876
Trans. by OBED JOHNSON, 1946
Anonymous
Meditatively
1. As pil - grims in this world where life is fleet - ing, We jour - ney
2. It mat - ters not that tri - als come and sor - rows, For soon the
3. The Lord is near; He is my source of pleas - ure, He shares with
4. Well may you ask if I can now be, tru - ly A child of
5. Then like the sun a-blaze in noon-day splen - dor, With light ce -
on to meet our dear-est Friend; Keep Thou, O Lord, our hearts from false af -
pil-grim-age will reach its goal; And then will God in more a - bun-dant
me my jour-ney ev - ery day; When I am sad He speaks to me of
God, the Lord's de - vot - ed bride; But here you see in me my hu - man
les - tial I shall bright-ly shine, When at the throne my praise to God I
fec - tions And lead us on - ward to the jour-ney's end.
meas-ure Give rest and glad-ness to the wea - ry soul.
Je - sus, Then joy re - turns, all sad-ness steals a - way.
frail-ties, Some day you'll see my spir - it glo - ri - fied.
ren - der, I tru - ly then shall live the life di - vine. A-men.

As Pilgrims in This World

The "pilgrim" theme was popular among our hymnists. "Vi bo ej här, vi blott här nere gästa" was written by Otto Ottander in 1876 and first appeared in *Östra Smålands Missionsblad* that year under the title "Thoughts on the Journey Home." Ottander had borrowed the theme and the greater part of the first stanza from a song in an issue of *Gotlands Missions-Tidning*.. A free translation is:

I do not live here.
I am only a guest for a short time on this side of the Jordan.

My friend dwells up there;
My heart is held there with strong bands of love.

The song was published in *Sionsharpan* and *Sions Basun*. Obed Johnson translated five of the seven stanzas for use in *The Hymnal* (1950).

VI BO EJ HÄR is a Swedish folk melody that has been the only setting for the text. But it had been used with a different text in *Hemlandssånger*, 1877.

601 Behold a Host Arrayed in White
Based on Revelation 7:9
Hans Adolph Brorson, 1694-1764
Tr. Carl Doving, 1867-1937, alt.
BEHOLD A HOST 8.8.8.6. 12L.
Norwegian Folk Song
Harm. by Edvard Grieg, 1843-1907
1 Be - hold a host ar - rayed in white, Like thou - sand
These are the ran - somed throng, the same That from the
2 O joy - ful saints, for - ev - er blest! Hail, ye who
The world ye did re - nounce of yore, The pre - cious
snow - clad moun - tains bright! With palms they stand— who
trib - u - la - tion came, And in the flood of
have at - tained your rest! In life and death ye
seed ye weep - ing bore; Now reap the joy with -
are this band Be - fore the throne of light?
Je - sus' blood Are cleansed from guilt and shame:
kept the faith, Though ye were sore op - prest.
out al - loy In bliss for - ev - er - more.
And now, ar - rayed in robes made white, They serve the
Lift up your voice, ye ran - somed throng, And swell the
Lord by day and night; And an - thems swell where
ev - er - last - ing song: Praise, hon - or, laud, to
God doth dwell With an - gels in the height.
thee, our God, And to the Lamb be - long.
LIFE EVERLASTING

Behold a Host Arrayed in White

This hymn appears in most hymnals of Scandinavian heritage. Based on Revelation 7:9, it is often sung on All Saints' Sunday. "Den store hvide flok vi se" was written by Bishop Hans Adolph Brorson, one of Denmark's foremost hymnists. In his *Den Kristna Psalmen* (Stockholm, 1916), E.N. Soderberg writes: "For the awaited future splendour, Brorson's harp had marvelous sounds. There rests a glorious brilliance over his hymn about God's chosen in heaven." It was published after his death by his son in *Hans Adolph Brorson's Swan-Song*, 1765. Carl Doving, a noted Norwegian hymnologist, is credited with the translation, but others may have been involved in the work as well. There are several versions. Doving was a member of the committee appointed by three Norwegian synods to prepare an English hymnal. This was published in 1913 as *The Lutheran Hymnary*. Here the hymn was included with two tunes—one by Ludwig Lindeman, and the other, the Grieg arrangement. The song came into Covenant usage through *The Hymnal* (1950), where all three stanzas were included. *The Covenant Hymnal* (1973) omits stanza two.

BEHOLD A HOST was arranged by Edvard Grieg from a Norwegian folk song. He had the ability more than any other Scandinavian to create out of national folk melodies a higher art music that could stand by itself.

Bright and Glorious Is the Sky

"Dejlig er den himmel blaa" is a lovely, childlike carol written in 1810 by the famous Danish hymnist, Nikolai Grundtvig. The author was in deep depression at the time and on the brink of insanity. Against this background the hymn comes as a burst of sunlight through a clouded sky. Grundtvig's constant emphasis upon the importance of the Word of God can be seen in stanzas five and six. The hymn was first published in Knud Lyhne Rahbek's *Sandsigeren* in 1811. It appeared in several Danish hymnals, and a translation by J.C. Aaberg was included in the *Hymnal for Church and Home* (Danish), Blair, Nebraska, 1927 and 1938. Our version is from the *Service Book and Hymnal*, where the translation is the work of commission members.

CELESTIA came to be used with this text in 1929. It is a Danish folk melody which was introduced in Henrik Rung's addition to the *Koralbog* of Christoph Weyse in 1857.

Built on the Rock

Of all the hymns that Grundtvig wrote, "Kirken den er et gammelt hus" (The Church Is an Old House) is the greatest. As a believer in objective Christianity, he stressed the God-given means of grace—the Word and the sacraments. He emphasized the divine character of the Church, for Christ founded it and as the Living Word is present in it. The hymn was first published in his own *Sang-Vaerk til den Danske Kirke*, 1837. It was translated into English by Carl Doving in 1909 and included in *The Lutheran Hymnary*, 1913. Our version is a revision by Fred C.M. Hansen, a pastor in the United Evangelical Lutheran Church.

KIRKEN DEN ER ET was composed for the text by Ludvig Mathias Lindeman in 1840 and first published in W.A. Wexel's *Christelige Psalmer*. The tune is in the Dorian mode and has some of the character of a folk song, like so many of his original melodies. But the tune also has the majesty of a chorale and has often been equated with EIN FESTE BURG.

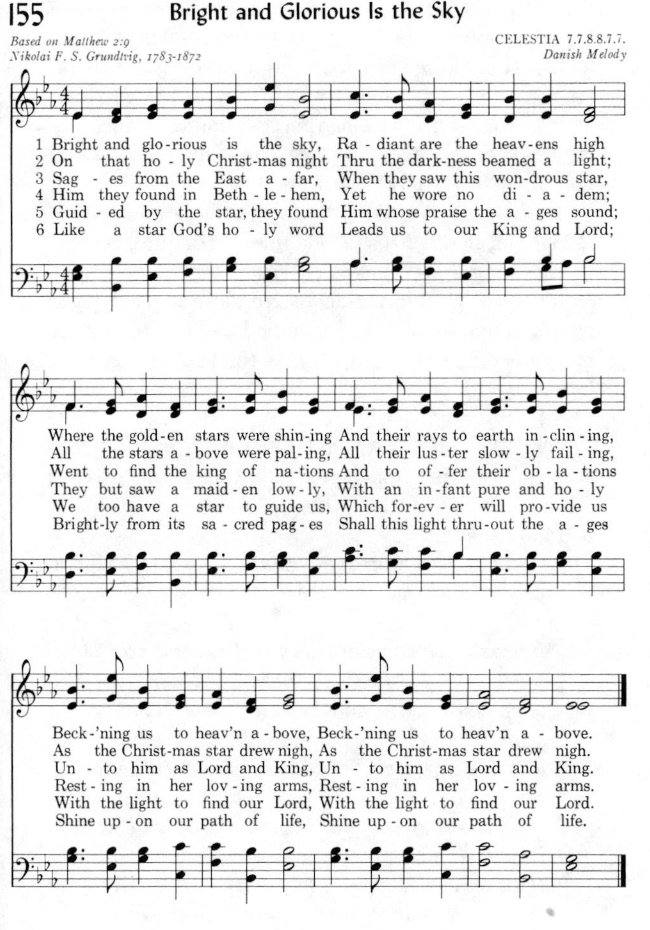
155
Bright and Glorious Is the Sky
Based on Matthew 2:9
Nikolai F. S. Grundtvig, 1783-1872
CELESTIA 7.7.8.8.7.7.
Danish Melody
1 Bright and glo-rious is the sky, Ra-diant are the heav-ens high
2 On that ho-ly Christ-mas night Thru the dark-ness beamed a light;
3 Sag-es from the East a-far, When they saw this won-drous star,
4 Him they found in Beth-le-hem, Yet he wore no di-a-dem;
5 Guid-ed by the star, they found Him whose praise the a-ges sound;
6 Like a star God's ho-ly word Leads us to our King and Lord;
Where the gold-en stars were shin-ing And their rays to earth in-clin-ing,
All the stars a-bove were pal-ing, All their lus-ter slow-ly fail-ing,
Went to find the king of na-tions And to of-fer their ob-la-tions
They but saw a maid-en low-ly, With an in-fant pure and ho-ly
We too have a star to guide us, Which for-ev-er will pro-vide us
Bright-ly from its sa-cred pag-es Shall this light thru-out the a-ges
Beck-'ning us to heav'n a-bove, Beck-'ning us to heav'n a-bove.
As the Christ-mas star drew nigh, As the Christ-mas star drew nigh.
Un-to him as Lord and King, Un-to him as Lord and King.
Rest-ing in her lov-ing arms, Rest-ing in her lov-ing arms.
With the light to find our Lord, With the light to find our Lord.
Shine up-on our path of life, Shine up-on our path of life.

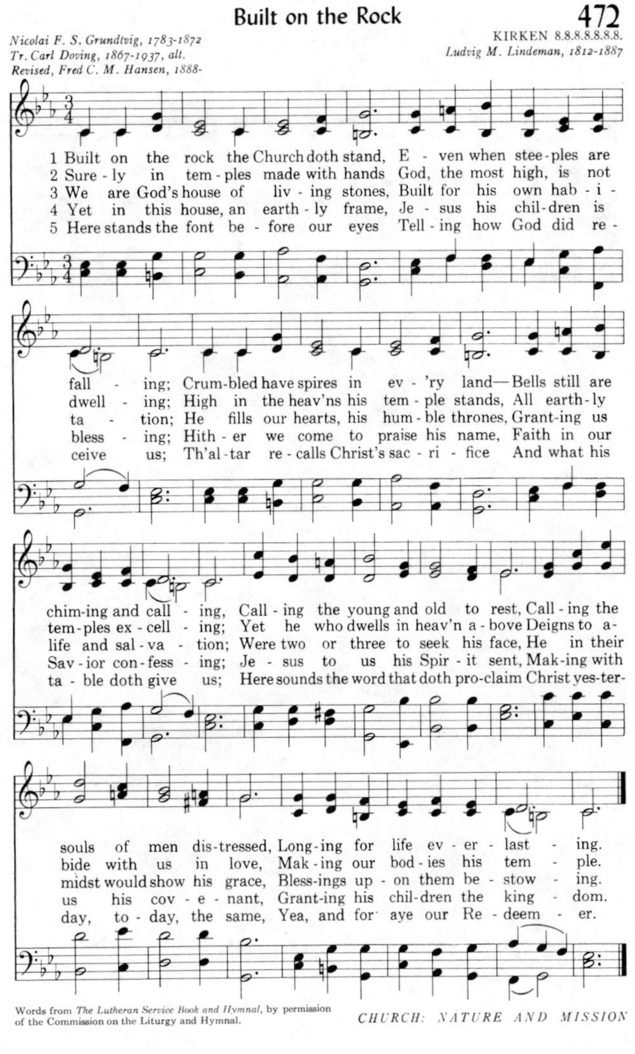
Built on the Rock
472
Nicolai F. S. Grundtvig, 1783-1872
Tr. Carl Doving, 1867-1937, alt.
Revised, Fred C. M. Hansen, 1888-
KIRKEN 8.8.8.8.8.8.8.
Ludvig M. Lindeman, 1812-1887
1 Built on the rock the Church doth stand, E-ven when stee-ples are
2 Sure-ly in tem-ples made with hands God, the most high, is not
3 We are God's house of liv-ing stones, Built for his own hab-i-
4 Yet in this house, an earth-ly frame, Je-sus his chil-dren is
5 Here stands the font be-fore our eyes Tell-ing how God did re-
fall-ing; Crum-bled have spires in ev-'ry land—Bells still are
dwell-ing; High in the heav'ns his tem-ple stands, All earth-ly
ta-tion; He fills our hearts, his hum-ble thrones, Grant-ing us
bless-ing; Hith-er we come to praise his name, Faith in our
ceive us; Th'al-tar re-calls Christ's sac-ri-fice And what his
chim-ing and call-ing, Call-ing the young and old to rest, Call-ing the
tem-ples ex-cell-ing; Yet he who dwells in heav'n a-bove Deigns to a-
life and sal-va-tion; Were two or three to seek his face, He in their
Sav-ior con-fess-ing; Je-sus to us his Spir-it sent, Mak-ing with
ta-ble doth give us; Here sounds the word that doth pro-claim Christ yes-ter-
souls of men dis-tressed, Long-ing for life ev-er-last-ing.
bide with us in love, Mak-ing our bod-ies his tem-ple.
midst would show his grace, Bless-ings up-on them be-stow-ing.
us his cov-e-nant, Grant-ing his chil-dren the king-dom.
day, to-day, the same, Yea, and for aye our Re-deem-er.
Words from The Lutheran Service Book and Hymnal, by permission of the Commission on the Liturgy and Hymnal.
CHURCH: NATURE AND MISSION

EPIPHANY

Music from *The Lutheran Service Book and Hymnal*, by permission of the Commission on the Liturgy and Hymnal.

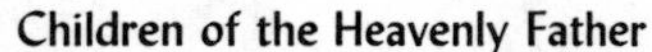
Children of the Heavenly Father
382

Lina Sandell, 1832-1903
Tr. Ernst W. Olson, 1870-1958
TRYGGARE KAN INGEN VARA 8.8.8.8.
Swedish Folk Melody, 1874
1 Chil - dren of the heav'n-ly Fa - ther Safe - ly in his bos-om gath - er;
2 God his own doth tend and nour - ish, In his ho - ly courts they flour - ish;
3 Nei - ther life nor death shall ev - er From the Lord his chil-dren sev - er;
4 Praise the Lord in joy - ful num-bers, Your Pro - tect - or nev - er slum-bers;
5 Though he giv - eth or he tak - eth, God his chil - dren ne'er for - sak - eth;
Tryg - ga - re kan ing - en va - ra Än Guds lil - la bar - na - ska - ra;
Nest-ling bird nor star in heav - en Such a ref - uge e'er was giv - en.
From all e - vil things he spares them, In his might - y arms he bears them.
Un - to them his grace he show - eth, And their sor - rows all he know - eth.
At the will of your De - fend - er Ev - 'ry foe - man must sur - ren - der.
His the lov - ing pur - pose sole - ly To pre - serve them pure and ho - ly.
Stjär - nan ej på him - la - fäs - tet, Få - geln ej i kän - da näs - tet.

Words from *The Lutheran Service Book and Hymnal*, by permission of the Commission on the Liturgy and Hymnal.

FAITH AND ASSURANCE

Children of the Heavenly Father

An old tradition in Fröderyd, where Lina Sandell lived, relates that she wrote "Tryggare kan ingen vara" while seated on the branch of a large ash tree that stood in the parsonage yard. (The tree is still there.) From that spot on warm summer evenings she could listen to the contented twitter of the birds as they hid in their nests among the green leaves. And from there she could watch the stars as they began to appear. Her impressions fortified the biblical concepts of the security of God's children. The first draft consisted of three stanzas, of which two became the first stanzas in the completed text. It first appeared in 1855 in her anonymous publication called *Andeliga daggdroppar* (Spiritual Dewdrops). Fredrik Engelke included her text in his *Lofsånger och andeliga wisor*, 1873, with the tune that has become so familiar. He added five stanzas of his own, one of which came to be included in the final form—"Lo, their very hairs he numbers. . . ." That stanza, however, is omitted in all modern hymnals.

A composite translation beginning "More secure is no one ever. . ." was published in *Mission Hymns* (1921) and *The Covenant Hymnal* (1931). Ernst Olson's version was used in *The Hymnal* (1950) and in our present volume. Until quite recently the song's use has been restricted primarily to churches of Scandinavian origin, but at least eight recent hymnals of other groups have included it. It has had some use in England as the result of a translation made in 1935, beginning, "Fear not, little flock, for surely. . . ."

TRYGGARE KAN INGEN VARA is purported to be a Swedish folk melody, but there are earlier German variant forms. One dates back to 1813, but it could be older.

In his *Den Segrande Sången* Oscar Lövgren relates the following incident:

> *It was a winter Saturday in Leksand early in 1939. Old John F. Hagstrom had just been buried. He had been active in Sunday school work all his life, and he loved and was loved by the children. About an hour after the committal service, the pastor chanced to pass the church yard, and he heard singing. As he came closer, he saw that several children had gathered around the fresh plot. They were singing "Tryggare kan ingen vara." In this way they wanted to thank the old Sunday school teacher and friend of children.*

Chosen Seed and Zion's Children

"Lammets folk och Sion's fränder" was one of the favorites of the "läsare." It had been written a good hundred years earlier by Anders Rutström, a State Church pastor who was active in Moravian circles. Two original handwritten copies, which are located in the Royal Library in Stockholm, omit the fourth stanza, "Faith and love. . . ." In a collection called *Twenne Andeliga Wijsor*, 1754, stanza three is omitted. The complete text with music was included in *Sions Nya Sånger*, 1854. It appeared in most of the Swedish-American hymnals. The translation by Claude W. Foss is found in all Covenant hymnals, beginning with *Mission Hymns*, 1921.

The source of LAMMETS FOLK is unknown. It has been attributed to Rutström since its first known appearance was in *Sions Nya Sånger*, a collection containing many of his songs. In the 1854 edition, the melody line was indicated by numerals.

During the revivals in the 1800s many people developed the habit of coming to church early to sing the songs of the "läsare." In an attempt to stop the practice, the church officials levied a fine against anyone who started to sing before the service. On the first Sunday following, Pastor Warrén was scheduled to preach at Bergkulla in Småland. Many parishioners were there an hour early as usual, but all was quiet. They wanted to sing, but they feared the consequence. It appeared that the ruling was effective. After a half-hour a farmer, who was sitting toward the front, stood and looked around the sanctuary. "Where are you sitting, Bäckstrom?" he asked. "Can't you sing a song while we wait?" "I'm too poor to sing here," answered the shoemaker. "Sing," said the farmer, "I'll pay." A holy hush swept over the group, and Bäckstrom began to sing so that it echoed in the rafters: "Lammets folk och Sions fränder. . . ."

He was so carried away with his singing that he did not notice Pastor Warrén standing at the altar rail with folded hands, listening intently. It was easy to preach after Bäckstrom had sung the coldness and listlessness out of the hearts of the people. He kept on for two hours, but no one left. And there was scarcely a dry eye in the congregation. When the farmer went to pay the fine, one of the church officials said, "Put your money away. If anyone is going to pay, I'm the man to do it." Not long after that the rule was rescinded; many of the church leaders wanted to sing as well.

473 Chosen Seed and Zion's Children
Anders Carl Rutström, 1721-1772
Tr. Claude W. Foss, 1855-1935
LAMMETS FOLK 8.7.8.7.D.
Attr. to Anders Carl Rutström, 1721-1772
"Sions Nya Sånger," 1854
1 Cho - sen seed and Zi - on's chil - dren, Ran - somed from e -
2 Still re - joice a - mid thy tri - als, Nor re - gard thy
3 Pleas - ant - ly thy lines have fall - en Un - der - neath the
4 Faith and love are the con - di - tions— All on faith and
5 And up - on this blest foun - da - tion, Lord, our Lord and
ter - nal wrath, Trav - 'ling to the heav'n - ly Ca - naan
lot a - miss, For the kind and lov - ing Sav - ior
tree of life, For the Lord is thy sal - va - tion
love de - pends; Love of law is the ful - fill - ment,
Sav - ior - King, May thy Spir - it e'er u - nite us,
On a rough and thorn - y path: Church of God, in
Is the source of all thy bliss. May he ev - er
And thy shield in all thy strife. Here the tim - id
Faith God's mer - cy ap - pre - hends: Who hath faith shall
To it may we ev - er cling. May we, mem - bers
Christ e - lect - ed, Thou to God art rec - on - ciled; But on earth thou
be thy por - tion, He who gave thee life and breath; In his keep - ing
bird finds shel - ter, Here the swal - low finds a nest, Trem - bling fu - gi -
see sal - va - tion, Who hath love shall life ob - tain; May, O Lord, thy
of one bod - y, Grow in - to a per - fect whole; Grant, O Lord, that
art a stran - ger, Per - se - cut - ed and re - viled.
fear no e - vil, Now or in the hour of death.
tive a ref - uge, And the wea - ry pil - grim rest.
love pos - sess us And thy Spir - it in us reign.
in thy peo - ple There may be one heart and soul. A - men.
CHURCH: NATURE AND MISSION
Words used by permission of Fortress Press.

164 Christ the Lord Is Risen!

Kristus är uppstånden
11. 11. 11. 11. with refrain

ANDERS NILSSON (1849-1912)
Trans. by JOSEPH E. ANDERSON, 1946

American folk melody

Joyously

1. Christ the Lord is ris - en! O re - joice my soul! Christ the Lord is
2. Lift your joy - ful voic - es on this Eas - ter - tide! Peace and hope and
3. Glo - ry, praise and hon - or to our ris - en King! Heav - en's gates are

ris - en! He has made you whole. O - ver death tri - um - phant;
glad - ness in our hearts a - bide, For the Lamb of God, who for
o - pen; hear the an - gels sing! There in scenes of glo - ry,

crushed the ser - pent's head; Sa - tan's pow - er van - quished thus the Lord has said.
sin - ful men was slain, Con - quer'd death's do - min - ion, and He lives a - gain!
soon he'll beck - on, "Come," And with Him we'll dwell in our e - ter - nal home.

REFRAIN

Sing, then, heir of heav - en! Je - sus lives a - gain! He is now your
broth - er, your re - deem - er, friend. Christ the Lord is ris - en—
sound the glad re - frain—Died for us on Cal - v'ry, but He lives a - gain!

Christ the Lord Is Risen!

The joyous Easter text "Kristus är uppstånden" was written by Anders Nilsson and first published in *Östra Smålands Missionsbladet* in April, 1881. Later the same year it appeared in several smaller publications. Its first use as a hymn was in *Evangelii Basun*, which was published in Minneapolis in 1886. Later it appeared in *Sionsharpan* and *Sions Basun*. In 1946, it was translated by Joseph E. Anderson for inclusion in *The Hymnal* (1950).

The tune, KRISTUS ÄR UPPSTÅNDEN, is actually an American folk melody arranged for use with the text by A.L. Skoog.

Come, Let Us Praise Him

Most of Lina Sandell's lyrics are gentle and intimate, but a brighter and more openly joyous note is sounded in "Låtom oss sjunga." Here she lets go and invites young and old to praise Jesus for his grace, love, and redemptive work. Oscar Ahnfelt was continually begging her for new texts till one day she said jokingly that she could find no peace so long as he was in town. This is one of at least twenty-five of her hymns that were first published in Ahnfelt's *Andeliga Sånger*. In the complete edition, which was finished in 1877, there are at least fifty-six Sandell texts. The American edition of this collection was published in Chicago in 1882. In this way many of Lina Sandell's songs were brought here, including the hymn in question. Later it appeared in *Sionsharpan, Hemlandssånger*, and *Sions Basun*. Karl Olsson translated it for the North Park College choir in 1967.

The source of LÅTOM OSS SJUNGA is unknown, but it is the tune that was originally published with the text.

Consecrated to Thy Service

Perhaps it was his almost constant poor health that made Emil Gustafson quiet and introspective. In his hymns he is concerned quite often with the soul's inner secret life and the consecration of the whole person. "Avskild för min Herres räkning" is a good example of this emphasis. It was first published in his *Hjärtesånger*, 1892. It was copyrighted in the United States the same year by A.L. Skoog and included in *Jubelklangen*, 1896. Later it appeared in *Sions Basun* and *De Ungas Sångbok*. The song was translated by Nathaniel Carlson in 1932 and used in his *Songs of Trust and Triumph.* The English version came into use in the Covenant through *The Hymnal* (1950). This was one of the hymns sung at the dedication of this hymnal at the Covenant Annual Meeting in Minneapolis.

Emil Gustafson composed the tune AVSKILD FÖR MIN HERRES RÄKNING as a setting for his text.

Come, Let Us Praise Him 244

Lina Sandell, 1832-1903
Tr. Karl A. Olsson, 1914-

LÅTOM OSS SJUNGA 5.6.5.6.6.
Ahnfelt's "Sånger," 1868
Harm. by A. Royce Eckhardt, 1937-

1 Come, let us praise him, Sing-ing of grace di-vine; Youths now and eld-ers Prais-ing his love's de-sign, Laud-ing his acts be-nign.
2 Earth and the heav-ens Show forth his glo-ry bright; Yet he was hum-bled, Stripped of his won-drous might, Shar-ing our hu-man plight.
3 Will-ing-ly stoop-ing Un-der my bur-den, he Pa-tient-ly car-ried All that op-press-es me, Set-ting the cap-tive free.
4 Bear-ing our an-guish, Nailed to a shame-ful tree, He died to save us From an e-ter-ni-ty Of deep-est mis-er-y.
5 All this he suf-fered For his be-lov-ed bride, That she for-ev-er, By his death sanc-ti-fied, Might in his house a-bide.
6 Let us be sing-ing Al-ways of him, our friend, Ev-er a-dor-ing Mer-cies with-out an end: Christ, we our prais-es lend.

DEDICATION AND CONSECRATION

259 **Consecrated to Thy Service**

Avskild för min Herres räkning
8.7.8.7. D. with refrain

EMIL GUSTAFSON (1862-1900)
Trans. by NATHANIEL CARLSON, 1932

EMIL GUSTAFSON (1862-1900)

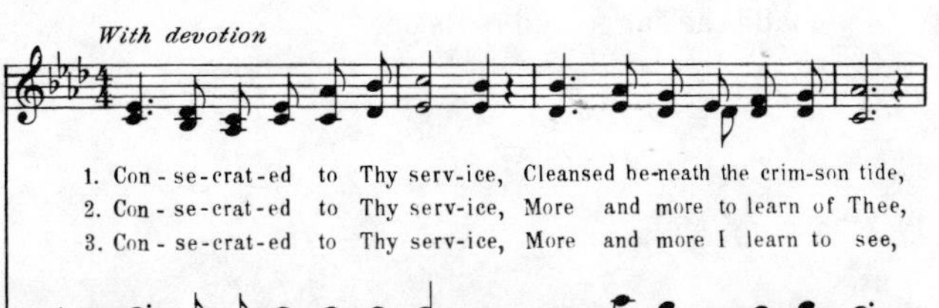

With devotion
1. Con-se-crat-ed to Thy serv-ice, Cleansed be-neath the crim-son tide,
2. Con-se-crat-ed to Thy serv-ice, More and more to learn of Thee,
3. Con-se-crat-ed to Thy serv-ice, More and more I learn to see,

All my sins and guilt for-giv-en, Now in Thee I will a-bide.
Of the depth and breadth of mer-cy, And Thy won-d'rous love for me.
Pass-ing all my un-der-stand-ing, Is Thy mer-cy wrought for me.
In Thy cross my joy and glo-ry, And my right-eous-ness I see,
Then the world with all its glit-ter, All the more as dross I see,
And the more my life is yield-ed, All the more Thy love fills me,
Let me fol-low Thee, my Sav-ior, Con-se-crate me, Lord, to Thee.
And my heart is filled with long-ing; Con-se-crate me, Lord, to Thee.
Keep me near the flow-ing foun-tain, Con-se-crate me, Lord, to Thee.
REFRAIN
Pre-cious Sav-ior, guide and keep me, Fer-vent in my love to Thee; That wher-ev-er I may jour-ney, Oth-ers may see Christ in me.
Pre-cious Sav-ior, guide and keep me, Fer-vent in my love to Thee; That wher-ev-er I may jour-ney,

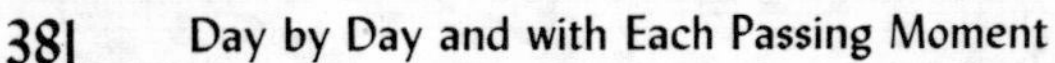
381 Day by Day and with Each Passing Moment

Lina Sandell, 1832-1903
Tr. A. L. Skoog, 1856-1934
BLOTT EN DAG 10.9.10.9.D.
Oscar Ahnfelt, 1813-1882
1 Day by day and with each pass - ing mo - ment, Strength I
2 Ev - 'ry day the Lord him - self is near me With a
3 Help me then in ev - 'ry trib - u - la - tion So to
find to meet my tri - als here; Trust - ing in my Fa - ther's
spe - cial mer - cy for each hour; All my cares he fain would
trust thy prom - is - es, O Lord, That I lose not faith's sweet
wise be - stow - ment, I've no cause for wor - ry or for fear.
bear, and cheer me, He whose name is Coun - sel - lor and Pow'r.
con - so - la - tion Of - fered me with - in thy ho - ly word.
He whose heart is kind be - yond all meas - ure Gives un -
The pro - tec - tion of his child and treas - ure Is a
Help me, Lord, when toil and trou - ble meet - ing, E'er to
to each day what he deems best— Lov - ing - ly, its part of
charge that on him - self he laid; "As thy days, thy strength shall
take, as from a fa - ther's hand, One by one, the days, the
pain and pleas - ure, Min - gling toil with peace and rest.
be in meas - ure," This the pledge to me he made.
mo - ments fleet - ing, Till I reach the prom - ised land. A-men.

FAITH AND ASSURANCE

Day by Day and with Each Passing Moment

Recently a well-known journalist in Sweden said that every Swede ought to begin each day with the song, "Blott en dag ett ögonblick i sänder." It would help in the pressure and hurry to meet each new day relaxed. Lina Sandell wrote these words of comfort and assurance. They first appeared in 1886 in the calendar *Korsblomman*, along with an allegory about an old wall clock that had stopped suddenly. The dial decided to investigate and discovered that the pendulum was at fault. It had become bored and tired of swinging back and forth 86,400 times each day. "Try swinging six times," said the dial. The pendulum agreed and admitted that this was not wearisome, "but it's not six times, or sixty; it's the thought of six million times that disturbs me." "But bear in mind," said the dial, "that while in a single moment you can think of the millions of swings you must make in a lifetime, only one at a time will be required of you. And no matter how often you must go through the same movements you will be given a moment for each one." The pendulum admitted that it had acted foolishly in going on strike and promptly resumed its work.

Lina then commented on the allegory, saying that it is foolish to put future burdens upon the present moment. We are given only a day at a time, and for each day new grace, new strength, new help. Then she quoted Leviticus 33:25: "Thy shoes shall be iron and brass; and as thy days, so shall thy strength be." The text of the song followed.

Oscar Ahnfelt intoduced the hymn in his *Andeliga Sånger*, 1872. Being one of the favorites, it appeared in most of the early Swedish hymnals published in this country. *Mission Hymns* and the Covenant hymnals of 1931 and 1973 made use of the A.L. Skoog translation, while the E.E. Ryden version (Day by Day Thy Mercies, Lord, Attend Me) was used in the *The Hymnal* (1950). It was believed that, while the Ryden version is more poetic, Skoog's is closer to the original.

BLOTT EN DAG was composed as a setting for the text by Oscar Ahnfelt. In the original lyric each line had one less syllable than it now has. Ahnfelt felt that the song would have a softer and more natural rhythm if each line were lengthened by one syllable. He shared his feeling with the writer, and she made the suggested revision.

Dearest Jesus, Draw Thou Near Me
64
Thomas Kingo, 1634-1703
Tr. C. K. Solberg, 1872-1954, alt.
WERDE MUNTER 8.7.8.7.7.7.8.8.
Johann Schop, c.1590-c.1664
1 Dear - est Je - sus, draw thou near me, Let thy Spir - it dwell with mine;
2 Un - der-neath thy wings a - bid-ing, In thy Church, O Sav - ior dear,
3 Thou earth's great-est joy and glad-ness And sal - va - tion, full and free;
O - pen now my ear to hear thee, Take my heart and seal it thine;
Let me dwell, in thee con - fid - ing, Hold me in thy faith and fear;
Let thy pres-ence cheer my sad-ness And pre-pare my soul for thee!
Keep me, lead me on my way, Thee to fol - low and o - bey,
Take a - way from me each thought That with wick - ed - ness is fraught,
In the hour when I de - part, Touch my spir - it, lips and heart,
E'er to do thy will and fear thee, And re-joice to know and hear thee.
Tempt-ing me to dis - o - bey thee, Root it out, O Lord, I pray thee.
With thy word as - sure, up-hold me Till the heav'n-ly gates en-fold me. A-men.
Reproduced from The Concordia Hymnal, copyright © 1932 and 1960, by permission of Augsburg Publishing House, Minneapolis, Minnesota, copyright owner.
PULPIT

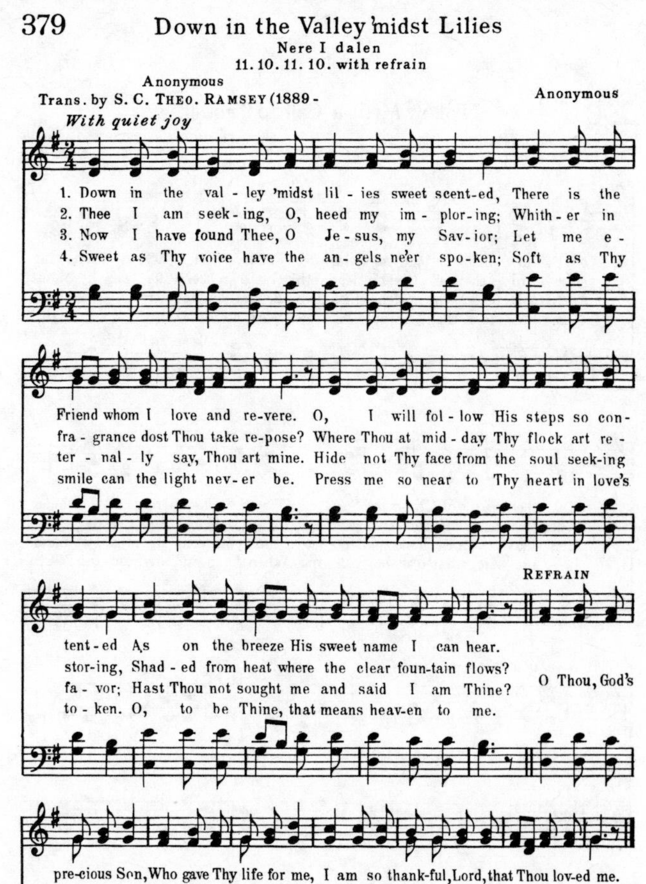
379
Down in the Valley 'midst Lilies
Nere I dalen
11. 10. 11. 10. with refrain
Anonymous
Trans. by S. C. Theo. Ramsey (1889 -
Anonymous
With quiet joy
1. Down in the val - ley 'midst lil - ies sweet scent-ed, There is the Friend whom I love and re-vere. O, I will fol - low His steps so con-tent-ed As on the breeze His sweet name I can hear.
2. Thee I am seek - ing, O, heed my im - plor-ing; Whith - er in fra - grance dost Thou take re-pose? Where Thou at mid - day Thy flock art re - stor-ing, Shad - ed from heat where the clear foun-tain flows?
3. Now I have found Thee, O Je - sus, my Sav - ior; Let me e - ter - nal - ly say, Thou art mine. Hide not Thy face from the soul seek-ing fa - vor; Hast Thou not sought me and said I am Thine?
4. Sweet as Thy voice have the an - gels ne'er spo - ken; Soft as Thy smile can the light nev - er be. Press me so near to Thy heart in love's to - ken. O, to be Thine, that means heav-en to me.
Refrain
O Thou, God's pre-cious Son, Who gave Thy life for me, I am so thank-ful, Lord, that Thou lov-ed me.
Words used by permission of S. C. Theo. Ramsey.

Dearest Jesus, Draw Thou Near Me

This prayer for the presence, guidance, and help of Jesus was written by Denmark's first great hymnist, Thomas Kingo. The hymn was published in 1699 in the official hymnal of the Danish church, commonly referred to as "Kingo's Hymnal." It has not had much use except among the Danes and Norwegians. C.K. Solberg translated it in 1908, and it was published in the *Lutheran Hymnody*, 1913. The hymn was included in our last two hymnals.

WERDE MUNTER was composed by Johann Schop in 1642 for Johann Rist's hymn "Sink Not Yet, My Soul, to Slumber," but it has been used with many different texts, especially in Lutheran hymnals. It became the tune for Bach's arrangement of "Jesu, Joy of Man's Desiring."

Down in the Valley 'midst Lilies

It is the imaginative metaphors of the biblical *Song of Solomon* that inspired the author of "Down in the Valley. . . ." Like many others he saw Christ in the bridegroom. The text, which was popular in gospel songbooks around the turn of the century, was the work of H.M. Bradly. The first lines read: "Down in the valley among the sweet grasses / Walks my Beloved—His footprints I see." It was published in J.R. Sweeney's *Songs of Redeeming Love* (Philadelphia, 1882). The Swedish-American Methodist pastor, Henrik Wilhelm Eklund (1848-1920), translated it into Swedish, and it appeared in Sweden in *"Sånger för Ungdomsföreningar samt Böne- och Väckelsemöten"* (Songs for Youth Groups As Well As Prayer and Revival Meetings). In America it was included in several of the privately published songbooks as well as in *De Ungas Sångbok* and *Sions Basun*. Our English version is a translation of "Nere i dalen bland doftande liljor," done by S.C. Theodore Ramsey (b. 1889).

The source of NERE I DALEN is unknown. Most likely it is an American tune, since it was associated with the original text.

290 "Follow Me!" a Call So Tender

Based on John 10:27, 28
A. L. Skoog, 1856-1934

TENDER CALL 8.7.8.7. *with Refrain*
A. L. Skoog, 1856-1934

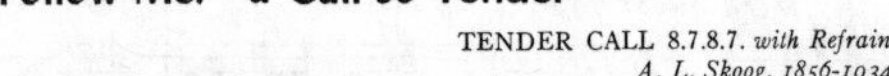

1 "Fol-low me!" a call so ten-der Falls up-on my lis-t'ning ear;
2 In - to pas-tures green he lead-eth, His own sheep he calls by name;
3 Lit - tle flock, fear not! he shields you From the dan-gers of the land;
4 In his steps, then, I would fol-low, Seek in him my all in all;
'Tis the voice of Christ, my Sav-ior, 'Tis the Shep-herd's call I hear.
When their feet are sore and wea-ry, In his arms he car-ries them.
Hear his pro-mise: none shall ev - er Pluck you from his might-y hand.
I am safe, what-e'er be-falls me, When I heed his ten-der call.
REFRAIN (after last stanza only)
O that call! lov-ing call! 'Tis the sweet - est voice of all! How it
draws me near-er to him, When I hear my Shep-herd's call.
draws me near - er hear my Shep - herd's call.

CALL OF CHRIST

"Follow Me!" a Call So Tender

This hymn, based on John 10:27 and 28 ("My sheep hear my voice, and I know them, and they follow me . . ."), was written in Swedish by A.L. Skoog—"'Följen mig!' en stämma ljuder." It was published in *Lilla Basunen*, 1890, and *Jubelklangen*, 1896. Then it appeared in *Mission Hymns*, 1921, in an English translation by the author.

TENDER CALL was composed by the author for use with this text.

75 For God So Loved All the World

Old Hundredth (Altered form)
8.8.9.6.

BETTY EHRENBORG (1818-1880)
Trans. by E. GUSTAV JOHNSON, 1946

LOUIS BOURGEOIS
Genevan Psalter, 1551

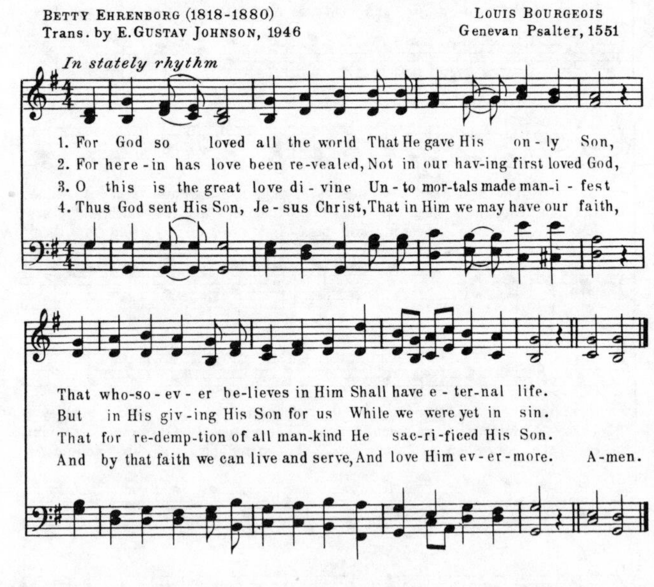

In stately rhythm
1. For God so loved all the world That He gave His on-ly Son,
2. For here-in has love been re-vealed, Not in our hav-ing first loved God,
3. O this is the great love di-vine Un-to mor-tals made man-i - fest
4. Thus God sent His Son, Je - sus Christ, That in Him we may have our faith,
That who-so-ev-er be-lieves in Him Shall have e - ter-nal life.
But in His giv-ing His Son for us While we were yet in sin.
That for re-demp-tion of all man-kind He sac-ri-ficed His Son.
And by that faith we can live and serve, And love Him ev-er-more. A-men.

For God So Loved All the World

"Så älskade Gud världen all" is a paraphrase of John 3:16 and 1 John 4:9-11. Upon the suggestion of Per Palmquist, Betty Ehrenborg-Posse translated several hymns from English and published them in a collection called *Andeliga Sånger för Barn* (Spiritual Songs for Children). In two later editions some of her original hymns were included. "Så älskade Gud världen . . ." appeared in the third and last edition in 1856. It was her most popular hymn and is still included in the *Psalmbok*. Most of the Swedish-American hymnals also printed it. It was translated by E.G. Johnson for *The Hymnal* (1950).

This arrangement of OLD HUNDREDTH is an alteration of the setting for Psalm 100 in the *Genevan Psalter*, 1551. The composer was Louis Bourgeois, whom Calvin had engaged to provide tunes for Marot's and Beza's metrical versions of the Psalms.

Give, O Lord, Unto Thy Servant

Lina Sandell never complained that God was severe or unfair, but she grieved over the fact that she often was rebellious and sinful. And more than anything else she wanted to live a life in submission to God. She discovered that she was unhappy so long as she felt that she was not resting in him. In this text she longs for that rest and peace which only Jesus can give. A literal translation of "Jesus, låt din rädda duva åter vila ut hos dig" is "Jesus, let your frightened dove once more rest with you." The figure is from Genesis 8:8 and 9 where the dove returns to the ark because she can find no other resting place. The song was first published in Ahnfelt's 1863 collection and it was included in the American edition of his songs and in most of the Swedish hymnals. E.G. Johnson translated the text for use in the *The Hymnal* (1950). It was believed that the hymn would have wider use if the word "weary" were eliminated. Hence the change in the present hymnal to "Give, O Lord, unto Thy Servant."

The tune, TILLFLYKT (Refuge), is a Swedish folk melody of unknown origin. This is not the melody used in Ahnfelt's 1863 edition but was the setting for the text in *Sionstoner*, 1889. Albert Lindström, music director in Jacob's Church, Stockholm, published several editions of *Ahnfelts Sånger* after the composer's death. Here the tune from *Sionstoner* was used, the one with which we are familiar.

Give, O Lord, unto Thy Servant
408
Lina Sandell, 1832-1903
Tr. E. Gustav Johnson, 1893-
TILLFLYKT 8.7.8.7.8.7.
Swedish Folk Melody
"Sionstoner," 1889
Harm. by A. Royce Eckhardt, 1937-
1 Give, O Lord, un - to thy serv - ant Rest and qui - et peace in thee, For the world's wild rush - ing cur - rent Has no rest - ing place for me. I am long - ing, I am long - ing, Safe with - in thy gates to be!
2 May thy ten - der Spir - it guide me And di - rect my ev - 'ry deed, Walk in love and grace be - side me, In thy pas - tures let me feed. Come, O Sav - ior! come, O Sav - ior, Give the strength I dai - ly need!
3 May not sin nor world - ly pleas - ure Lure me from thy path a - stray; Help me on - ly thee to treas - ure And thy pres - ence seek each day. Lead me, Sav - ior! lead me, Sav - ior, On the right-eous road, I pray!
4 Make me calm and still be - fore thee, Hide me in thy shel - ter mild; There no e - vil can come o'er me. There I'm safe from tem - pests wild. In that shel - ter, in that shel - ter, Is the ref - uge for thy child! A-men.
Words copyright 1950 by Covenant Press.
Harm. copyright 1973 by Covenant Press.
COMFORT AND PEACE

God, My God, in Heaven Above
90
Nils Frykman, 1842-1911
Tr. E. Gustav Johnson, 1893-
GUDS GODHET 7.7.7.3.
Oscar Ahnfelt, 1813-1882
1 God, my God, in heav'n a - bove, How a - bun - dant is thy love,
2 Thy com - pas - sion and thy grace, Great - er than my thought can trace,
3 E - ven when I can - not see What thy pur - pose is for me,
4 O my soul, with glad - ness sing, E - ven death has lost its sting;
5 Oth - er com - forts have I none, Earth's al - lure - ments now I shun;
For thy good - ness full and free Reach - es me!
O - ver all the earth ex - tend To the end.
I my trust can al - ways place In thy grace.
Mer - cy with its heal - ing ray Comes each day.
Grace thou hast for me in store Ev - er - more! A - men.
Words copyright 1950 by Covenant Press.
GOD'S LOVE AND FATHERHOOD
FAITH AND ASSURANCE

God, My God, in Heaven Above

The celebration of God's love and grace was a common theme of the pietists, and it is often found in the hymns of Nils Frykman. There is no reference to "Gud, min Gud och fader kär" in any of the writings about him, but evidently it was written especially for *Sions Basun*, Frykman being a member of the editorial committee. Both the original text and the translation by E.G. Johnson were printed in *The Hymnal* (1950).

GUDS GODHET was composed by Oscar Ahnfelt in 1850 as the setting for the allegorical text entitled, "Guds barn i mörker och ljus" (God's Children in Darkness and Light).

324
God's Name Is a Refuge to Hide Me
Guds namn
9. 8. 9. 8.
A. G. LINDQVIST, 1878
Trans. by JOSEPH E. ANDERSON, 1946
Anonymous
With assurance
1. God's name is a ref - uge to hide me; A
2. Sweet com - fort it brings in my sor - row, A
3. When sin and the world would as - sail me, This
4. When doubts and temp - ta - tions un - num - bered Like
5. His name spans the cold, surg - ing riv - er; A -
6. And there in the man - sions of glo - ry, The
shel - ter se - cure in the storm; A light in the val - ley, to
har - bor of bliss for my soul. It hap - pi - ness bodes for the
name is a ha - ven for me. It cour - age and strength will a -
le - gions a - gainst me were 'rayed; With fears though my heart were en -
cross to e - ter - ni - ty's shore It safe - ly will bear me for -
home of the heav - en - ly throng, It will be the theme of my
guide me When shad - ows of night round me form.
mor - row Though trou - bles like bil - lows may roll.
vail me If I to its shel - ter but flee.
cum - bered, My faith on this pow - er is stayed.
ev - er To dwell when my jour - ney is o'er.
sto - ry, The joy - ful re - frain of my song.
Words copyright, 1950, by The Covenant Book Concern.

God's Name Is a Refuge to Hide Me

Anders Lindqvist's lyric "Guds namn är ett fäste i nöden" speaks of the power of the name of God and the security in life and death under that name's protection. The song appeared first in *Sanningsvittnet* in 1878 under the title "Guds namn." J.A. Hultman included it in *Cymbalen*, 1888, and later it was published in *Sionsharpan*, *Evangelii Basun*, and *Sions Basun*. In 1946, it was translated by Joseph Anderson for inclusion in *The Hymnal* (1950).

The melody, GUDS NAMN, goes back to a song about the legendary Fingal, "Ensam I skuggrika dalen" (Alone in the Dark Valley). It is known through August Bondeson's *Visbok*, 1873.

Great Hills May Tremble

Lina Sandell was only eighteen when she wrote "Bergen må vika och högarna falla." She had written an article on the theme "Christianity's Power in Life and Death." She concluded with the words, "Truly, our God is a faithful God." Then she added two stanzas beginning, "Great hills may tremble. . . ." Later she revised the text, and it was published simultaneously in *Pilgrims-Sånger* and in B. Wadstrom's *Andeliga Sånger*. Many of the Swedish hymnals in America included the song. The English translation was the work of E. Lincoln Pearson. Bryan Jeffery Leech penned two additional stanzas for the 1973 hymnal.

The original tune, BERGEN MÅ VIKA, composed by Joel Blomqvist, is the tune commonly used in Sweden, but our tune of the same name—the source of which is unknown—seems to have appeared first in this country in *Hemlandssånger*, 1892. A.L. Skoog arranged it for inclusion in *Evangelii Basun*, 1894. There the song has a chorus, no doubt added by Skoog. In *Sions Basun* the song appeared with a different harmonization and without the chorus.

Great Hills May Tremble
102
Based on Isaiah 54:10
Lina Sandell, 1832-1903
Tr. E. Lincoln Pearson, 1917- , Sts. 1,4, alt.
Bryan Jeffery Leech, 1931- , Sts. 2,3
BERGEN MÅ VIKA 11.10.11.10.
Source unknown
1 Great hills may trem - ble and moun - tains may crum - ble,
2 Though peace be shat - tered by war's ag - i - ta - tion,
3 Strong to pre - serve us in mo - ments of dan - ger,
4 Teach us, O Lord, thy com - mand-ments to pon - der,
God's lov - ing - kind - ness re - main - eth se - cure;
Though change and ten - sion give birth to great fears,
Strong when frus - tra - tion and frail - ty in - crease;
Help us to heed them wher - ev - er we roam,
Peace he will give to the con - trite and hum - ble:
God still re - mains an un - shak - en foun - da - tion,
Strong to e - quip us for lov - ing the stran - ger,
Wait - ing the day thou shalt call us up yon - der,
Thus saith the Lord— his prom - ise is sure.
Strong to sup - port us through tur - bu - lent years;
Strong where our hu - man re - sourc - es may cease.
Trust - ing thy prom-ise to car - ry us home. A - men.
Words copyright 1950, 1973 by Covenant Press.
GOD'S ABIDING PRESENCE

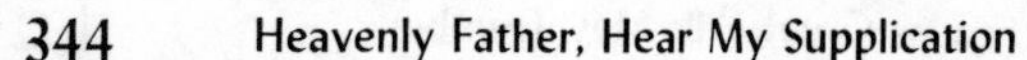
344 Heavenly Father, Hear My Supplication

Joel Blomqvist, 1840-1930
Tr. Carl E. Backstrom, 1901-
FLEMMING 11.11.11.6.
Friedrich F. Flemming, 1778-1813
1 Heav - en - ly Fa - ther, hear my sup - pli - ca - tion;
2 Draw me, Re - deem - er, I would seek thee sole - ly,
3 Dwell thou, O Sav - ior, in my heart for - ev - er,
I bow be - fore thee in thy con - gre - ga - tion Hum - ble and
Help me to cher - ish, love, o - bey thee whol - ly, Ful - ly sur -
Thou who hast prom - ised noth - ing shall us sev - er, Com - fort and
need - y, seek - ing thy sal - va - tion, Hear thou my prayer, O God!
ren - dered, live a life that's ho - ly, Hear thou my prayer, O God!
lead me, I would leave thee nev - er, Hear thou my prayer, O God! A-men.
A higher setting may be found at No. 274

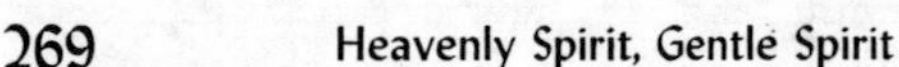
269 Heavenly Spirit, Gentle Spirit

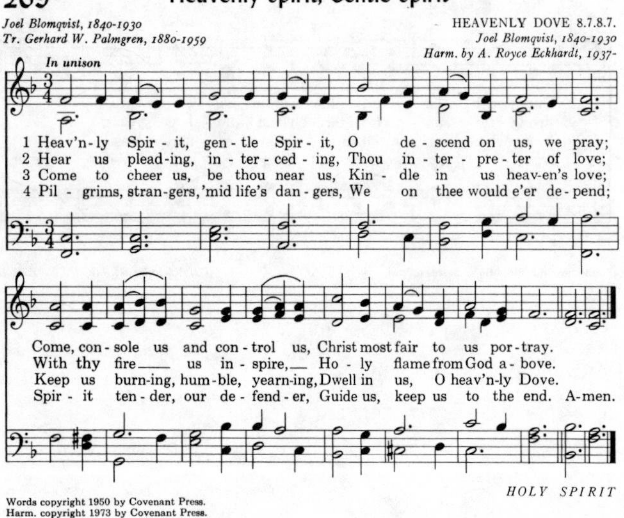
Joel Blomqvist, 1840-1930
Tr. Gerhard W. Palmgren, 1880-1959
HEAVENLY DOVE 8.7.8.7.
Joel Blomqvist, 1840-1930
Harm. by A. Royce Eckhardt, 1937-
In unison
1 Heav'n-ly Spir - it, gen - tle Spir - it, O de - scend on us, we pray;
2 Hear us plead - ing, in - ter - ced - ing, Thou in - ter - pre - ter of love;
3 Come to cheer us, be thou near us, Kin - dle in us heav-en's love;
4 Pil - grims, stran-gers, 'mid life's dan - gers, We on thee would e'er de - pend;
Come, con - sole us and con - trol us, Christ most fair to us por - tray.
With thy fire us in - spire, Ho - ly flame from God a - bove.
Keep us burn-ing, hum - ble, yearn-ing, Dwell in us, O heav'n-ly Dove.
Spir - it ten - der, our de - fend - er, Guide us, keep us to the end. A-men.
HOLY SPIRIT

Heavenly Father, Hear My Supplication

An important theme in Joel Blomqvist's hymns was sanctification—longing for total consecration and discipleship. This is the prayer in "Helige Fader, böj ditt öra neder" (. . . Bow Down Your Ear). It was published first in his *Sabbatsklockan*, 1878, with the Flemming tune. Most of the Swedish hymnals of all denominations in America carried the song. It was translated by Carl E. Backstrom for *The Covenant Hymnal* (1931).

FLEMMING gets its name from the composer, Friederich Ferdinand Flemming (1778-1813), a Berlin physician. It was written in 1811 for male voices, to the ode of Horace's "Integer vitae."

Heavenly Spirit, Gentle Spirit

"Himladuva, Ande ljuva" is the work of Joel Blomqvist. It was published in his *Sabbatsklockan*, 1887, under the title "Pingstpsalm" (Pentecost Hymn). Evidently it was not used in Sweden, for it is not to be found in any of their hymnals and Oscar Lövgren makes no mention of it. It was included in most of the Swedish hymnals in this country except those of the Augustana Lutheran Church. In 1946, Gerhard Palmgren translated it for inclusion in *The Hymnal* (1950).

The rather unusual tune, HEAVENLY DOVE (formerly, HIMLADUVA), was composed by Blomqvist and has always been associated with this text. It is very easily sung in unison, having a range of only five notes.

Hide Not Thy Face, O My Savior

There is a tradition which says that "Herre, fördölj ej ditt ansikte för mig" was written in sorrow by Lina Sandell immediately after the tragic death of her father. Oscar Lövgren believes that if it had been written after the tragedy, it could not have been ready for publication in *Budbäraren*, October,1858. There was also the report that this was one of the fourteen songs that B. Wadstrom received from "a pastor's daughter in Småland" late in 1857 and early in 1858, which would point to an earlier date.

The song is based on a folk love song about a girl awaiting her lover—"Fjärran han dröjer . . ." (Far Away He Delays . . .). And the last line is "Are you coming? Are you coming soon?" Lövgren makes a further point for an earlier date by insisting that at the time of her father's death Lina Sandell was in no mood to choose a secular love song as a basis for her hymn. The hymn found its way into most of the Swedish hymnals (except the *Psalmbok*) in Sweden and America, including *Hemlandssånger*, 1881. The English translation by Joseph Anderson was first published in *The Hymnal* (1950).

LOST IN THE NIGHT was the name given the tune by the 1973 Hymnal Commission because of its popularization by F. Melius Christiansen in the anthem of that name. It is taken from *Karelen*, a Finnish collection published by K. Collan and R. Lagi in 1857. In that book it served as the setting for the folk love song mentioned above.

235 Hide Not Thy Face, O My Savior
Lina Sandell, 1832-1903
Tr. Joseph E. Anderson, 1890-1954
LOST IN THE NIGHT 11.11. with Refrain
Finnish Folk Melody
"Karelen," 1857
1 Hide not thy face, O my Sav - ior— be near me;
2 Still far re - moved from my home - land, I wan - der;
3 While thou dost tar - ry, my path wouldst thou bright - en;
4 Grant, then, O Lord, that I fear thee, a - dore thee;
5 Help me the bur - den to bear thou hast giv - en;
Com - fort and bless— while I pray, wilt thou hear me:
Here but a pil - grim and stran - ger, I pon - der:
Sor - rows and cares of my heart wouldst thou light - en.
Hum - bly in spir - it I bow down be - fore thee.
Give me at last, Lord, a crown in thy heav - en.
REFRAIN
Bless - ed Re - deem - er, my Sav - ior and Com - fort - er,
Art thou com - ing soon? Art thou com - ing soon? A - men.
COMING IN GLORY
Words copyright 1950 by Covenant Press.

5 Holy Majesty! Before Thee
Samuel J. Hedborn, 1783-1849
Tr. Composite
WACHET AUF Irregular
Philipp Nicolai, 1556-1608
Harm. by Norman E. Johnson, 1928-
1 Ho - ly Maj - es - ty! be - fore thee We bow to wor - ship and a -
2 Bless us, Lord, and keep us ev - er, Re - veal thy face and show thy
dore thee; Our hearts thy sov-'reign-ty ac - claim. Bound-less are thy
fa - vor; Up - on thy peo - ple smile with peace. Here we sing thy
might and glo - ry, All heav'n and earth re - peat thy sto - ry;
name re - joic - ing, Un - til thy praise we shall be voic - ing
Lo! all thy works ex - alt thy name. To thee all cher - u - bim
In loft - ier strains that nev - er cease, And with thy cher - u - bim
And all thy ser - a - phim Sing ho - san - na! Ho - ly is God,
And all thy ser - a - phim Sing ho - san - na! Ho - ly is God,
Our Lord of pow'r, Of grace and wis - dom ev - er - more!
Our Lord of pow'r, Of grace and wis - dom ev - er - more! A - men.
ADORATION
Harm. copyright 1973 by Covenant Press.

Holy Majesty! Before Thee

"Höga Majestät, vi alla" is one of the most majestic of the Swedish hymns. It appeared in the writer's own publication, *Psalmer av Hedborn*, 1812. About his hymns Samuel Hedborn had the following to say:

> *The language of my hymns is not modern, but I hope it is Christian. The fountains are Moses and the prophets, the evangelists and the apostles. If anyone thinks that this language is too sophisticated, let him consider the common folk. The Bible is their only education. I, who was born and until my fourteenth year lived among them, know that they understand enough of the Bible for that which is most essential—to seek the Kingdom of God and his righteousness. I look upon religion as a divine revelation which defends itself, and from which it is reprehensible to take away one letter or add thereto. In this spirit ought churchly hymns be created—Christlike, simple, and sublime.*

Originally there were eight stanzas, but only seven were included in the 1819 *Psalmbok*. The hymn appeared in most Swedish hymnals in this country. It was published in the Augustana *Hymnal*, 1925, in a translation by August W. Kjellstrand (1864-1930). Kjellstrand's translation begins with "glorious" instead of "holy." All English hymnals of the Covenant print only two stanzas in a composite translation.

WACHET AUF is Nicolai's melody for this so-called "King of Chorales." Although attributed to Nicolai, the tune is generally thought to be an adaptation of older material. Bach used the melody in three movements of *Cantata 140*.

How Beautiful, Serene, and Grand

"Hur skönt att vandra på livets stig" is exclusively a song of the Evangelical Covenant Church of America. It is found in none of the hymnals in Sweden, and Lövgren makes no mention of it in his lexicon or in his biography of Frykman. Its initial appearance was in *Sions Basun*, 1908, and evidently Frykman, one of the editors, wrote the text for inclusion there. The translation by E.G. Johnson was first published in *The Hymnal* (1950).

The name of the tune, HEM DET GÅR (Homeward Bound), is taken from the first words of the chorus. It was written by William Kirkpatrick (1838-1921), a Philadelphia musician who composed many song tunes and was associated with the publication of at least one hundred collections of gospel songs. Among his musical settings in our present hymnal are: "Away in a Manger" (second tune), "King of My Life I Crown Thee Now," and "A Wonderful Savior Is Jesus My Lord."

How Glad I Am Each Christmas Eve

This delightful Christmas carol by Marie Wexelsen is one of the few songs we have from the Norwegian. The original, "Jeg er saa glad hver julekveld," had nine stanzas. It was published in *Nynorsk Salmebog*, 1926. An English translation appeared in the *Concordia Hymnbook* (Norwegian Edition), 1918. Peter Andrew Sveeggen made a new translation for the *Concordia Hymnal* (Augsburg Publishing House), 1932, in which stanzas seven and eight were omitted. This was the source for our version of the song. *The Hymnal* (1950) had a quite different translation by J. Prudence Kearney. The beginning line was "When Lights Are Lit on the Christmas Tree."

CHRISTMAS EVE is by Peder Knudsen. It was composed toward the close of his life while he was organist at Åresund.

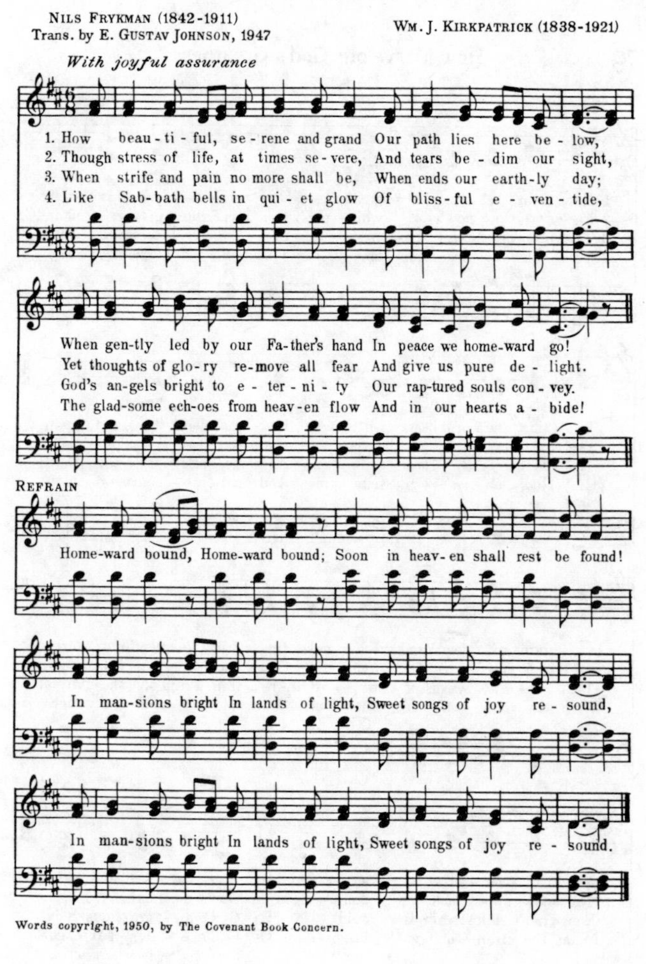
HEAVEN AND HOMELAND
508 How Beautiful, Serene and Grand
Hem det går
8. 6. 9. 6. with refrain
NILS FRYKMAN (1842-1911)
Trans. by E. GUSTAV JOHNSON, 1947
WM. J. KIRKPATRICK (1838-1921)
With joyful assurance
1. How beau-ti-ful, se-rene and grand Our path lies here be-low,
2. Though stress of life, at times se-vere, And tears be-dim our sight,
3. When strife and pain no more shall be, When ends our earth-ly day;
4. Like Sab-bath bells in qui-et glow Of bliss-ful e-ven-tide,
When gen-tly led by our Fa-ther's hand In peace we home-ward go!
Yet thoughts of glo-ry re-move all fear And give us pure de-light.
God's an-gels bright to e-ter-ni-ty Our rap-tured souls con-vey.
The glad-some ech-oes from heav-en flow And in our hearts a-bide!
REFRAIN
Home-ward bound, Home-ward bound; Soon in heav-en shall rest be found!
In man-sions bright In lands of light, Sweet songs of joy re-sound,
In man-sions bright In lands of light, Sweet songs of joy re-sound.
Words copyright, 1950, by The Covenant Book Concern.

How Glad I Am Each Christmas Eve
131
Marie Wexelsen, 1832-1911
Tr. Peter A. Sveeggen, 1881-1959
CHRISTMAS EVE C.M.
Peder Knudsen, 1819-1863
1 How glad I am each Christ-mas Eve, The night of Je-sus' birth!
2 The lit-tle child in Beth-le-hem, He was a king in-deed;
3 He dwells a-gain in heav-en's realm, The Son of God to-day;
4 How glad I am each Christ-mas Eve! His prais-es then I sing;
Then like the sun the star shone forth, And an-gels sang on earth.
He came from his high state in heav'n, Down to a world in need.
But he knows all the lit-tle ones, And hears them when they pray.
He o-pens then for ev-'ry child The pal-ace of the King.
Reproduced from The Concordia Hymnal, copyright © 1932 and 1960, by permission of Augsburg Publishing House, Minneapolis, Minnesota, copyright owner.
BIRTH

79 How Marvelous God's Greatness
Valdimar Briem, 1848-1930
Tr. Charles Venn Pilcher, 1879-1961
BLOMSTERTID 7.6.7.6.D.
Swedish "Koralbok," 1697
1 How mar - vel - ous God's great - ness, How glo - ri - ous his might!
2 Each ti - ny flow'r-et whis - pers The great life - giv - er's name;
3 The o - cean's vast a - byss - es In one grand psalm re - cord
4 The star - ry hosts are sing - ing Thru all the light-strewn sky
To this the world bears wit - ness In won - ders day and night.
The might - y moun - tain mass - es His maj - es - ty pro - claim;
The deep mys - te - rious coun - sels And mer - cies of the Lord;
Of God's ma - jes - tic tem - ple And pal - ace - courts on high;
In form of flow'r and snow - flake, In morn's re-splend-ent birth,
The hol - low vales are hymn - ing God's shel - ter for his own;
The i - cy waves of win - ter Are thun-d'ring on the strand;
When in these out - er cham - bers Such glo - ry gilds the night,
In af - ter - glow at e - ven, In sky and sea and earth.
The snow-capped peaks are point - ing To God's al - might - y throne.
E'en grief's chill stream is guid - ed By God's all - gra - cious hand.
What the tran - scend - ent bright - ness Of God's e - ter - nal light!

Words from *The Lutheran Service Book and Hymnal*, by permission of the Commission on the Liturgy and Hymnal.

GOD IN NATURE

How Marvelous God's Greatness

Our only Icelandic hymn, "Hve dyralegur er Drottinn," was written by Valdimar Briem, a pastor and vice-bishop. It appeared in the Icelandic hymnal of 1886 along with 102 original texts and thirty-nine translations by Briem. The hymn beautifully pictures some of the rugged scenes from the rocky coasts and mountainous terrain of the country. The translator was Charles Venn Pilcher, an Anglican clergyman. The song was introduced to America through *The Lutheran Service Book and Hymnal*, 1958.

BLOMSTERTID is from the Swedish *Koralbok* of 1697, where it was the setting for "Den blomstertid nu kommer" (The Season of Flowers Is Now Coming). This was a song by I. Kolmodin about spring, along with a prayer that Jesus would be our joy and light and kindle love in our hearts. But the melody is older; it is the setting for a thirty-one-verse "visa" about a Roman count who desired to visit the grave of Christ. Though his wife discouraged him, he went, was taken captive by the Turks, and was put to work as a slave. His wife, dressed as a monk, went to the king, and through her pleasing appearance and beautiful harp music was able to win his favor and the freedom of her husband, though neither he nor the king knew her identity.

How Wonderful It Is

Although the practice was not in accord with the law of the Church of Sweden, free communion services with lay ministration became quite common during the Rosenian revival. It was out of this experience that "Det är en härlig ting" was born. One Sunday afternoon Nils Frykman was on his way to a meeting. "To write was like a game," he wrote later. "I sat on the seat of the cart and sang in my heart, as though we were sitting as brothers and sisters at the Lord's table. O, how we sang it later!" Per Olsson, a pastor who was born in Sunne, related that as an eighteen-year-old he participated in a communion service in the Magnus Olsson home in Torvnäs. Frykman led the service, and the new song was sung. It was published in *Hemlandssånger*, 1877, and has been included in the hymnals of the Swedish Covenant ever since. In this country it has been limited to hymnals used in the Covenant. The English translation in *The Hymnal* (1950) was by E.G. Johnson.

Frykman composed the music for his text. The name of the tune was changed from DET ÄR EN HÄRLIG TING to GEMENSKAP (Fellowship).

I Have a Friend, So Patient, Kind, Forbearing

"Jag har en vän, så huld, så mild, så tålig" first appeared in *Pietisten*, 1851. In 1859, it was included in *Pilgrims-Sånger*, which was published by the author, Gustaf Palmquist, and his brother, Per. In this hymnal credit was given to Carl Rosenius for reworking the text. The song proved to be quite popular and was included in most Swedish collections on both sides of the Atlantic. Its first appearance in translation, by John Jesperson, was in the Augustana *Hymnal*, 1901. It has been included in all English Covenant hymnals except the current one.

JAG HAR EN VÄN was adapted from a Swedish folk melody for use with the text. It was published in the music edition of *Pilgrims-Sånger*, 1860.

520 How Wonderful It Is
Nils Frykman, 1842-1911
Tr. E. Gustav Johnson, 1893-
GEMENSKAP 6.6.7.6.
Nils Frykman, 1842-1911
1 How won-der-ful it is To come in per-fect bliss, With saints in sweet com-mun-ion, To such a feast as this.
2 Of great-er joy to me No oth-er thing can be, Than shar-ing with God's chil-dren This love and har-mo-ny.
3 I know that he is near, Our friend and Sav-ior dear; I feel his ho-ly pres-ence, His lov-ing words I hear.
4 My soul is now at ease, My bless-ings here in-crease, Since from all guilt the Sav-ior Has giv-en me re-lease.
5 His full a-bun-dant grace In truth I can em-brace, And there-fore in his keep-ing My life and soul I place.
6 O broth-ers, sing with joy, With praise your tongues em-ploy; The good-ness of his bless-ing The world can-not de-stroy.
7 No mor-tal here be-low Can ev-er see or know The glo-ry that in heav-en The Fa-ther will be-stow.
Words copyright 1950 by Covenant Press.

380 I Have a Friend, So Patient, Kind, Forbearing

Jag har en vän

11. 10. 11. 10. Iambic

GUSTAF PALMQVIST, 1851, and
CARL OLOF ROSENIUS (1816-1868)
Trans. by JOHN JESPERSON (1858-1943)

Swedish folk melody

In quiet trust

1. I have a Friend, so pa-tient, kind, for-bear-ing, Of all my
2. He is my Lord, my Friend, yea, He's my Broth-er; And Je-sus
3. My poor and wretch-ed soul He bought so dear-ly, And freed from
4. Thus I'm re-deemed; no more the law pre-vail-eth, For Christ, the
5. With hal-le-lu-jahs here I'd tell the sto-ry, My Lord to

friends this Friend doth love me best; Though I am weak and sin-ful,
Christ is His most bless-ed name. He loves more ten-der-ly than
con-dem-na-tion, death, and hell; The old and bit-ter foe He
Lord, is my Re-deem-er's name; His pre-cious blood more than my
praise, to laud and mag-ni-fy; And praise His name for-ev-er-

yet when shar-ing His love and mer-cy I am ev-er blest.
an-y moth-er: To rest in Him is more than wealth and fame.
crushed com-plete-ly: My soul, re-joice and sing, for all is well!
sin a-vail-eth; And cleans-eth me from all my guilt and shame.
more in glo-ry, Be-fore His throne with all the saints on high.

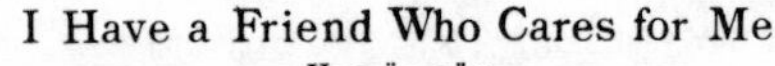
367 I Have a Friend Who Cares for Me

JOY
Han är när
8. 7. 8. 7. with refrain
A. L. Skoog, 1892
Trans. by Joseph E. Anderson, 1946
A. L. Skoog, 1892
Joyfully
1. I have a Friend who cares for me, He is every moment near;
2. Though His lov-ing face I can - not see, He is ev-ery mo-ment near;
3. My hap-py hours with praise o'er-flow, He is ev-ery mo-ment near;
4. This as - sur-ance cheers me on the way; He is ev-ery mo-ment near;
In love He leads me con - stant-ly, He is ev-ery moment near.
I hear Him whis - per ten - der - ly: "I am ev-ery mo-ment near."
In dan - ger how se - cure to know He is ev-ery mo-ment near.
When eve-ning shad-ows end my day, He is ev-ery mo-ment near.
Refrain
He is near, ev-er near, Ev-ery bur-dened heart to cheer,
He is near, ev-er near,
Ev-ery mo-ment to the jour-ney's end Is my Sav-ior ev - er near.
Words copyright, 1950, by The Covenant Book Concern.
Music used by permission of the A. L. Skoog Estate.

I Have a Friend Who Cares for Me

In one of his letters A.L. Skoog wrote:

> *How did I come to write any certain song? . . . Some came easily and without any effort; others required not so little thought and patience. I sat one night by myself on a railroad train and gazed out over the moonlit landscape. The atmosphere together with the rhythmic music of the wheels teased a melody out of my mind, which I notated. I wrote immediately a few verses, and there stood "Han är när."*

I Have a Friend Who Loveth Me 416
Nils Frykman, 1842-1911
FRYKMAN L.M. with Refrain
Nils Frykman, 1842-1911
Harm. by A. Royce Eckhardt, 1937-
1 I have a friend who lov-eth me, He gave his life on Cal-va - ry;
2 My Sav-ior's love, so full and free, Doth light the wea - ry way for me;
3 I have a friend, a might-y friend, Up - on his pow'r I may de - pend;
4 O broth-er, join us in our song! This friend to you would fain be - long;
Up - on the cross my sins he bore, And I am saved for ev - er - more.
It fills with joy each pass-ing day And drives my sor - rows all a - way.
He reign-eth o - ver ev - 'ry land, O'er val - ley, hill, o'er sea and strand.
Tho far from what you'd like to be, His grace suf - fi - cient is for thee.
REFRAIN
O hal - le - lu - jah, he's my friend! He guides me to the jour-ney's end;
He walks be-side me all the way And will be-stow a crown some day.
Harm. copyright 1973 by Covenant Press.
JOY

This was the title of the song. The original opening line was "O jag har en vän som älskar mig." It was published in *Sionsharpan* and *Sions Basun*. It was translated in 1946 by Joseph Anderson for *The Hymnal* (1950).

The tune, HAN ÄR NAR (He Is Near), gets its name from the first phrase of the refrain.

I Have a Friend Who Loveth Me

"Jag har en vän some älskar mig," one of the best loved of Frykman's songs, was written when he was pastor of the Salem circuit in Minnesota. In a little booklet entitled "Mina Sångers Historia" (The History of My Songs), he wrote:

> *How long has it taken to write a song? There is great variation. Sometimes, but very seldom, it takes only a little while or several hours. . . ."Jag har en vän" was written at Salem when I was riding from the town. Both words and music were ready in less than twenty minutes.*

The exact date of composition is not known, but the song was included in the first edition of *Sionsharpan*, 1890. This would place it during the time a revival swept through the circuit of churches. The identity of the translator is not known, but *The Covenant Hymnal* (1931), where the song first appeared in English, gave the initials "E.H.J."

In the 1950 hymnal the tune was given two names—JAG HAR EN VÄN or FRYKMAN. Since this is perhaps his best known melody, the Hymnal Commission of 1973 decided on FRYKMAN.

I Have a Future All Sublime

Frykman once was asked which of his songs he considered to be the best. Without hesitation he answered, "Min framtidsdag är ljus och lång." In his biography of the hymnist, Oscar Lövgren relates an interesting account about the writing of the song. In the winter of 1883, the singer-preacher was on an evangelistic tour. One day he was the guest of Enoch Olsson in the town of Hugnvik. The visit was a high point in the life of the family, and forty years later one of the sons related his memory of the experience:

> *Soon after his arrival our guest was left alone for a while, and we heard him playing the organ. I became curious and carefully watched through the open door. I saw him standing, playing a short line, after which he turned to his writing board, and still standing, wrote on a sheet of paper. After persistently working this way for a while, it appeared that he was*

I Have a Future All Sublime **609**

Nils Frykman, 1842-1911
Tr. A. L. Skoog, 1856-1934, St. 1
Tr. Gustaf Frykman, 1873-1953, Sts. 2-5

MIN FRAMTIDSDAG L.M.
Nils Frykman, 1842-1911

1 I have a future all sublime, Beyond the realms of space and time, Where my Redeemer I shall see And sorrow nevermore shall be.
2 A precious heritage is mine, In heaven kept by love divine; What serves me best, while here below, My Father will provide, I know.
3 Praised be the Lord! he planned for me— I need have no anxiety; He would alone my burden bear And make me free from earthly care.
4 Now peace and joy within me dwell, I sing with gladness, "All is well!" Protected, guided by his might, He leads me to the land of light.
5 Dear Lord, I pray that I may be More wholly yielded unto thee, While on the way I yet remain, Before my heav'nly home I gain. Amen.
Min framtidsdag är ljus och lång, Den räcker bort om tidens tvång, Där Gud och Lammet säll jag ser Och ingen nöd skall vara mer.

Words copyright 1950 by Covenant Press. *LIFE EVERLASTING*

> *satisfied that his work was complete. And before he left our home, he played and sang his new song, "Min framtidsdag. . . ."*

It was ready also to send to *Sanningsvittnet*, where it was published November 8, 1883. Soon it made its way into most of the free church hymnals in Sweden as well as America. The text was translated by A.L. Skoog for use in *Mission Hymns* and later in *The Covenant Hymnal* (1931). The translation of the first stanza by Skoog was retained in *The Hymnal* (1950), but the remaining stanzas were the work of Gustaf Frykman.

As noted above, the tune, MIN FRAMTIDSDAG, was composed by the author of the text.

I Sing of the Savior

In many of the songs of the "Sunshine Singer," J.A. Hultman gives expression to his unbounded joy in Christ, the Savior. The songs are reminiscent of the Moravian spirit one meets in *Sions Nya Sånger*; "O nu vill jag sjunga en fröjdefull sång" is definitely in this vein. It was written under the inspiration of a spiritual awakening in the Covenant church in Omaha, where the writer was the pastor from 1881 to 1895. The song appeared first in his *Cymbalen*, 1885, and later in *Sionsharpan* and *Sions Basun*. Its first publication in English was in *The Hymnal* (1950), in a translation by E.G. Johnson.

The tune, O NU VILL JAG SJUNGA, was composed for the text by Hultman.

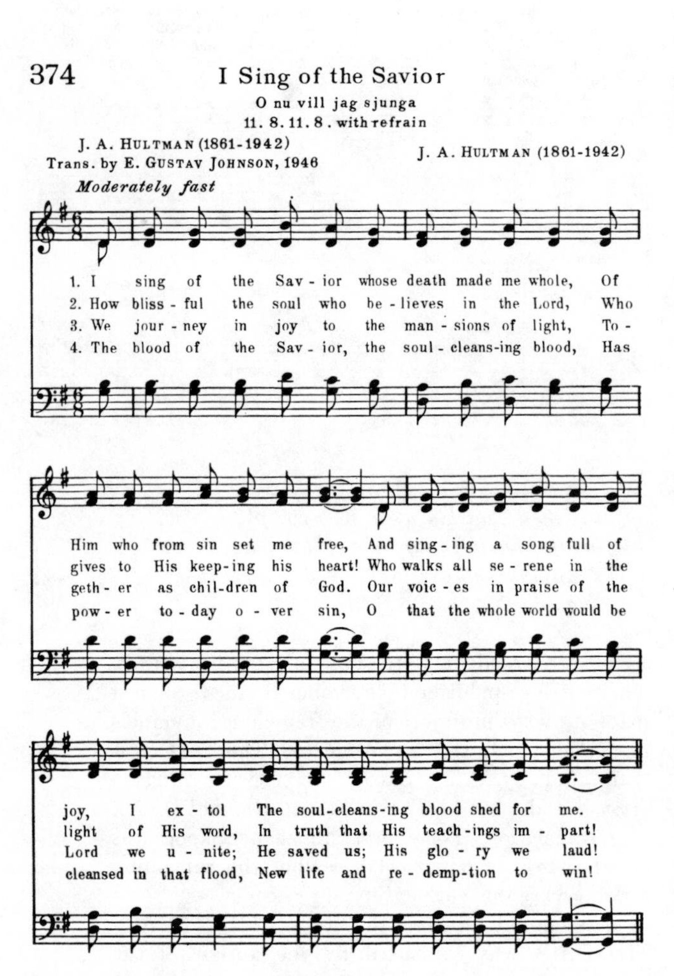
374
I Sing of the Savior
O nu vill jag sjunga
11. 8. 11. 8. with refrain
J. A. Hultman (1861-1942)
Trans. by E. Gustav Johnson, 1946
J. A. Hultman (1861-1942)
Moderately fast
1. I sing of the Sav - ior whose death made me whole, Of
2. How bliss - ful the soul who be - lieves in the Lord, Who
3. We jour - ney in joy to the man - sions of light, To -
4. The blood of the Sav - ior, the soul - cleans-ing blood, Has
Him who from sin set me free, And sing - ing a song full of
gives to His keep-ing his heart! Who walks all se - rene in the
geth - er as chil-dren of God. Our voic - es in praise of the
pow - er to - day o - ver sin, O that the whole world would be
joy, I ex - tol The soul-cleans-ing blood shed for me.
light of His word, In truth that His teach-ings im - part!
Lord we u - nite; He saved us; His glo - ry we laud!
cleansed in that flood, New life and re - demp-tion to win!
Words copyright, 1950, by The Covenant Book Concern.
Music used by permission of Mrs. J. A. Hultman.

Refrain
The blood of the Sav - ior re-deemed me, In right - eous-ness
now I a - bide! In mer - cy and love He es -
teemed me As worth - y of be - ing His bride!

I Sing with Joy and Gladness

Nils Frykman relates that it was during the time he was being harassed by the school board for his activities as a lay preacher and singer that he wrote this song. It is easy to understand that he should be depressed at this time, but he never spent much time nursing his ills. "I felt so happy one day," he wrote, "as I sat in my rocking chair and thought about God's goodness toward me. And then came the song, words, and melody at the same time: 'Nu är jag nöjd och glader. . . .' " He added that the fourth stanza—beginning, "The evil adversary . . ."—was written with the school board in mind. "Then I was not afraid or easily frightened."

When he submitted the song to *Sanningsvittnet* (May 5, 1881), he sent along a three-verse poem in which he likened the text and melody of the song to little children. The final lines bore this message to the editor: "Send the children home in the event you find them too small to go out into the world." Later he wrote, "But he thought the children were big enough, and so sent them out. Since then they have journeyed about . . . and have been well received, because they have not come to beg, but to give, to serve, and to be profitable." This was true, because the song was published in many of the free church hymnals in Sweden and the United States. In *The Hymnal* (1950) it is one of the many translations of E.G. Johnson.

For *The Covenant Hymnal* (1973) the tune name was changed from NU ÄR JAG NÖJD to JOYFUL PILGRIM.

I Sing with Joy and Gladness
418
Nils Frykman, 1842-1911
Tr. E. Gustav Johnson, 1893-
JOYFUL PILGRIM 13.13.13.8.
Nils Frykman, 1842-1911
1 I sing with joy and glad - ness, my soul has found re - lease;
2 My for - mer res - o - lu - tions to lead a bet - ter life
3 When thoughts of guilt op - press me and I thru weak-ness fail,
4 The e - vil ad - ver - sar - y may in his fu - ry smite;
5 Thus march - ing on cou - ra - geous, with joy I see my goal—
Now free from sin and sad - ness, with God I live in peace:
Were on - ly vain il - lu - sions—my soul was still at strife:
The Sav - ior yet will bless me, his mer - cy does pre - vail:
I fear not, for I car - ry God's ar - mor in the fight:
The bless - ing of the a - ges, the ha - ven of my soul:
His ev - er - last - ing mer - cy to me has been re -
Now on the love of Je - sus com - plete - ly I re -
For - give - ness for the sin - ner his lov - ing heart pro -
The word, di - vine and might - y, shall vic - to - ry ob -
And on the pil - grim jour - ney my voice in song I
vealed, His truth in my heart has been sealed.
ly— For me he was will - ing to die.
vides, His faith - ful - ness ev - er a - bides.
tain, Its strength shall for - ev - er re - main.
raise, My God and my Sav - ior to praise.
Words copyright 1950 by Covenant Press.
JOY

159 I Think of That Star of Long Ago
A. L. Skoog, 1856-1934
BETLEHEMS STJÄRNA 9.10.10.11. with Refrain
A. L. Skoog, 1856-1934
1 I think of that star of long a - go That light - ed the
2 "A child un - to us is born"– O joy! To sin - blight - ed
3 It sheds on the world its peace - ful rays, And greets ev - 'ry
wan - der - ers' path be - low; In faith I look up, and
earth comes high heav'n's en - voy; Now o - ver my path that
mor - tal with heav'n - ly grace; To Beth - le - hem's babe I
o'er me I see That star in its beau - ty— still shin - ing for me.
dear mem - o - ry— A star in its beau - ty— is shin - ing for me.
has - ten with thee, O star in thy beau - ty— still shin - ing for me.
REFRAIN (after last stanza only)
O star that once shone o - ver Beth - le - hem! Thy beams yet to
mor - tals great joy pro - claim; The Lord to a - dore, I
has - ten with thee, O star in thy beau - ty— still shin - ing for me.
EPIPHANY

I Think of That Star of Long Ago

"Som fordom i fjärran österland" is one of A.L. Skoog's songs first written in Swedish and later translated into English by the author. The Swedish version first appeared in *Evangelii Basun* and later in *Jubelklangen* and *Sions Basun*. An English version was printed in *Ancora*, 1901, one of Skoog's collections of anthems. There the words "beautiful guide-star" were used instead of "star in its beauty," and there were differences in the chorus as well. The present version first appeared in *Mission Hymns*.

BETLEHEMS STJÄRNA was composed by Skoog in 1889 for this text.

I with Thee Would Begin

Lina Sandell's "Låt mig börja med dig" has often been called a New Year's prayer. But it may serve also as an opening hymn or at any "beginning" occasion. It has been used at weddings, with a change from the singular to the plural. The text was first published in *Barnens Tidning* (The Children's Magazine) in 1875. As a hymn it appeared first in *Hemlandstoner*, 1884. Though not as popular as some of her works, it was used in several free church hymnals in Sweden and was introduced to American Covenant congregations through *Sionsharpan* and *Sions Basun*. It was translated by A. Samuel Wallgren for publication in *The Covenant Hymnal* (1931).

The tune, BEGYNNELSE (Beginning), formerly known by the opening words of the first line, was composed by Wilhelm Theodor Söderberg for the Sandell text.

I with Thee Would Begin

353

Lina Sandell, 1832-1903
Tr. A. Samuel Wallgren, 1885-1940
BEGYNNELSE 12.9.12.9.9.
Wilhelm Theodor Söderberg, 1845-1922
Harm. by James P. Davies, 1913-
1 I with thee would be - gin, O my Sav - ior so dear,
2 I with thee would be - gin— and go forth in thy name,
3 Let thy word all - di - vine be my lamp, in whose light
4 I with thee would be - gin— yea, and hear one more prayer,
On the way that I still must pur - sue; I with thee would be -
Which a - lone doth sal - va - tion be - stow; Fold me close to thy
I may con - stant - ly keep to thy way; And each day wouldst thou
I would close with thee too my brief day; And when day - light has
gin ev - 'ry day grant-ed here, As my ear - nest re - solve I re -
breast, where found joy all who came: There is ref - uge for me too, I
cleanse me a - new, make me white In the blood shed for me on that
failed let me sleep in thy care, Un - til wak - ing thy child thou dost
new: To be and re - main thine for - ev - er.
know, Though all in this world is con - fu - sion.
day The cross thou didst suf - fer, Lord Je - sus.
say, "Come, live with me ev - er in heav - en!" A - men.

Harm. copyright 1973 by Covenant Press. *ASPIRATION*

If Asked Whereon I Rest My Claim 388

"Brödraförsamlingen," Copenhagen, 1748
Tr. A. Samuel Wallgren, 1885-1940
SALIGHETSGRUND 8.6.8.6.8.8.8.6.
Swedish Folk Melody
"Sions Nya Sånger," 1874
1 If asked where-on I rest my claim To full sal - va - tion's joy,
2 This is my hope's foun-da - tion firm, Which ev - er shall en - dure;
If noth - ing more I need to name Or oth - er words em - ploy
And, at the end of life's brief term, I'll rest there-on se - cure:
Be - sides our Sav-ior's blood and wounds, To me all - sat - is - fy-ing grounds,
Then dread-ed death shall lose its sting As of my Sav-ior's wounds I sing;
I an - swer then, "My claim is good! 'Tis based on Je - sus' blood."
His pre-cious blood shall be the key That o - pens heav'n for me.

If Asked Whereon I Rest My Claim

This is an example of a text from Denmark that has come to us through Sweden. "Om nogen mig nu spørge vil" is from the Herrnhut collection, *Guds Børnssende Bryllups-Glaede over Brudgummens Naervaerelse,* which was published in Copenhagen in 1748. The Moravian emphasis upon the blood of Christ is basic in the theme of the song. "Om Någon mig åtspörja vill," the Swedish translaion by Fredrik Engelke, was published in his *Lofsånger och Andeliga Wisor*, 1872. It sould be noted that although several hymnals credit Erik Pontoppidan (1699-1764) with the text, there is no valid basis for this. The hymn appeared in several hymnals in Sweden, but it seems that here it has been limited to use in the Covenant. It was included in *Sions Basun* and then translated by A. Samuel Wallgren for *Mission Hymns.*

SALIGHETSGRUND (The Grounds of Blessedness) was a Swedish folk melody used with a different text in *Sions Nya Sånger*, 1874. In *Svenska Missionsförbundets Sångbok*, 1894, it was the setting for the text in question.

441
If I Gained the World
Anna Ölander, 1861-1939
Tr. composite
TRUE RICHES 10.9.10.9.D.
Swedish Melody
1 If I gained the world but lost the Sav - ior, Were my life worth liv - ing for a day? Could my yearn-ing heart find rest and com - fort In the things that soon must pass a - way? If I gained the world, but lost the Sav - ior, Would my gain be worth the life-long strife? Are all earth-ly pleas-ures worth com-par - ing For a mo - ment with a Christ-filled life?
2 Had I wealth and love in full - est meas - ure, And a name re - vered both far and near, Yet no hope be - yond, no har - bor wait - ing Where my storm-tossed ves - sel I could steer— If I gained the world, but lost the Sav - ior, Who en-dured the cross and died for me, Could then all the world af - ford a ref - uge, Whith - er in my an - guish I might flee?
3 O what emp - ti - ness with-out the Sav - ior Mid the sins and sor - rows here be - low! And e - ter - ni - ty, how dark with-out him— On - ly night and tears and end - less woe! What tho I might live with-out the Sav - ior, When I come to die, how would it be? O to face the val-ley's gloom with-out him! And with-out him all e - ter - ni - ty!
4 O the joy of hav - ing all in Je - sus! What a balm the bro - ken heart to heal! Ne'er a sin so great but he'll for - give it, Nor a sor - row that he does not feel! If I have but Je - sus, on - ly Je - sus, Noth - ing else in all the world be - side, O then ev - 'ry - thing is mine in Je - sus— For my needs and more he will pro - vide.

If I Gained the World but Lost the Savior

"Om jag ägde allt men icke Jesus" has been Anna Ölander's most appreciated song. In a simple but effective way she expounds on the richness of the life in Christ. The text was first published in her collection of poems, *Vallfärdssånger* (Pilgrimage Songs), in 1900. It was included in *Sions Basun* and *De Ungas Sångbok*. Hultman printed it in his first edition of *Solskenssånger*, 1911. It first appeared in English in *Mission Hymns*. No doubt the translation was the work of several members of the editorial committee.

OM JAG ÄGDE ALLT, renamed TRUE RICHES, is a folk melody of unknown origin. It appeared in *Sanningsvittnet* November 8, 1887, and in *Pilgrimstoner*, 1888, but not with this text. In the present hymnal of the Swedish Covenant it is the setting for lyrics by A.G. Lindqvist, "Aftonsolen sjunker bakom bergen" (The Evening Sun Is Setting behind the Mountain).

In Heaven Above

"I himmelen, i himmelen" was written in 1620 by Laurentuis L. Laurinus upon the death of his wife. At a service in the home a pastor colleague of Laurinus, Isak Erici, preached a lengthy sermon. He likened death to being invited to sleep in a comfortable bed and to a homegoing after a long prison term. The sermon was published in 1622 in a little octavo along with three poems, the last of which was "I himmelen. . . ." The original text had seven stanzas. It was revised by John Åstrom for the 1814 and 1816 proof editions of the *Psalmbok* and later was included in many of the Swedish hymnals. In *The Story of Christian Hymnody* Ernest E. Ryden calls this All Saints' Day hymn "one of the finest of Swedish sacred lyrics."

The English translation was done by William Maccall, a Scotchman, who published *Hymns of Sweden Rendered into English*, 1868. He was able to preserve much of the original beauty of the Swedish text. The hymn was published in *The Lutheran Hymnary*, 1913, the Augustana *Hymnal*, 1925, the Lutheran *Service Book and Hymnal*, 1958, and the last two Covenant hymnals. They all print four stanzas except *The Lutheran Hymnary*, which has six.

The tune originally used with the text, and still used in Sweden, was a folk melody from the *Koralbok*, 1697. *The Lutheran Hymnary* has a melody by Lindeman. HAUGE is a Norwegian folk melody which now seems to be the accepted tune in America.

Some years ago a group of two to three hundred Swedish young people (not necessarily believers) were taking a course which touched on all types of problems. Someone suggested that they determine which hymn in the *Psalmbok* was best loved. "I himmelen . . ." received the most votes.

604
In Heaven Above
Laurentius L. Laurinus, 1573-1655
Revised by John Åstrom, 1767-1844
Tr. William Maccall, 1812-1888
HAUGE 8.6.8.6.8.8.6.
Norwegian Folk Melody
1 In heav'n a - bove, in heav'n a - bove, Where God our Fa - ther dwells,
2 In heav'n a - bove, in heav'n a - bove, What glo - ry deep and bright!
3 In heav'n a - bove, in heav'n a - bove, No tears of pain are shed,
4 In heav'n a - bove, in heav'n a - bove, God hath a joy pre - pared
How bound-less there the bless - ed - ness! No tongue its great-ness tells;
The splen-dor of the noon-day sun Grows pale be - fore its light:
For naught can yon - der fade or die—Life's full - ness round is spread;
Which mor - tal ear had nev - er heard Nor mor - tal vis - ion shared,
There face to face, and full and free, For - ev - er,
The heav'n - ly light that ne'er goes down, A - round whose
And, like an o - cean, joy o'er - flows, And with im -
Which nev - er en - tered mor - tal breast, By mor - tal
ev - er - more we see Our God, the Lord of hosts!
ra - diance clouds ne'er frown, Is God, the Lord of hosts!
mor - tal mer - cy glows Our God, the Lord of hosts!
lips was ne'er ex - pressed: 'Tis God, the Lord of hosts!
LIFE EVERLASTING

In Heaven All Is Gladness
605
Johan N. Brun, 1745-1816
Tr. Composite
GLÄDJE 7.6.7.6.D.
Oscar Ahnfelt, 1813-1882
1 In heav-en all is glad-ness—Here trou-bles press, and fears;
2 This world is not my home-land, In tents I pass my days;
3 Would I ex-change con-di-tions With one whose all's be-low?
4 My hope for life e-ter-nal Rests on foun-da-tion sure;
Here, oft-en bowed and sigh-ing, I eat "the bread of tears."
T'ward yon-der shore of glo-ry With yearn-ing eyes I gaze.
No, rath-er I'd be sow-ing Good seed, tho tears may flow,
My cross I there-fore glad-ly Will yet a-while en-dure.
Here joy and sor-row min-gle For Christ's be-lov-ed bride;
While seeks the world its fol-ly, I view the cit-a-del
If at my jour-ney's end-ing I but in joy may reap,
Soon there shall be no sor-row, No plaints nor sighs for me,
But 'tis not so up yon-der, For there doth joy a-bide.
Where, free from care and sor-row, For-ev-er I shall dwell.
When world-ly joys are o-ver And some, too late, must weep.
When, with un-cov-ered vi-sion, My Sav-ior I shall see.
LIFE EVERLASTING

In Heaven All Is Gladness

A Norwegian hymnologist wrote:

Within the revival circles of former days there was not a hymn or song that expressed joy in fellowship with God as this text by Brun. Actually in times of spiritual awakening it was sung at almost every meeting. In the humble cottages many a Norwegian Christian has made his confession by singing the line "I would not change my lot with fools who have their happiness here."

[The final sentence is a literal translation of the first line of stanza three.]

The song came into use much later in Sweden and proved to be as popular there. In Norway, "Hos Gud er idel glade" was sung to a Norwegian folk melody; in Sweden it was sung to an Ahnfelt tune. Oscar Ahnfelt made several tours in Norway, and it is believed that he brought the text back to Sweden where he asked Lina Sandell to translate it into Swedish. "Hos Gud är idel glädje" was published in the tenth part of *Ahnfelts Sånger*, 1872. The song found its way into most of the hymn collections in Sweden. In America it was included in most of the free church hymnals as well as the early Augustana songbooks. The English translation (composite) can be found in all four Covenant hymnals. There is a version in three stanzas by O.H. Smeby in *The Lutheran Hymnary.*

GLÄDJE is a shortening of the first line, HOS GUD ÄR IDEL GLÄDJE, by which the Ahnfelt tune has been known.

394 In Tenderness, Jesus, Enfold Me

Ack, göm mig
9. 8. 9. 8.

J. E. SETH (1865-1923)
Trans. by E. GUSTAV JOHNSON, 1946

N. L. RIDDERHOF

Meditatively

1. In ten-der-ness, Je-sus, en-fold me, With Thee I would
2. Life speed-i-ly reach-es its meas-ure, Its joys are but
3. O Lord, in Thy faith-ful-ness lead me, Thy will for my
4. Thy pres-ence, my Sav-ior, I cher-ish, My soul is se-
5. I long for the heav-en-ly por-tals, I yearn for the
ev-er a-bide. Give strength to my faith to up-
fleet-ing and vain. The things of this world that I
guid-ance re-veal; With heav-en-ly nour-ish-ment
cure in Thy hand. When earth and its van-i-ties
man-sions of rest; The griefs and the striv-ings of

hold me, And keep me in grace at Thy side.
treas-ure, No bliss for my soul can ob-tain.
feed me; Thine im-age with-in me make real.
per-ish, With Thee tru-ly saved I shall stand.
mor-tals Are banned from the home of the blest. A-men.

298 In the Springtime Fair

Lina Sandell, 1832-1903
Tr. Karl A. Olsson, 1914-

SPRINGTIME 8.7.8.7. *with Refrain*
Swedish Folk Melody
Harm. by Norman E. Johnson, 1928-

In unison

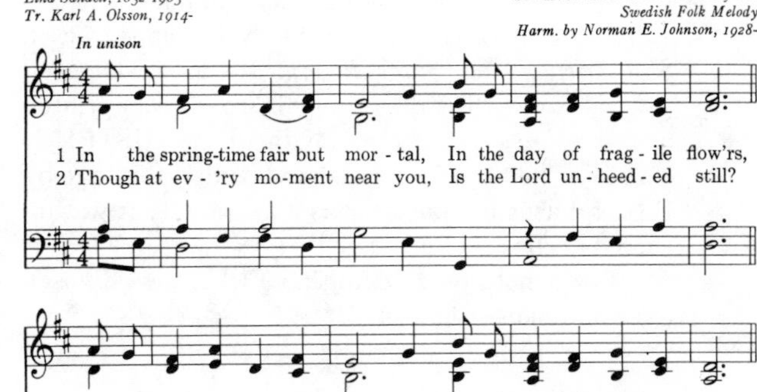
1 In the spring-time fair but mor-tal, In the day of frag-ile flow'rs,
2 Though at ev-'ry mo-ment near you, Is the Lord un-heed-ed still?

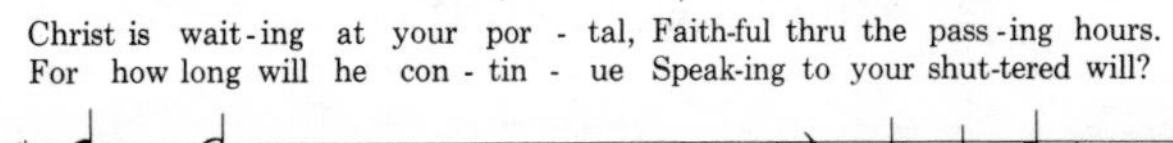
Christ is wait-ing at your por-tal, Faith-ful thru the pass-ing hours.
For how long will he con-tin-ue Speak-ing to your shut-tered will?

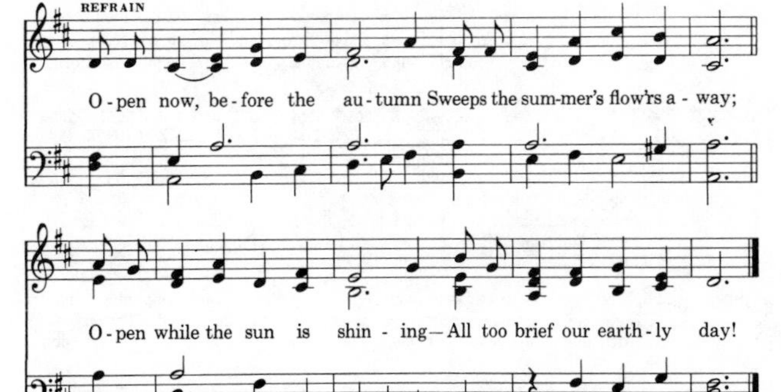
REFRAIN
O-pen now, be-fore the au-tumn Sweeps the sum-mer's flow'rs a-way;

O-pen while the sun is shin-ing—All too brief our earth-ly day!

ANSWERING CHRIST'S CALL

In Tenderness, Jesus, Enfold Me

"Ack göm mig, O Jesus, i såren," written by J.E. Seth, appeared in several of the privately published Swedish hymnals in this country under the title "En lärjunges bön" (A Disciple's Prayer). It was included in *Sions Basun* and then in *The Hymnal* (1950). It had been translated by E.G. Johnson in 1946 for inclusion in *Pegasus*, an annual literary publication of students and faculty at North Park College and Theological Seminary. The song is quite typical of pietistic works, with its emphasis upon close fellowship with Jesus, the impermanence of this world, and longing for heaven.

ACK, GÖM MIG was composed by Nicholas Ridderhof as a setting for this text.

In the Springtime Fair

The gentle song of invitation, "Medan allting ler och blommar" (literally, While All Things Smile and Blossom), was written by Lina Sandell. It was first published in 1876 in *Sångbok for Söndagsskolan*, edited by C.A.V. Lundholm. Karl Olsson translated it for use by the North Park College choir in 1967, and then it was chosen for *The Covenant Hymnal* (1973). The original can still be found in most of the free church hymnals in Sweden, but thus far I have been unable to discover it in any of the Swedish songbooks in the United States.

SPRINGTIME is the name the hymnal commission gave to the Swedish folk melody which has been associated with the text from the outset. The tune was used in *Sions Basun* as the setting for a similar Sandell text, "I den ljusa morgonstunden" (In the Bright Morning Hour). Here the invitation is to come to Jesus in the morning time of life.

In Thy Temple Courts, O Father

Although David Nyvall's claim to fame is not as a hymnist, several of his fine lyrics appeared in *Sionsharpan* and *Sions Basun.* He also composed several tunes. "Uti dina tempelgårdar" was printed in *Sions Basun* with the Haydn tune, AUSTRIAN HYMN. The text was translated some years ago by E.G. Johnson but not used as a hymn until it was included in our present hymnal.

For a note on LAMMETS FOLK see "Chosen Seed and Zion's Children."

In Thy Temple Courts, O Father
54
David Nyvall, 1863-1946
Tr. E. Gustav Johnson, 1893-
LAMMETS FOLK 8.7.8.7.D.
Attr. to Anders Carl Rutström, 1721-1772
"Sions Nya Sånger," 1854
1 In thy tem - ple courts, O Fa - ther, Once a - gain as - sem - bled now,
2 For the hour of mer - cy grant - ed We pre - sent our heart - felt praise;
3 Help us now thy word to cher - ish, Sanc - ti - fy our serv - ice, Lord!
Sing we prais - es as we gath - er, In con - tri - tion hum - bly bow.
Thanks, O Lord, for truths im - plant - ed, Thanks for to - kens of thy grace.
That thy truth our souls may nour - ish, Be thy will in us re - stored!
Here a fore - taste we are giv - en Of the ho - ly sab - bath peace
Thanks for warn - ings, for in - struc - tion, Thanks for new - born hope re - ceived;
Help us in our dai - ly liv - ing, As we face the days a - head,
Which for us is stored in heav - en, When life's woes and strife shall cease.
Thanks for light—blind fear's de - struc - tion, For anx - i - e - ty re - lieved.
That we may be al - ways giv - ing Room to thee, by thee be led. A - men.
OPENING

Jerusalem, Lift Up Thy Voice!

This Advent hymn by Johan Wallin first appeared in the proof edition of the *Psalmbok* in 1813. "Jerusalem, häv upp din röst" was omitted from the edition of 1816 but included in 1819, where it was reduced from eight stanzas and reflected various improvements on the text. Later the hymn was published in most of the hymnals in Sweden, but until the inclusion of Ernst Olson's translation in *The Hymnal* (1950) its use in this country had been restricted to the churches of the Augustana Synod.

VON HIMMEL HOCH first appeared in Valter Schumann's *Geistliche Lieder* (Leipzig, 1539), set to Luther's Christmas Carol, "From Heaven High to Earth I Come." The story is told that on Christmas Eve, 1534, Luther took down his lute and began to hum and sing beside the cradle of his young son, Paul. Using the pattern and tune of the popular folk song, "From Foreign Lands I Have Come Here," he sang the Christmas story. The song appeared in *Klug's Hymnbook* in 1543 with the subtitle "A Children's Hymn of the Christ Child for Christmas Eve." Bach used the melody three times in his *Christmas Oratorio* and in several organ numbers.

Jerusalem, Lift Up Thy Voice!
105
Johann Olof Wallin, 1779-1839
Tr. Ernst W. Olson, 1870-1958
VOM HIMMEL HOCH L.M.
"Geistliche Lieder," Leipzig, 1539
1 Je - ru - sa - lem, lift up thy voice! Daugh - ter of Zi - on,
2 He comes to ev - 'ry tribe and race, A mes - sen - ger of
3 In God's e - ter - nal cov - e - nant, He comes for our sal -
4 Let all the world with one ac - cord Now hail the com - ing
now re - joice! Thy King is come, whose might - y hand
truth and grace; With peace he comes from heav'n a - bove,
va - tion sent; The star of hope moves on be - fore,
of the Lord: Praise to the prince of heav'n-ly birth,
Hence - forth shall reign o'er ev - 'ry land.
On earth to found his realm of love.
And hosts as - sem - ble to a - dore.
Who bring - eth peace to all the earth! A - men.
ADVENT

Jesus, in Stillness, Longing I Wait

The period between her father's death in 1858 and her move to Stockholm in 1861 was a time of sadness, unrest, and indecision for Lina Sandell. Besides this, her health was poor and much of her time was spent in bed. It was a period of severe trouble and inner struggle. In her diary she confessed her impatient and unloving spirit toward members of her own family, but ended with a prayer that God would not allow her to take one step back from his way. It was during this period that she wrote "Herre, mitt hjärta längtar i stillhet." It was published in *Pilgrims-Sånger*, 1859, and later in the collections used by most of the Swedish free church groups on both sides of the Atlantic as well as in the early Augustana hymnals. E.G. Johnson translated the text into English for the North Park College magazine, *Pegasus*, in 1946.

HERRE, MITT HJÄRTA, or STILLNESS, by which the tune now is known, is the work of Carl Erik Sjögren. It was composed as a setting for Tegner's "Sjärnorna blinka" (The Stars Are Twinkling). Shortly thereafter the melody gained popularity and became the setting for Sandell's text in *Pilgrims-Sånger*.

Jesus, in Stillness, Longing I Wait
327
Lina Sandell, 1832-1903
Tr. E. Gustav Johnson, 1893-
STILLNESS 5.7.5.7.
Carl Erik Sjögren, 1799-1877
1 Je - sus, in still - ness, Long - ing I wait for thy peace;
2 Hope - ful and yearn - ing Ev - er to be at thy side—
3 Je - sus, O lead me Forth on my fal - ter - ing way;
4 Safe from temp - ta - tion Keep me and hide me, O Lord;
5 Keep me, dear Sav - ior, Bless me and sanc - ti - fy me;
Heal my soul's ill - ness, Bid thou my an - guish to cease.
Keep me from turn - ing, Help me in grace to a - bide.
Teach me to heed thee Will - ing - ly, al - ways, I pray.
In trib - u - la - tion Sol - ace and glad - ness af - ford.
In lov - ing fa - vor Let me thy coun - te - nance see. A - men.
Words copyright 1950 by Covenant Press.
CONSECRATION

Jesus, Jesus, Name Most Precious

Carl Boberg is best known for "O Store Gud," but another beautiful text from his pen is "Jesus, Jesus, O det ordet." The impulse to write this came when he was reading a passage from the poetry of E.J. Stagnelius: "Jesus! Jesus! sighs this heart, oppressed, broken-hearted, bowed with pain, / Wasted by want and suffering—Jesus! Jesus! answer mountain and valley." These mystical writings often had interested Boberg, but he wanted to present a clearer, more personal biblical witness to Christ than had the bishop's morbid son from Kalmar. Both text and music were published in *Sanningsvittnet*, 1884, and later in the hymn collections of the Swedish Covenant. In this country its publication has been restricted to *Sions Basun* and, in translation, to the 1973 hymnal. The translation, which faithfully retains the beauty and spirit of the original, was done by Karl Olsson for the North Park College choir in 1969. Only three of the original eight stanzas have been translated.

The tune, JESU NAMN, was composed for the words by Amanda Sandborg-Waesterberg.

Jesus, Jesus, Name Most Precious
252
Carl Boberg, 1859-1940
Tr. Karl A. Olsson, 1914-
JESU NAMN 8.7.8.7.8.7.
Amanda S. Waesterberg, 1842-1918
Harm. by A. Royce Eckhardt, 1937-
1 Je - sus, Je - sus, name most pre - cious—Like a song that an - gels sing!
2 It is like a star a - bove me, Set to guide my steps a - right,
3 Won - drous name! O may I hear it Dai - ly on my pil - grim way!
It my thirst - y heart re - fresh - es Like a gush - ing wood - land spring;
'Mid con - fus - ion and temp - ta - tion, Thru earth's mis - er - y and night;
May it bring me bless - ed ti - dings From the world of end - less day;
It my thirst - y heart re - fresh - es Like a gush - ing wood - land spring.
'Mid con - fus - ion and temp - ta - tion, Thru earth's mis - er - y and night.
May it bring me bless - ed ti - dings From the world of end - less day.
Words and harm. copyright 1972 by Covenant Press.
PRAISE TO CHRIST

Jesus, Lord and Precious Savior
433
Jakob Arrhenius, 1642-1725
Tr. Augustus Nelson, 1863-1949
KALMAR 8.7.8.7.7.7.
Swedish Melody, 1676
1 Je - sus, Lord and pre-cious Sav - ior, All my com-fort and my joy,
2 All I do, O let me ev - er, Je - sus, in thy name be - gin;
3 Let my words and thoughts, O Sav - ior, To thy praise and glo - ry tend;
4 When my days on earth are o - ver, Let me en - ter in - to rest;
Gra-cious-ly ex - tend thy fa - vor, Let thy word my soul em - ploy:
Give suc - cess to my en - deav - or, Fi - nal vic - to - ry there - in:
Help me, Lord, that I may gath - er Trea-sures that shall nev - er end:
Bear me home, O bless - ed Sav - ior, When to thee it seem - eth best:
Je - sus, come, a - bide with me, Let me ev - er be with thee. A-men.
Words from The Lutheran Service Book and Hymnal, by permission of the Commission on the Liturgy and Hymnal.
Another harmonization in a higher setting may be found at No. 56
LOVE AND COMMUNION

163
Jesus of Nazareth Passes By
Anders Frostenson, 1906-
Tr. Glen V. Wiberg, 1925-
NORDQVIST 9.6.9.6.7.
Gustaf L. Nordqvist, 1886-1949
1 Je - sus of Naz - a - reth pass - es by— Now, as in
2 Wealth in a - bun-dance he gives the poor, Brings to the
3 O - pen your heart in re - pent - ant prayer, Un - lock each
an - cient time, Frees the op-pressed who for par - don cry,
sick re - lief; Souls that are emp - ty, in bond - age sore,
se - cret place; Ask him to en - ter, do not de - spair,
Giv - ing his peace sub - lime: Lo, the king-dom is near us!
Free-dom and joy re - ceive: Lo, the king-dom is near us!
Take of his bound-less grace: Lo, the king-dom is near us!
Words copyright 1972 by Covenant Press. Music copyright © 1949 by AB Nordiska Musikförlaget, Stockholm, Sweden. Reprinted by permission.

Jesus, Lord and Precious Savior

"Jesus, du min fröjd och fromma" is a translation by Jakob Arrhenius of the German "Jesu, meine lust und wonne." It was written by an unknown author sometime in the seventeenth century and published in *Lüneburgisches Gesangbuch*, 1686. The Swedish translation first appeared in a trial edition of the Swedish hymnal put out by Arrhenius in 1691. Since then it has been included in most hymn collections in Sweden. "That this hymn has been so dear to us and so often used," wrote Lövgren, "can be due only to its extreme simplicity." And then he added that it is not the grandest but the simplest hymns that have been the most popular. The Swedish emigrants brought the hymn with them to this country and included it in many of their songbooks. Four of the five original stanzas were translated by Augustus Nelson for the Augustana *Hymnal*, 1901. It came into use in the Covenant through *The Hymnal* (1950).

KALMAR is a melody dating from before 1676. There is a handwritten copy of the tune which came from Kalmar in the library in Västerås, hence the tune name. The exact source is not known, but it is thought to be German. The tune has commonly been used with the words "Hela världen fröjdes Herren" (Praise the Lord, Each Tribe and Nation), but it was first used with the Arrhenius translation as noted above. KALMAR is no longer associated with this text in Sweden.

Jesus of Nazareth Passes By

"Jesus från Nasaret går här fram" was written by Anders Frostenson for the 1937 edition of the *Psalmbok*. The hymn has had great popularity, especially during Advent. It is now included in the free church collections. It was translated by Glen Wiberg for *The Covenant Hymnal* (1973).

The music was composed for the text by Gustaf L. Nordqvist; hence the tune name, NORDQVIST.

Jesus Stands Outside the Door

Because it was first published in *Sabbatsklockan* (1877), "Herren står vid hjärtats dörr" often has been attributed to Joel Blomqvist. He always placed his signature at the bottom of his lyrics, however, and there is none for this song. The message of invitation is based on Revelation 3:20: "Behold, I stand at the door and knock," and Matthew 11:28: "Come unto me . . . for I am meek. . . ." The song was used widely in free church circles. In this country it was published in the first edition of *Evangelii Basun*, 1880, and then in several hymnals used in Augustana and Covenant churches. It has been a favorite of male choruses. Again it is being sung in Covenant churches in a translation by Herbert Palmquist.

The melody, RÖSLEIN, was composed in 1827 by Heinrich Werner, a German music teacher and composer. It was the music for Goethe's *Heidesröslein: Sah ein Knab ein Röslein stehn*, 1829. It provides an appropriate setting for the appealing message of the text.

292 Jesus Stands Outside the Door
Based on Revelation 3:20
Source unknown
Tr. Herbert E. Palmquist, 1896-
RÖSLEIN 7.6.7.7.6.7.6.
Heinrich Werner, 1800-1833
Harm. by A. Royce Eckhardt, 1937-
1 Je - sus stands out - side the door— Why not bid him en - ter?
2 With a wea - ry, trou - bled race Hear the Sav - ior plead - ing:
3 Come to me, O Je - sus good, O - pen now your treas - ure,
Though your weight of sin be sore, He can life and
"Come to me and my em - brace, I am meek and
Cleanse me in your pre - cious blood, That life - giv - ing,
strength re - store: Hear his voice so ten - der. Trou - bled soul, I
full of grace That your souls are need - ing." Sons of men, what-
heal - ing flood Flow - ing with - out meas - ure. Je - sus, Je - sus,
do im - plore, Will you let him en - ter?
e'er your place, Will you spurn his plead - ing?
Je - sus good, Be my last - ing treas - ure. A - men.
CALL OF CHRIST
Words and harmonization copyright 1973 by Covenant Press.

Joy Bells Are Ringing
143
Nils Frykman, 1842-1911
Tr. E. Gustav Johnson, 1893-
JULEN ÄR INNE 5.5.6.D.
Wilhelm Theodor Söderberg, 1845-1922
1 Joy bells are ring - ing, Christ - mas is bring - ing
2 Light is as - cend - ing, Night - time is end - ing,
3 O what a treas - ure God in his pleas - ure
4 Come to the man - ger, Kin - dred and stran - ger,
5 Ban ish all sad - ness, Fill me with glad - ness
Ti - dings of Je - sus' birth. Can - dles are gleam - ing,
Sun - shine from God ap - pears. Hope of the a - ges,
Lov - ing - ly gives to - day! Grace to the low - ly,
Hail now the new - born King! In ad - o - ra - tion,
Je - sus, whom I a - dore! All else may per - ish,
Glad - ness is stream - ing Out o - ver all the earth.
Fore - told by sag - es, Comes to dis - pel all fears.
Peace pure and ho - ly, An - gels to men con - vey.
With ju - bi - la - tion, Peo - ples and na - tions sing!
Thee will I cher - ish Now and for - ev - er - more!
Words copyright 1950 by Covenant Press.
BIRTH

Joy Bells Are Ringing

Under the title "Julmorgonen," this happy carol appeared in *Sanningsvittnet*, December 22, 1881. It was the celebration of Christmas in his home community of Sunne in Värmland that inspired Nils Frykman to pen these words. We can see the candles shining from the windows of the cottages as the people make their way to the Julotta service, and we hear the sound of voices as they sing praises to the newborn king. The carol ends with a prayer and a promise.

The song became popular among the free church people and is still included in their hymnals. In the United States its use has been largely restricted to the Covenant. It is interesting to note that the first two phrases were reversed when the song was published in *Sionsharpan*. The original version begins: "Fröjdas vart sinne, Julen är inne" (Rejoice everyone, Christmas is here). Frykman must have approved of the change, because it was printed this way in *Sions Basun*, a publication he helped to compile. Although the first line is not a literal rendering of the text, E.G. Johnson has caught the spirit of the carol in his excellent translation, which was prepared for the 1950 hymnal.

Wilhelm Söderberg was the composer of the joyful tune, JULEN ÄR INNE, which has always been associated with this text.

List to the Gospel Resounding

As a member of the editorial committee of *Sions Basun*, Nils Frykman was asked to submit some of his own songs. We do not know how many he submitted, but no less than 123 were credited to him. "Hör huru fridsropet skallar" was one of them. It had already been published in the 1901 edition of *Pilgrimstoner*. It did not appear in any of the hymnals in Sweden, and Lövgren does not refer to it. The song was translated by Frykman's son, Andrew, and appeared in *The Covenant Hymnal* (1931).

The tune, HEAVENLY VOICE (formerly JESUS DIG KALLAR), was composed by Carl Frykman, another of the hymnist's sons.

List to the Gospel Resounding

293

Nils Frykman, 1842-1911
Tr. Andrew T. Frykman, 1875-1943
HEAVENLY VOICE 8.7.8.7. with Refrain
Carl M. Frykman, 1880-1930
1 List to the gos-pel re-sound-ing, Beau-ti-ful mes-sage of love;
2 Why not, O why not, re-pent-ing, Turn from your per-il-ous course,
3 Life, like the dew of the morn-ing, Van-ish-eth quick-ly a-way;
4 Touch'd by the Spir-it so ten-der, Call-ing as ev-er be-fore,
Je-sus, in mer-cy a-bound-ing, Call-eth for you from a-bove.
End-ing in woe un-re-lent-ing, An-guish, dis-grace and re-morse?
Death bring-eth sor-row and mourn-ing, Wail-ing for-ev-er and aye.
Will-ing-ly, free-ly sur-ren-der, O-pen, yes, o-pen your door.
REFRAIN
List to the heav-en-ly voice Ten-der-ly urg-ing your choice;

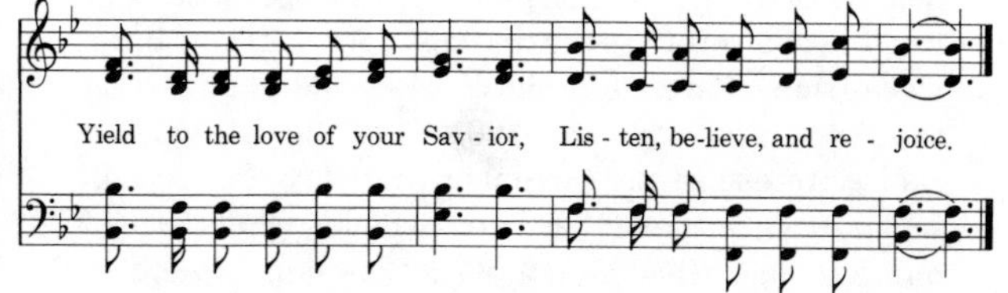

Yield to the love of your Sav-ior, Lis-ten, be-lieve, and re-joice.

462

Lord, As a Pilgrim

Wilhelmi Malmivaara, 1854-1922
Paraphrase, Ernest Edwin Ryden, 1886-
Based on tr. by Aino Lilja Kantonen-Halkola, 1901-
PILGRIM SONG 9.9.5.5.4.
Ernest August Hagfors, 1827-1913
Harm. by Norman E. Johnson, 1928-
1 Lord, as a pil-grim on earth I roam, By foes sur-round-ed, far from my home; What-e'er be-tide me, Walk thou be-side me, Shep-herd di-vine!
2 Though friends for-sake me, thou art the same, Faith-ful for-ev-er is thy blest name; Thou wilt not leave me, Oft though I grieve thee, Thou friend di-vine!
3 Thou art my ref-uge: grant me, I pray, Strength for each bur-den, light on my way, Balm in my sor-row, Grace for to-mor-row, Sav-ior di-vine!
4 Lord, let thy pres-ence lead all the way, Un-til the dawn-ing of that great day When I shall see thee Throned in thy glo-ry, God blest for aye! A-men.
Words from The Lutheran Service Book and Hymnal, by permission of the Commission on the Liturgy and Hymnal.
Harm. copyright 1973 by Covenant Press.

Lord, As a Pilgrim

In Finland this is known as "The Pilgrim Song." "Oi Herra, jos mä matkämies maan" was written by Wilmelmi Malmivaara, a Lutheran provost. He was a leader in a pietistic movement in Ostrobothnia in the late 1800s. The hymn was written during a period of great sorrow, after the death of his wife and two children in the short space of two weeks. His biographer says:"This is one of the few religious songs that has found its way to every corner of our Fatherland. . . . The Finnish Christian piety, which is characterized by a spirit of quiet sorrow and sadness, has found in this hymn its most beautiful expression." During the fearful days of the 1940 Russo-Finnish conflict this hymn was a source of hope and consolation in thousands of bereaved homes. The song appeared first in Malmivaara's *Hymns of Zion*, 1893. Ernest Ryden's paraphrase of a translation by Aino Lilja Kantonen-Halkola was published in the Lutheran *Service Book and Hymnal*, 1958.

The tune, PILGRIM SONG, was composed for secular words by Ernest August Hagfors, and it was well known when the hymn was written. It was chosen by Malmivaara because he wanted a song the pietists would love to sing.

83 Mine Eyes Look toward the Mountains

Bohemian Hymn
7. 6. 7. 6. D.

PSALM 121
From the Swedish version

From "Brödraförsamlingen"

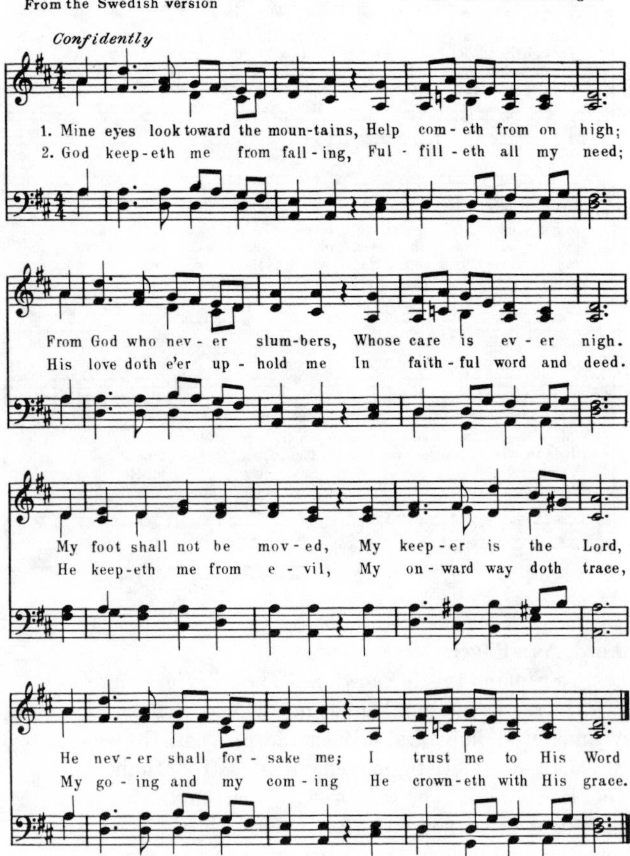
Confidently
1. Mine eyes look toward the moun-tains, Help com - eth from on high;
2. God keep-eth me from fall - ing, Ful - fill - eth all my need;
From God who nev - er slum-bers, Whose care is ev - er nigh.
His love doth e'er up - hold me In faith - ful word and deed.
My foot shall not be mov - ed, My keep - er is the Lord,
He keep-eth me from e - vil, My on - ward way doth trace,
He nev - er shall for - sake me; I trust me to His Word
My go - ing and my com - ing He crown-eth with His grace.

Mine Eyes Look toward the Mountains

This hymn is based on Psalm 121, but neither the author nor the translator is known. *The Hymnal* (1950) states that it is "from the Swedish version." There is a well-known text by J. Arrhenius dating from the seventeenth century, "Jag lyfter mina händer." This was published in *Sions Basun* with a tune by E. August Skogsbergh. If this is the source of our hymn, the English text is more of a paraphrase than a translation. The original song had three stanzas, but our version has only two.

FAR OFF LANDS is the name now used for BOHEMIAN HYMN. It has its roots among the Herrnhuters in the eighteenth century and is taken from the Bohemian Brethren's songbook.

My Crucified Savior

"Min blodige Konung" (actually, "My Bleeding King") from its outset has been called "Lenten Song." It is the work of Fredrika Falck, a pastor's wife who was greatly influenced by the Herrnhuters. Witness the emphasis upon the blood, suffering, and finished work of Christ on the cross. The hymn was published in *Sions Nya Sånger*, 1778, in four eight-line stanzas. Later, in almost all of the free church hymnals in Sweden and America it appeared in five to eight four-line stanzas. The text has been altered several times. All eight stanzas were translated by Claude W. Foss and published in the Augustana *Hymnal*, 1901. The English version came into use in the Covenant first through *Mission Hymns*. Since then it has been included in all three of our hymnals, though not with the same choice of stanzas. In order to bring stanza two more in line with traditional Covenant theology, the word "appeased" was changed to "obeyed."

Although the tune is called RUTSTRÖM, there is no proof that Anders Rutström was the composer. Actually, there are no extant tune books from that period. The melody appeared in numbered notes in four editions of *Sions Nya Sånger* in the 1870s and in regular notation in *Sionstoner*, 1889. Although most of the collections in Sweden now use a Blomqvist melody, in America we have preferred RUTSTRÖM.

My Soul Now Magnifies the Lord

"Min själ berömmer Gud med fröjd" is Carl Boberg's version of the Magnificat, the song of Mary as found in Luke 1:46-55. The first publication of the song was in *Mönsterås-Tidningen*, January 3, 1885. It was sung by most of the free church groups in Sweden, but here it appeared only in *Sionsharpan* and *Sions Basun* until the English translation by Obed Johnson was included in *The Hymnal* (1950).

MARIAS LOVSÅNG is a Swedish folk melody which appeared in J. Hammarlund's songbook for schools. The first time it was used as a setting for a hymn was in *Hemlandstoner*, 1884, in which it is the melody for a Sandell translation of "Jag har en vän, en trofast vän." It is the setting for Boberg's text in *Sionstoner* and the 1894 edition of the Swedish Covenant's hymnal.

My Crucified Savior
195
Fredrika E. Falck, 1719-1749
Tr. Claude W. Foss, 1855-1935, alt.
RUTSTRÖM 11.11.11.11.
Anders Carl Rutström, 1721-1772
1 My cru - ci - fied Sav - ior, de - spised and con - temned, Thou in - no - cent
2 Our Sav - ior thus fin - ished God's plan for our race, And laid the foun -
3 Re - stored to the bliss that was lost in the fall, Yes, great - er, for
4 Yes, come, trem - bling sin - ner, come just as thou art, Thy cares and thy
Lamb for all sin - ners con - demned, In thir - ty years' an - guish our
da - tion for par - don and grace; And then rose tri - umph - ant, the
Je - sus pre - pared for us all E - ter - nal sal - va - tion and
sor - rows to Je - sus im - part; In him seek sal - va - tion from
path thou hast trod, And di - est at last to re - deem us to God.
con - quer - ing Lord, O - beyed the Cre - a - tor and man - kind re - stored.
man - sions a - bove: Come, poor, bur - dened sin - ner, re - joice in his love.
death and the grave, For Je - sus is will - ing and might - y to save.
Words used by permission of Fortress Press.
A higher setting may be found at No. 301
PASSION

421 My Soul Now Magnifies the Lord

Based on Luke 1:46-55
Carl Boberg, 1859-1940
Tr. Obed Johnson, 1881-1970

MARIAS LOVSÅNG C.M.D.
Swedish Folk Melody

1 My soul now magnifies the Lord, With joy his praise I sing; For God my Savior unto me Has done a wondrous thing: This child of dust he richly blessed, His mercy fills my soul; For me he opened heaven's gate—His love will I extol.

2 The power of his righteous arm Amazing things has wrought; Earth's mighty men he has subdued, Like dust they've come to naught: The proud of spirit he has sent With empty souls away; To depths of need have haughty men Been brought within a day.

3 His mercy is indeed so great Its length cannot be spanned; For those who trust his promises His help is near at hand: The covenant that he has made, As in our fathers' day, Forever steadfast shall remain When earth shall pass away.

4 His wisdom cannot be discerned By carnal-minded man; But he who truly loves the Lord Shall know his sacred plan: The man whose heart is filled with pride Will God, the Lord, bring low; To him who humbly serves his God Shall streams of mercy flow.

5 My soul now magnifies the Lord, With joy his praise I sing; For God my Savior unto me Has done a wondrous thing: This child of dust he set apart For blessedness sublime; His answer to my prayer extends Beyond the realms of time.

JOY

 Now Before Thee, Lord, We Gather

Lina Sandell, 1832-1903
Tr. A. L. Skoog, 1856-1934
MONTCLAIR 8.7.8.7.8.8.8.7.
William B. Bradbury, 1816-1868
1 Now be - fore thee, Lord, we gath - er To re - ceive thy pre-cious word;
2 May thy word, to us now giv - en, Be re - tained in hearts con - trite;
3 Of the time may we a - vail us, When to seek us thou art near;
Let thy grace in show'rs, O Fa - ther, On our parch - ed hearts be poured.
On the nar - row way to heav - en Lead us in thy per - fect light.
Soon the day of grace may fail us, And no mes - sage more we hear.
Send thy Ho - ly Spir - it o'er us, With thy quick-'ning fire re - store us,
Hush with - in us all com - mo - tion, Si - lence each dis - turb-ing no - tion;
Turn our minds to med - i - ta - tion On our need of thy sal - va - tion;
At thy ta - ble spread be - fore us Fill our hun-g'ring souls, dear Lord.
May we, Lord, with true de - vo - tion Use this hour of grace a - right.
Urge on all thine in - vi - ta - tion—To our prayer in-cline thine ear. A-men.

PULPIT

Now before Thee, Lord, We Gather

"Herre, samla oss nu alla" is an excellent hymn for use at the beginning of a service or before the sermon. This was written by Lina Sandell soon after her husband, Oscar Berg, had purchased an old Jewish synagogue and converted it into a seamen's mission. They went together to the chapel every Sunday afternoon, and perhaps it was one of these services that inspired the hymn. It was published with the tenth edition of *Ahnfelts Sånger*, 1872, and later could be found in almost all Swedish collections on both sides of the Atlantic. The translation by A.L. Skoog has been included in all of our hymnals since 1921.

The Swedish text has appeared with several different tunes, but MONTCLAIR (HERRE SAMLA OSS), written by the American hymn composer and editor, William Bradbury, now is the melody most commonly used.

Now Hail We Our Redeemer

This hymn has been credited erroneously to St. Ambrose. It was written by Elisabet Cruciger, the wife of the headmaster of Wittenberg University during the time of Luther. One night she had a dream that she stood in the pulpit of the church in Wittenberg. Upon hearing of the dream, her husband said that perhaps "the good God thinks you are worthy to have your songs sung in church." She laughed; the thought was too humorous. No woman's song had ever been accepted. But her husband was right, because her Advent song, "Herr Christ, der einig Gottes Sohn," was published in Luther's second collection of hymns, the *Erfurt Enchiridion*, 1524. By 1526 the Swedish reformer Olavus Petri had published his translation of the song in the first collection of Reformation hymns in Sweden. The opening phrase was "Förlossningen är vunnen" (Redemption is won). The text was revised by J. Åstrom for publication in the *Psalmbok*, 1826. In the many Swedish hymnals in which the hymn has appeared the number of stanzas has varied from five to ten. Four of the stanzas were translated by Ernst Olson for the Augustana *Hymnal*, 1925.

The tune, ENCHIRIDION, is named for Luther's hymnal of 1524, in which it was the setting for this text, but the melody is older. It was used with a secular text in *Lochheimers Liederbuch*, a manuscript from the fifteenth century.

114 Now Hail We Our Redeemer

St. Ambrose, 340-397
Olavus Petri, 1493-1552
Tr. Ernst W. Olson, 1870-1958

ENCHIRIDION 7.6.7.6.7.7.6.
"Enchiridion," Erfurt, 1524

1 Now hail we our Re - deem - er, E - ter - nal Son of
2 A man, of God be - got - ten, Bro't in the age of
3 O Je - sus, grant us mer - cy, And grace on us be -
4 In - to thy hand the Fa - ther Gave all, that we might

God, Born in the flesh to save us And cleanse us
grace; Lo, all the earth is ra - diant With light and
stow, To walk by thine own guid - ance, Thy sav - ing
be In bonds of faith u - nit - ed, And ded - i -

in his blood. The morn - ing star as - cend - eth, Light to the
hope and peace. Our pris - on he de - mol - ished, Death's pow-er
truth to know. For thee our hearts are yearn - ing, From world - ly
cate to thee: A peo - ple through thy mer - it En - ti - tled

world he lend - eth— Our guide in grief and gloom.
he a - bol - ished And o - pened heav - en's gate.
pleas - ures turn - ing Un - to thy right - eous - ness.
to in - her - it Thy realm e - ter - nal - ly. A - men.

ADVENT

Now Shine a Thousand Candles Bright

The delightful Christmas carol "Nu tändas tusen juleljus" was written by Emmy Köhler, a frequent contributor of children's stories and articles to various publications. It appeared in *Korsblomman* for 1899 and then in many song and hymn collections, especially for schools. Evidently it had never been published in the United States until it was included in the 1973 hymnal. Desiring to use the song at a North Park Seminary Christmas party, I submitted the text to Karl Olsson with the request that he translate it if he could find the time. Meanwhile I tried my hand at translating. Since Dr. Olsson's version came too late for the party, mine was used. Later, when the 1973 Hymnal Commission considered the song, they chose a combination of both versions.

CHRISTMAS CANDLES is the name given to the tune, which also was the creation of Emmy Köhler.

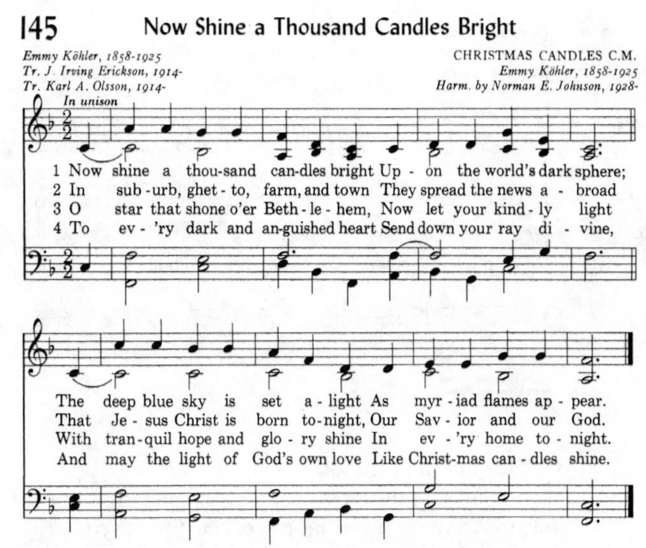
145 Now Shine a Thousand Candles Bright
Emmy Köhler, 1858-1925
Tr. J. Irving Erickson, 1914-
Tr. Karl A. Olsson, 1914-
CHRISTMAS CANDLES C.M.
Emmy Köhler, 1858-1925
Harm. by Norman E. Johnson, 1928-
In unison
1 Now shine a thou-sand can-dles bright Up - on the world's dark sphere;
2 In sub-urb, ghet-to, farm, and town They spread the news a - broad
3 O star that shone o'er Beth-le-hem, Now let your kind - ly light
4 To ev - 'ry dark and an-guished heart Send down your ray di - vine,
The deep blue sky is set a - light As myr - iad flames ap - pear.
That Je - sus Christ is born to-night, Our Sav - ior and our God.
With tran-quil hope and glo - ry shine In ev - 'ry home to - night.
And may the light of God's own love Like Christ-mas can - dles shine.
BIRTH
Words and harm. copyright 1972 by Covenant Press.

O Bride of Christ, Rejoice!
115
Johann Olof Wallin, 1779-1839
Tr. Victor O. Peterson, 1864-1929
AUF MEINEN LIEBEN GOTT 6.6.7.7.7.7.
Jacob Regnart, 1540-c.1600
Harm. by A. Royce Eckhardt, 1937-
In unison
1 O Bride of Christ, re - joice! Ex - ul - tant raise thy
2 Let shouts of glad - ness rise Tri - um - phant to the
3 He wears no king - ly crown, Yet as a king he's
4 Thy heart now o - pen wide, Bid Christ with thee a -
5 E'en babes with one ac - cord With thee shall praise the
voice To hail the day of glo - ry, Fore -
skies; Here comes the King most glo - rious To
known; Though not ar - rayed in splen - dor, He
bide; He gra - cious - ly will hear thee And
Lord, And ev - 'ry gen - tile na - tion Re -
told in sa - cred sto - ry.
reign o'er all vic - to - rious.
still makes death sur - ren - der. Ho - san - na, praise and
be for - ev - er near thee.
spond with ex - ul - ta - tion.
glo - ry: Our King, we bow be - fore thee. A - men.
Words used by permission of Fortress Press.
Harm. copyright 1973 by Covenant Press.
ADVENT
O Lamb of God, Most Holy
519
Nikolaus Decius, c.1490-1541
Tr. Olof Olsson, 1841-1900
O LAMM GOTTES 7.7.7.7.7.7.7.7.
"Christliche Kirchen Ordnung," 1542
O Lamb of God, most ho - ly, On Cal - va -
ry an of - f'ring, De - spis - ed, meek and low - ly,
Thou in thy death and suf - f'ring Our sins didst
bear, our an - guish, The might of death didst
van - quish: Grant us thy peace, O Je - sus! A - men.
Words from The Lutheran Service Book and Hymnal, by permission
of the Commission on the Liturgy and Hymnal.
LORD'S SUPPER

O Bride of Christ, Rejoice!

"Gläd dig, du Kristi brud" has been credited to Johan Wallin because he reworked the text for the *Psalmbok*, 1819. It was published in A.R. Gryderup's *Psalmebog* in 1631, and it is assumed to be of Danish origin. Its first appearance in Sweden was in *Tree Sköna Andeliga Historiske Wijsor* (Three Beautiful Spiritual Historic Songs), 1642. S.J. Hedborn revised it for his *Psalmer*, 1812. It became a standard Advent hymn among Scandinavians everywhere. The song came into early use in the English hymnals of Lutheran Scandinavian groups in America through the translation by Victor Peterson in 1899. Although it appeared in *Sionsharpan* and *Sions Basun*, the English version was not published in the Covenant until 1950.

AUF MEINEN LIEBEN GOTT was composed by Jacob Regnart, a German organist, and was published in his *Schöne kurzweilige teutsche Lieder* in 1574. It was first used as a chorale by G. Gesius in 1605.

O Lamb of God Most Holy

This is an example of a hymn that was translated three times before coming to us in English. The original was the "Agnus Dei" of the Latin mass, which is based on John 1:29. Nikolaus Decius (d. 1541), a German monk, musician, and preacher who converted to Lutheranism, translated the text into German early in the sixteenth century. "O Lamm Gottes unschuldig" appeared first in low German in Joakim Slüter's *Geystlycke Leder* in Rostock, 1531, and later in high German in Valentin Schumann's *Gesangbuch*, Leipzig, 1539. The hymn was sung by the congregation at communion during the distribution of the elements. Although there are several English translations, our version comes from a Swedish rendering, perhaps by Olavus Petri; it was included in his collection of hymns in 1536. It has appeared in most Swedish hymnals abroad and in the United States, including those of the Covenant. Olof Olsson translated the text for the first English hymnal of the Augustana Synod. This is the version that was included in all four English Covenant hymnals.

The tune, O LAMM GOTTES, is also by Decius. It was first printed in *Geistliche Lieder und Psalmen*, Magdeburg, 1540.

O Let Your Soul Now Be Filled with Gladness

"Så hav nu, själ, ett muntert sinne" is a good example of a type of Moravian hymnody popular in the mid-1700s. It speaks of a spirit that is freer and more joyous than that of the average pietist. In fact, Lövgren says we find in the song "an almost thoughtless happiness." It first appeared in the handwritten *Sions Evangeliska Sånger* under the title "Själens frimodiga tröstevisa" (The Soul's Genuine Song of Trust), and bore the date of August 4, 1757. The song has been quite well known in the free churches of Sweden, but not in America, even though it was printed in some of the early hymnals (e.g., *Sionsharpan* and *Evangelii Basun*). The song is one of several that Karl Olsson translated especially for the North Park College choir, and it has proved to be one of the most popular in the present hymnal. The original text had four stanzas.

The folk melody most commonly used with the text has been given the name RANSOMED SOUL. It is taken from Joel Blomqvist's *Melodier till Sions Nya Sånger*, 1873.

423 O Let Your Soul Now Be Filled with Gladness
Peter Jönsson Aschan, 1726-1813
Tr. Karl A. Olsson, 1914-
RANSOMED SOUL 10.8.10.8.8.10.10.8.
Swedish Folk Melody
Harm. by A. Royce Eckhardt, 1937-
1 O let your soul now be filled with glad-ness, Your heart re-deemed, re -
2 If you seem emp - ty of an - y feel - ing, Re - joice- you are his
3 It is a good ev - 'ry good tran-scend - ing That Christ has died for
joice in - deed! O may the thought ban - ish all your sad - ness That
ran - somed bride! If those you cher - ish seem not to love you, And
you and me! It is a glad - ness that has no end - ing Therein his blood you have been freed, That God's un - fail - ing love is yours,
dark as - sails from ev - 'ry side, Still yours the prom - ise, come what may,
in God's won-drous love to see! Praise be to you, O spot-less Lamb,
That you the on - ly Son were giv - en, That by his
In loss and tri - umph, in laugh - ter, cry - ing, In want and
Who thru the des - ert my soul are lead - ing To that fair
death he has o-pened heav-en, That you are ran-somed as you are.
rich - es, in liv - ing, dy - ing, That you are pur-chased as you are.
cit - y of joy ex - ceed - ing, For which you bought me as I am.
JOY
Copyright 1972 by Covenant Press.

O Lord, Give Heed unto Our Plea

It would be difficult to find a pulpit hymn that gathers up the concerns of the congregation so well as "O Gud, som hörer allas rost." The hymn was written about 1570 by Johann Utenhovius, a pastor in Holland, and published in *Sontags-Evangelia Gesangweise*, Amberg, 1608. The original text, "O Gott, du unser Vater bist," was translated into Swedish by Jesper Swedberg for the 1694 songbook. In Sweden the song has been used mostly in the State Church. As far as I can determine, the Swedish text was not included in any of the Augustana hymnals, but it did appear in *Sionsharpan*. Ernst Olson translated the hymn for the Augustana *Hymnal*, 1925.

HEAVENLY HOST, a Swedish melody of unknown origin, was first known through the *Koralbok* of 1697.

O Lord, Give Heed unto Our Plea **68**

Jesper Swedberg, 1653-1735

HEAVENLY HOST 8.7.8.7.8.8.7.
Swedish Melody, 1697

1 O Lord, give heed un - to our plea, O Spir - it, grant thy grac - es,
2 Touch thou the shep-herd's lips, O Lord, That in this bless-ed hour
3 Let heart and ear be o-pened wide Un - to thy word and plead - ing;

That we who put our trust in thee May right - ly sing thy
He may pro - claim thy sa - cred word With unc - tion and with
Our minds, O Ho - ly Spir - it, guide By thine own light and

prais - es. Thy word, O Christ, un - to us give, That grace and
pow'r. What thou wouldst have thy serv - ant say, Put thou in -
lead - ing. The law of Christ we would ful - fill, And walk ac -

pow'r we may re - ceive To fol - low thee, our Mas - ter.
to his heart, we pray, With grace and strength to say it.
cord - ing to his will, His word our rule of liv - ing. A - men.

Used by permission of Fortress Press.

PULPIT

O Mighty God, When I Behold the Wonder

"O store Gud, när jag den värld beskådar" was published in *Mönsteras-Tidningen*, March 13, 1886. It had been written the previous summer. Carl Boberg and some friends were returning home to Mönsterås from Kronobäck, where they had participated in an afternoon meeting. Nature was at its peak that radiant afternoon. Presently a thunder cloud appeared on the horizon, and soon sharp lightning flashes shot across the sky. Strong winds swept over the meadows and billowing fields of grain. The thunder pealed in loud claps. Then the rain came in cool fresh showers. In a little while the storm was over, and a rainbow appeared.

When Boberg arrived home, he opened the window and saw the bay of Mönsterås like a mirror before him. He hummed Nicander's "Welcome, Welcome, Clear, Calm, and Sweet Eventide." From the woods on the other side of the bay he heard the song of the thrush. There had been a funeral that afternoon, and now the church bells were tolling in the quiet evening. It was this series of sights, sounds, and experiences that inspired the writing of the song. After appearing in several periodicals it seems that the poem was forgotten. But several years later the author heard it sung in Värmland to an old Swedish melody. In 1891 he published the song in *Sanningsvittnet*. Soon it appeared in several hymnals in Sweden and America, among them *Evangelii Basun, Sionsharpan,* and *De Ungas Sångbok*. All nine stanzas were translated by E.G. Johnson in 1925 and published in *The Children's Friend*, organ of the Cromwell Children's Home. *The Covenant Hymnal* (1931) printed it with five stanzas. Our present hymnal includes all nine.

The version "How Great Thou Art" is the work of Stuart K. Hine, an English missionary who had settled in Western Ukraine in 1923. He had learned the Russian version, which was based on a German translation of Boberg's text: "Wie gross bist Du." When Hine returned to England in 1939, he made use of the three stanzas he had translated in his gospel campaigns. In 1949, he published the Russian and English words together in his Russian gospel magazine, *Grace and Peace*, distributing it to refugees in fifteen countries. But it was Dr. J. Edwin Orr of Fuller Theological Seminary who first brought the Hine text to the United States. He had heard it sung in Deolati, India, by a choir of Naga tribesmen from the jungles of Assam. On his tours in

19 O Mighty God, When I Behold the Wonder
Carl Boberg, 1859-1940
Tr. E. Gustav Johnson, 1893-
O STORE GUD 11.10.11.10. with Refrain
Swedish Folk Melody
Harm. by Norman E. Johnson, 1928-
1 O might - y God, when I be - hold the won - der
2 When I be - hold the heav - ens in their vast - ness,
3 And when I hear the roar of storms and thun - der,
4 When sum - mer winds o'er ver - dant fields are play - ing,
5 And when I see, in ho - ly Scrip - ture read - ing,
Of na - ture's beau - ty, wrought by words of thine,
Where gold - en ships in az - ure is - sue forth,
When light - ning cleaves the heav - y sky in twain,
When flow - ers bloom by cool - ing wa - ters' edge,
Thy deeds, O God, on earth since birth of man,
And how thou lead - est all from realms up yon - der,
Where sun and moon keep watch up - on the fast - ness
And rain - bow fair, the sign of prom - ise ten - der,
When sing - ing birds on ev - 'ry tree are sway - ing
Thy grace and wis - dom that is shown in lead - ing
Sus - tain - ing earth - ly life with love be - nign,
Of chang - ing sea - sons and of time on earth,
Re - veals it - self when ends re - fresh - ing rain,
And fill with mel - o - dy each grove and hedge,
Thy peo - ple ev - er safe a - cross life's span,

America he introduced it to various Christian groups. Dr. Cyrus Nelson of Gospel Light Publications copyrighted the song in 1954 and published it on broadsides. Subsequently, he relinquished the copyright to Manna Music, Inc., of North Hollywood, California, and it is through this company that the song has been distributed.

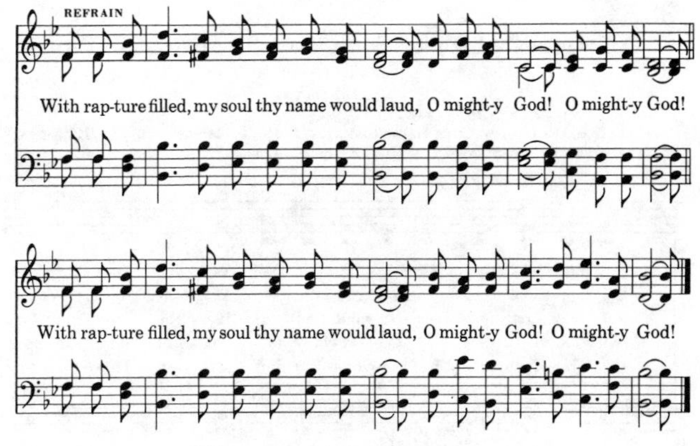
REFRAIN
With rap-ture filled, my soul thy name would laud, O might-y God! O might-y God!
With rap-ture filled, my soul thy name would laud, O might-y God! O might-y God!

6 When I hear fools in ignorance and folly
Deny thee, God, and taunt thy holy word,
And yet perceive that thou supplieth wholly
Their ev'ry need, thy love in grace conferred,

7 When I behold thy Son to earth descending,
To heal and save and teach distressed mankind,
When evil flees and death is seen recoiling
Before the glory of the Lord divine,

8 When crushed by guilt of sin, before thee kneeling
I plead for mercy and for grace and peace,
I feel thy balm and, all my bruises healing,
My soul is filled, my heart is set at ease.

9 And when at last the mists of time have vanished
And I in truth my faith confirmed shall see,
Upon the shores where earthly ills are banished
I'll enter, Lord, to dwell in peace with thee. Amen.

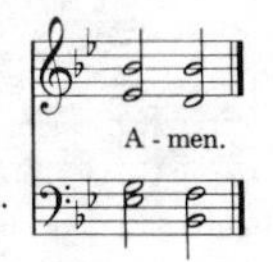
A - men.

O Store Gud, originally written in the summer of 1885 by the Rev. Carl Boberg of the Mission Covenant Church of Sweden, was first published in *Mönsterås-Tidningen*, March 3, 1886.

All nine stanzas included here are from E. Gustav Johnson's translation of the Swedish original poem, first published in *The Children's Friend*, 1925. A shorter version of the words and music first appeared in *The Covenant Hymnal*, published and copyrighted in 1931.

The text widely known as *How Great Thou Art* is an English translation of a Russian version based on an earlier German translation of the original.

ADORATION

The old Swedish melody, O STORE GUD, is the tune to which Boberg's text was first sung and with which it was first published in *Sanningsvittnet*. The original source is unknown, but the arrangement was the work of Erik Adolf Edgren, a musician who later emigrated to America. The setting was in three-quarter time with guitar and piano accompaniment. In 1894 it appeared in *Svenska Missionsförbundets Sångbok* in four beats, much as in "How Great Thou Art" and as in our present hymnal. The arrangements in our Swedish hymnals were in three beats. Various changes have been made from time to time in both the rhythm and the melody line.

337

O Precious Thought! Some Day the Mist Shall Vanish

O sälla land

11. 10. 11. 10.

WILHELM ANDREAS WEXELS, 1841
Trans. (from the Danish) CARL OLOF ROSENIUS, 1848
Trans. (from the Swedish) ANNA HOPPE (1889-1941)

OSCAR AHNFELT (1813-1882)

Quietly, without dragging

1. O precious thought! Some day the mist shall vanish; Some day the web of gloom shall be unspun. A day shall break whose beams the night shall banish, For Christ, the Lamb, shall shine, the glorious Sun!
2. O precious thought! No more will faith be anguished By doubt's uncertainties, by trembling fears. The pangs that wound the heart shall all be vanquished, And light shall flood the gloom of bygone years.
3. Some day each mystery shall find solution, Each troublous question an undimmed reply. The hidden deeps that now seem all confusion My God will open up and clarify.
4. Some day I'll see my ever-faithful Savior, Who pardoned all my sin in boundless grace. Here clouds of trial oft obscure His favor, There I'll behold the brightness of His face.
5. I pray Thee, O my precious Savior, waken These hallowed thoughts of Paradise in me, And let them solace me, till I am taken To dwell in Salem evermore with Thee.

O Precious Thought! Some Day the Mist Shall Vanish

The Danish lyric "Taenk naar engang den Taage er forsvunden" was born out of the writer's life of tragedy—and hope. When Wilhelm Wexels was but a child, his mother died; not many years later, he lost his older brother; after having been happily married only seven years, he lost his wife. After that he turned more and more to thoughts of life beyond death. He wondered whether or not unbelievers would be given a second chance. The more he considered it, the more he became convinced of the possibility. In spite of ridicule and charges of heresy, he sometimes preached it publicly. But his convictions did not prevent him from preaching the need of accepting the grace of God in Christ. It is out of this background that he could write the hymn.

The immediate occasion was the death of his sister's husband in 1841. He wrote the verses in her poetry album in the hope that it would bring her comfort. In 1845, it was published in *Religiøse Digte*. Carl Rosenius translated the text into Swedish—"Tänk när en gång den dimma är försvunnen." This was published in *Pietisten* in 1848. Oscar Ahnfelt set the words (twelve stanzas) to music and included the hymn in his *Andeliga Sånger*, 1850. Later it appeared in many Swedish songbooks in Sweden and America. Anna Hoppe translated eight stanzas for use in the Augustana *Hymnal*, 1925. Miss Hoppe had no knowledge of Swedish, but composed a poem out of a prose translation made by her friend Dr. Adolf Hult.

O SÄLLA LAND (O Happy Land) is the name given to Ahnfelt's tune.

O Savior, Thou Who for Us Died

"Kom huldaste förbarmare" (literally, Come, Most Gracious, Compassionate One) is one of Anders Rutström's most widely sung hymns. Its first appearance was in the handwritten *Sions Evangeliska Sånger*, 1767. Later it was included in most collections of Swedish hymns with the exception of the *Psalmbok*. In America it was printed in most Swedish collections. The translation by E.G. Johnson was prepared for *The Hymnal* (1950).

NUN FREUT EUCH, sometimes called LUTHER and ALTDORF, is probably by Luther. Tradition says that he wrote the tune after hearing it sung by a traveling artisan. It was the setting for his first hymn, "Nun freut euch, liebe Christen g'mein," written in 1523. It appeared in *Etlich Christliche lieder*, Wittenberg, 1524. The usual source is Joseph Klug's *Geistliche lieder*, Wittenberg, 1535. The tune has been the setting for many different texts. It is used four times in our 1973 hymnal.

O That Pearl of Great Price

"Har du funnit den kostliga pärlan?" is based on Jesus' parable as found in Matthew 13:45 and 46. The identity of the writer is uncertain. In his master's thesis, *A.L. Skoog, Pioneer Musician of the Covenant Church,* Oscar Olson assumes that Skoog is the original author. But in *Evangelii Basun* and *Sions Basun,* hymnals of which Skoog was the co-editor, there is no author credit. *Mission Hymns* indicates that Skoog translated from an anonymous Swedish source. The problem with this is that there is no indication of such a text having been used in Sweden. Although the original source remains a mystery, the song is in the spirit and style of Skoog. The hymn was first published in *Evangelii Basun.*

Skoog composed the tune, PEARL OF GREAT PRICE, for the text in 1893. The name is a translation of that used in *The Hymnal* (1950)—DEN KOSTLIGA PÄRLAN.

O Savior, Thou Who for Us Died
461
Anders Carl Rutström, 1721-1772
Tr. E. Gustav Johnson, 1893-
NUN FREUT EUCH 8.7.8.7.8.8.7.
Joseph Klug's "Geistliche Lieder," Wittenberg, 1535
1 O Sav-ior, thou who for us died, Come be our shep-herd ten - der;
2 O love un-bound-ed, pour thy balm Up - on our hu-man an - guish;
Thy flock to liv-ing wa-ters guide, Be thou our true de - fend - er.
With strength of peace our fears be-calm, Our dark fore-bod-ings van - quish.
To Zi - on's ver-dant slopes now lead, Where all thy sheep may
O thou whose mer - cy is com-plete, Trans-form our cold to
safe - ly feed— Thus in thy keep-ing hold us.
fer - vent heat, That we may serve thee whol - ly. A-men.
Words copyright 1950 by Covenant Press.
GUIDANCE AND CARE
294
O That Pearl of Great Price!
Based on Matthew 13:45, 46
From the Swedish
Tr. A. L. Skoog, 1856-1934
PEARL OF GREAT PRICE 10.9.10.9.D.
A. L. Skoog, 1856-1934
1 O that Pearl of great price! have you found it? Is the
2 Have you come to the liv - ing Re - deem - er, Him that
3 Has the Sav - ior, the right - eous, the ho - ly, Cast the
Sav - ior su-preme in your love? O con - sid - er it well, ere you
bore all your sins on the tree? Has he gra-cious-ly par-doned and
beams of his all-search-ing light In - to all of your heart's deep re -
an - swer, As you hope for a wel-come a - bove. Have you
cleansed you In the blood shed for you and for me? At his
cess - es, And trans-formed in - to day their dark night? O then
giv - en up all for this Treas - ure? Have you count - ed past
feet as one dead, have you fall - en, And been quick-ened a -
an - swer these ques-tions so press - ing, Be - fore God, ere time's
gains as but loss? Has your trust in your-self and your
new by his voice, Till, en-tranced by his rich - es of
fa - vor shall cease, Is the Pearl of great price yours for -
mer - its Come to naught be - fore Christ and his cross?
good - ness, In his pres - ence you live and re - joice?
ev - er? Have you Je - sus, and in him your peace?

118
O Zion, Acclaim Your Redeemer!
Mary Elizabeth Servoss, 1849-?
Tr. Erik Nyström, 1842-1907
Tr. E. Gustav Johnson, 1893-
GÅ SION 9.8.9.8. with Refrain
James McGranahan, 1840-1907
Harm. by Norman E. Johnson, 1928-
1 O Zi - on, ac-claim your Re-deem-er! Je - ru - sa-lem, wel-come your King!
2 He comes from the joys of the a - ges, He leaves his do-min - ion sub-lime;
3 He comes as a ran-som most ho - ly, He dies on the cross for the world;
4 He comes from the tomb as a vic - tor, The shad-ows of death clear a - way;
5 He comes to the sor - row-ing spir - it And life is re-newed by his hand;
Strew palms on the way for the Sav - ior, His prais - es ex - ul - tant - ly sing.
From glo - ry to Beth - le - hem's man - ger He comes in the full-ness of time.
Re - demp - tion from sin is ac-com-plished, His ban - ner of light is un-furled.
The slum - ber - ing saints are a - wak - ened, A - roused from their sleep in the clay.
He comes to es - tab - lish a king - dom That shall thru e - ter - ni - ty stand.
REFRAIN
Re - joice! Re - joice! Re - joice in your Sav - ior and King!
Re - joice! Re - joice! Ac - claim him your Sav - ior and King!
Words copyright 1950 by Covenant Press.
Harm. copyright 1973 by Covenant Press.
ADVENT
151
Our Day of Joy Is Here Again
A. L. Skoog, 1856-1934
YULETIDE C.M. with Refrain
A. L. Skoog, 1856-1934
1 Our day of joy is here a - gain With love and peace and song;
2 When dark - ness lay up - on this earth, A glo - rious light did shine;
3 Now to the man - ger let us go To wor - ship and a - dore
4 How won - der - ful that God's own Son Should so him - self a - base!
Come, let us join th' an - gel - ic strain With voic - es clear and strong.
God sent a gift of price - less worth And showed his love di - vine.
The ten - der babe up - on the straw, Our Sav - ior ev - er - more.
He thrust the might - y from their throne And gave the low - ly grace.
REFRAIN
Glo - ry to our God, we sing, Glo - ry to our Lord and King;
Peace, good will with all a - bide This ho - ly Christ - mas - tide.
BIRTH

O Zion, Acclaim Your Redeemer!

It would not be erroneous to say that Erik Nyström is the author rather than the translator of "Gå, Sion, din konung att möta." This is a song for Advent, while the text by Mary Servoss is a general hymn of praise. No doubt Nyström had the latter in mind when he wrote, since the tune is the same and the refrain begins with "Rejoice, rejoice." Nyström wrote the song for *Svenska Missionsförbundets Sångbok*, 1894, a hymnal of which he was the chief editor. It was included in *Sions Basun* and translated by E.G. Johnson for *The Hymnal* (1950).

GÅ SION is the name given to the tune which was composed by James McGranahan for the Servoss text and published in 1877.

Our Day of Joy Is Here Again

In "Nu glädjens timme inne är" A.L. Skoog caught the joy of Christmas in simple fashion. In a few common and almost all monosyllabic words, he told the basic story of the Gospel. The song was written in 1892 and published in *Evangelii Basun,* 1894. The English version, also the work of the author, was first published in *The Covenant Hymnal* (1931).

The joyful tune YULETIDE was composed as a setting for this text by Skoog.

Our Mighty God Works Mighty Wonders

Nils Frykman wrote "Vår store Gud gör stora under" during a revival meeting in a country cottage in 1876. He was preaching in a crowded room, and the people sang and rejoiced, sobbed and wept. A believer who had traveled a long distance to see and hear what was taking place in these meetings stood near the door. He had a puzzled look on his face, as much as to say, "What in the world is going on here?" Frykman took notice of this, and the answer came to him in a flash: "It is our great God who does wonderful things." After he concluded his sermon, another schoolteacher began to preach. Frykman sat at a little table behind the preacher with pen in hand, and the song was born. It was first published in *Sanningsvittnet,* April 13, 1877. Soon the song became a favorite among Swedish free church people on both sides of the Atlantic. All six stanzas were translated by A.L. Skoog for use in *Mission Hymns.* Later some revisions were made by Frykman's son, Andrew, and the new version of five stanzas was printed in our last two hymnals.

The tune name, VÅR STORE GUD, was altered to CELEBRATION in the present hymnal. This has come to be the accepted melody, although the text has had several settings. It is taken from Joel Blomqvist's *Melodier till Sions Nya Sånger,* 1873, where it is used with different words.

72 Our Mighty God Works Mighty Wonders
Nils Frykman, 1842-1911
Tr. A. L. Skoog, 1856-1934
Tr. Andrew T. Frykman, 1875-1943
CELEBRATION 9.8.9.8.8.8.
Swedish Folk Melody
1 Our might - y God works might - y won - ders— What joy to see them all a - round! Men's i - dols fall be - fore his thun - ders, Their al - tars crum - bling to the ground. He breaks the fet - ters, frees the slaves, His fall - en chil - dren still he saves.
2 His might - y word goes forth to con - quer, Its pow'r de - stroys the forts of doubt; The war - riors bold yield up their ar - mor To him who will not cast them out. They cleans - ing find in Je - sus' blood And laud and mag - ni - fy our God.
3 Be - hold the host of breth - ren near - ing The gates of heav'n with might - y tread; With ban - ners wav - ing, sing - ing, cheer - ing, They hail in joy their roy - al Head; And man - y more shall own his reign, His won - drous love the vic - t'ry gain.
4 Dear Lord, as throngs thy king - dom en - ter, May not my heart thy love de - cline; Teach me my faith on thee to cen - ter, Thy grace shall make me whol - ly thine. Take thou my hand and hold it fast, Un - til I reach thy heav'n at last.
5 O God be praised! the day is near - ing, When to our ears a voice shall come, "Look up! the Lord is now ap - pear - ing, To gath - er all his loved ones home!" O bless - ed day of ju - bi - lee! For thee I wait! I wait for thee!
GOD'S ETERNITY AND POWER

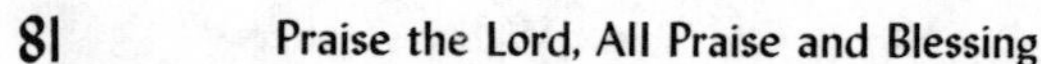
81 Praise the Lord, All Praise and Blessing

Joel Blomqvist, 1840-1930
Tr. Gerhard W. Palmgren, 1880-1959
LOVEN HERREN 8.7.8.7.7.7.
Joel Blomqvist, 1840-1930
1 Praise the Lord, all praise and bless - ing Ren - der
2 He cre - at - ed earth and heav - en, Deep - est
3 Stars a - bove in bril - liant glo - ry, Sun that
4 Yet of all that God cre - at - ed Man to
5 God so loved this world of sin - ners That his
to his might - y name; Thank him ev - er for his good-ness,
sea and all there - in; Small - est crea - ture, high - est be - ing,
scat - ters wide its gold, Birds a - loft, all join the cho - rus,
him most pre - cious is; O what won - der - ful de - vo - tion,
on - ly Son he gave To en - dure death's bit - ter an - guish
Now and ev - er - more the same. Come, my soul, your
Let your an - thems now be - gin. Bless him in this
Ev - 'ry crea - ture, young and old, Sing to him who
How it fills my heart with bliss! With a child - like
And the lost to seek and save. Let our prais - es
trib - ute bring, Praise him ev - 'ry liv - ing thing.
glad - some hour, Bless his maj - es - ty and pow'r.
reigns su - preme, Chant that ev - er - joy - ful theme.
joy I sing Prais - es to my God and King!
rend the sky, Glo - ry be to God on high. A - men.

GOD IN NATURE

Praise the Lord, All Praise and Blessing

Praise is not a common or strong note in Joel Blomqvist's writings, but it is there, nonetheless. And "Loven Herren, ty att lova" is a good example. It was first published in his *Fridstoner*, 1879. The hymn has been used almost exclusively among Covenanters here and in Sweden. It was translated by Gerhard Palmgren for the 1950 hymnal.

Blomqvist's strong and stately melody, LOVEN HERREN, is an appropriate setting for his text.

Praise the Lord, Each Tribe and Nation

"Hela världen fröjdas Herren" is the Swedish version of Johann Franck's "Alle Welt, was kreucht und webet," which was first published in Germany in 1653. Franck was a German lawyer and writer who sounded a new note through his warm-hearted "Jesus songs." These hymns were closely related to those of the pietists. This particular one was translated for use in *Psalme-Profwer*, 1691, by Jakob Arrhenius and revised by Swedberg for the 1694 *Psalmbok*. It found its way into most Swedish collections in Sweden and the United States. The English translation by Ernst Olson first appeared in the Augustana *Hymnal*, 1901. Our first publication of the hymn was in *Mission Hymns*.

For a note on KALMAR see "Jesus, Lord and Precious Savior."

Many years ago a Swedish newspaper carried an article about a religious conference. It read in part: "With what should a 'läsarfolkets' conference begin if not with the hymn of praise, 'Praise the Lord, Each Tribe and Nation'? The leader announced the song, whereupon a thousand voices made the rafters ring, assisted by the mighty rumble of the organ."

Praise the Lord, Each Tribe and Nation
56
Johann Franck, 1618-1677
Tr. Ernst W. Olson, 1870-1958
KALMAR 8.7.8.7.7.7.
Swedish Melody, 1676
1 Praise the Lord, each tribe and na - tion, Praise him with a joy - ous heart;
2 He's our God and our Cre - a - tor, We his flock and cho - sen seed;
3 Give him thanks with - in his por - tals, In the courts his deeds pro - claim;
Ye who know his full sal - va - tion, Gath - er now from ev - 'ry part:
He, our Lord and lib - er - a - tor, Us from sin and per - il freed:
Hith - er come, ye ran-somed mor - tals, Glo - ri - fy our Sav - ior's name:
Let your voic - es glo - ri - fy, In his tem - ple, God on high.
And at last his flock shall rest In the man - sions of the blest.
Ev - er lov - ing Lord is he, Keep - ing faith e - ter - nal - ly. A - men.

Words used by permission of Fortress Press.
Another harmonization in a lower setting may be found at No. 433

OPENING

Praise the Lord with Joyful Song
73
A. L. Skoog, 1856-1934
Tr. E. Gustav Johnson, 1893-
LOVEN GUD 7.6.7.6. with Refrain
A. L. Skoog, 1856-1934
1 Praise the Lord with joy - ful song, U - nite with full ac - cord!
2 Praise him for his maj - es - ty, His great and glo - rious pow'r!
3 Praise him with the sound of harps, With mu - sic loud and clear!
4 Praise him with har - mo - nious chimes, With chords of joy pro - claim!
For his glo - ry and his might Sing prais - es to the Lord!
Hail him with a wor - thy hymn, Ex - alt his name this hour!
With glad strains of mel - o - dy Our gra - cious God re - vere!
Great and ho - ly is the Lord: Sing prais - es to his name!
REFRAIN
Sing his prais - es, ev - 'ry liv - ing thing, Un - to him de - vo - ted hom - age bring,
Of his love and good - ness ev - er sing! Hal - le - lu - jah! Praise the Lord!

Words copyright 1950 by Covenant Press.

GOD'S ETERNITY AND POWER

Praise the Lord with Joyful Song

The joyful, rhythmic song "Loven Gud med glädjesång" is, no doubt, one of A.L. Skoog's best works. It came out under the title "Uppmaning till lov" (Exhortation to Praise) and cited Psalm 150 as the source. It was written in 1890 and published that year in *Söndagsskolvännen,* a children's paper edited by Skoog. After its publication in *Herde-Rösten* in 1890, it appeared in most of the Swedish free church collections in America. The translation into English was done by E.G. Johnson for *The Hymnal* (1950).

Skoog was also the composer of the tune, LOVEN GUD. In several of the early publications this note appeared below the song: "This song can also be sung as a fugue (canon), if one group begins the first stanza after another has reached the chorus, and so turn about without a break to the end of the song. If this is done with two choirs, a better effect is realized if they stand opposite each other."

Prepare the Way, O Zion!
119
Frans Michael Franzén, 1772-1847
Tr. Augustus Nelson, 1863-1949
MESSIAH 7.6.7.6.7.7.6.6.
Swedish Melody, 1694
1 Pre - pare the way, O Zi - on! Ye aw - ful deeps, rise high;
2 O Zi - on, he ap - proach - es, Your Lord and King for aye;
3 Fling wide your por - tals, Zi - on, And hail your glo - rious King;
4 The throne which he as - cend - ed Is fixed in heav'n a - bove;
Sink low, ye loft - y moun-tains, The Lord is draw - ing nigh.
Strew palms where he ad - vanc - es, Spread gar-ments in his way.
His ti - dings of sal - va - tion To ev - 'ry peo - ple bring,
His ev - er - last - ing king - dom Is light and joy and love.
The right-eous King of glo - ry, Fore - told in sa - cred sto - ry:
God's prom - ise fail - eth nev - er, Ho - san - na sound for - ev - er:
Who, wait - ing still in sad - ness, Would sing his praise with glad - ness:
Let us his praise be sound - ing For grace and peace a - bound - ing:
O blest is he who came In God the Fa - ther's name. A - men.
Words from The Lutheran Service Book and Hymnal, by permission of the Commission on the Liturgy and Hymnal.
ADVENT

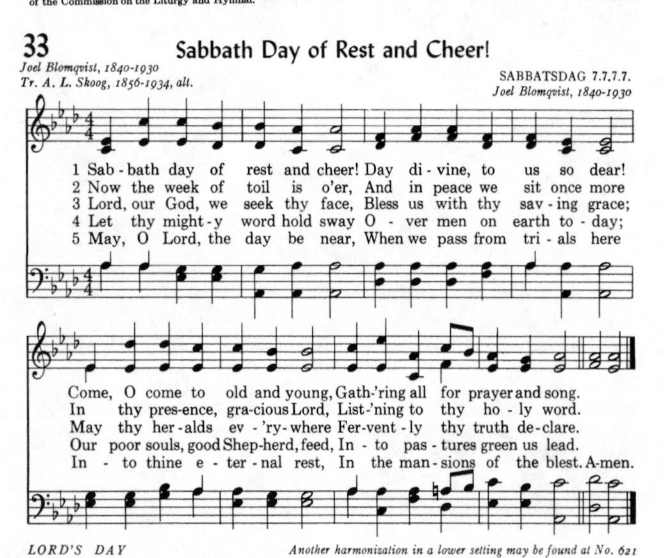
33
Sabbath Day of Rest and Cheer!
Joel Blomqvist, 1840-1930
Tr. A. L. Skoog, 1856-1934, alt.
SABBATSDAG 7.7.7.7.
Joel Blomqvist, 1840-1930
1 Sab - bath day of rest and cheer! Day di - vine, to us so dear!
2 Now the week of toil is o'er, And in peace we sit once more
3 Lord, our God, we seek thy face, Bless us with thy sav - ing grace;
4 Let thy might - y word hold sway O - ver men on earth to - day;
5 May, O Lord, the day be near, When we pass from tri - als here
Come, O come to old and young, Gath - 'ring all for prayer and song.
In thy pres - ence, gra - cious Lord, List - 'ning to thy ho - ly word.
May thy her - alds ev - 'ry - where Fer - vent - ly thy truth de - clare.
Our poor souls, good Shep - herd, feed, In - to pas - tures green us lead.
In - to thine e - ter - nal rest, In the man - sions of the blest. A - men.
LORD'S DAY
Another harmonization in a lower setting may be found at No. 621

Prepare the Way, O Zion

"Bereden väg för Herren" is considered by many to be Frans Mikael Franzen's finest lyric—and perhaps has been Sweden's most-loved Advent hymn. It is replete with biblical pictures and filled with holy anticipation. It sounded the missionary note long before the movement took hold. Stanza three reads:

> *His tidings of salvation*
> *To ev'ry people bring,*
> *Who, waiting still in sadness,*
> *Would sing his praise with gladness.*

In its original form it met with criticism in *Litteratur Tidningen,* 1812. After revision it was given a favorable review in *Stockholms Posten,* 1817. The hymn was first published in *Prof-Psalmer,* 1812, an edition prepared by Franzen and Wallin. The hymn has had wide use among Scandinavians the world over. The English translation by Augustus Nelson was first published in the Augustana *Hymnal,* 1901.

MESSIAH is an old Swedish melody. In 1694, it was included in a handwritten "koralbok" used in the Riddarholm Church in Stockholm.

Sabbath Day of Rest and Cheer

In his diary, colporteur Joel Blomqvist often expressed his joy over the sabbath, not only because it gave him a chance to rest, but also because it gave him an opportunity to listen to the preaching of the Word of God. He caught this joy in "Sabbatsdag, hur skön du är" (literally, Sabbath Day, How Beautiful You Are). It appeared first in his *Sabbatsklockan,* 1877, and later it was published in many free church songbooks in Sweden and the United States and in early Augustana collections. It was translated for *Mission Hymns* by A.L. Skoog.

The author of the lyrics was also the composer of the tune, which takes its name from the first word, SABBATSDAG. Although it is simple, it is interesting and enduring; it is used three times in our present hymnal.

Savior, in Thy Love Abiding

"Jesus, gör mig nöjd och stilla" (literally, Jesus, make me content and calm) came from the pen of Selma Lagerström. This prayer of consecration was first published in *Sanningsvittnet*, December, 1885, and soon was picked up by most of the free church groups in Sweden and the United States. The translation for *The Hymnal* (1950) was done by E.G. Johnson.

The tune, PROCH, is named after the Austrian composer, Heinrich Proch. It was the melody for a vocal solo entitled "High from the Alps Sounds the Horn." The hymn makes use of only the first two scores of music. *Sions Basun* had a setting of six scores in which the first two were identical to the last two, but scores three and four introduced a new ascending melody line. In this version there were three twelve-line stanzas. Most hymnals have used five four-line stanzas. In the original music there was a difficult-to-sing triplet at the beginning of the last line. The second note of the triplet has been eliminated in most versions to make the song more singable.

Sing the Glad Carol of Jesus, Our Lord

Someone has described "Sången om Jesus, o sjung den igen" as "a blend of joy-tempered Värmlandish and frank, go-go Americanism." It is a free and fresh expression of praise to God for Jesus Christ. The song was included in *Sionsharpan* and *Sions Glädjebud* and then in *De Ungas Sångbok*. The translation was one of the many done by E.G. Johnson for the 1950 hymnal. In 1954, Covenant Press published a collection of hymns and choruses for special occasions. It was named *Sing It Again* after the first song in the booklet.

GLAD CAROL is the name given to the tune which Skoog composed as a setting for his text.

Savior, in Thy Love Abiding 399

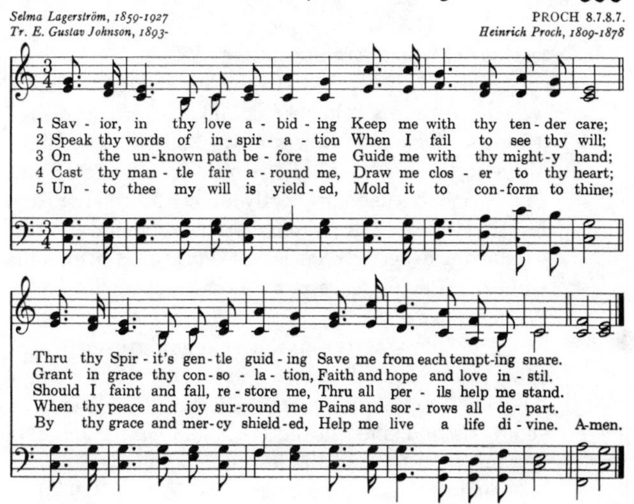
Selma Lagerström, 1859-1927
Tr. E. Gustav Johnson, 1893-
PROCH 8.7.8.7.
Heinrich Proch, 1809-1878
1 Sav - ior, in thy love a - bid - ing Keep me with thy ten - der care;
2 Speak thy words of in - spir - a - tion When I fail to see thy will;
3 On the un - known path be - fore me Guide me with thy might - y hand;
4 Cast thy man - tle fair a - round me, Draw me clos - er to thy heart;
5 Un - to thee my will is yield - ed, Mold it to con - form to thine;
Thru thy Spir - it's gen - tle guid - ing Save me from each tempt - ing snare.
Grant in grace thy con - so - la - tion, Faith and hope and love in - stil.
Should I faint and fall, re - store me, Thru all per - ils help me stand.
When thy peace and joy sur - round me Pains and sor - rows all de - part.
By thy grace and mer - cy shield - ed, Help me live a life di - vine. A - men.

Words copyright 1950 by Covenant Press.

FAITH AND ASSURANCE

255 Sing the Glad Carol of Jesus, Our Lord
A. L. Skoog, 1856-1934
Tr. E. Gustav Johnson, 1893-
GLAD CAROL 10.4.4.10.6. with Refrain
A. L. Skoog, 1856-1934
1 Sing the glad car - ol of Je - sus, our Lord, Sing it a - gain, sing it a - gain!
2 Faith and new cour - age are in this re - frain, Sing it a - gain, sing it a - gain!
3 Sing it for all who God's love hold in scorn, Sing it a - gain, sing it a - gain!
4 Sing with God's chil - dren a - round you to - day, Sing it a - gain, sing it a - gain!
No oth - er song can such bless - ing af - ford, Sing it a - gain, a - gain!
Free - dom it of - fers, it breaks ev - 'ry chain, Sing it a - gain, a - gain!
For through its pow - er can souls be re - born, Sing it a - gain, a - gain!
Let us our joy in the Sav - ior dis - play, Sing it a - gain, a - gain!
REFRAIN
Je - sus, our friend! Hap - py and bless - ed cho - rus!
Je - sus, our friend! our friend!
O - ver the earth let its mes - sage ex - tend, Sing it a - gain, a - gain!

PRAISE TO CHRIST

Words copyright 1950 by Covenant Press.

Springs of Grace Are Streaming

A Swedish Methodist minister, Carl Stenholm, was the author of "Hälsokällan flödde." He published it in *Lilla Sändebudet*, February 2, 1874 (The Little Messenger), a periodical of which he was the editor. The hymn was used primarily among Methodists and Baptists in Sweden, which may have been due to its similarity, especially in the melody, to "Här en källa rinner," Betty Ehrenborg-Posse's translation of William Cowper's "There Is a Fountain Filled with Blood." This was the hymn commonly used in the State Church and in the Covenant. Both songs, however, appeared in *Sions Basun*. The Stenholm song was published in the 1931 *Covenant Hymnal* in a translation by J.B. Linderholm. A new translation was made by E.G. Johnson for *The Hymnal* (1950).

The tune, LIVING WATER, seems to be a somewhat altered form of the melody used with the above-mentioned "Här en källa rinner," but the source is unknown.

510 Springs of Grace Are Streaming
Carl A. Stenholm, 1843-1884
Tr. E. Gustav Johnson, 1893-
LIVING WATER 6.5.6.5.
Source unknown
1 Springs of grace are stream - ing From the cross of Christ,
2 Sooth - ing balm is pour - ing In - to hearts that grieve,
3 When my heart is sink - ing 'Neath the load of care,
4 When the morn is glow - ing, And at e - ven - tide,
5 By this fount of bless - ing Is my rest - ing place;
Where for man's re - deem - ing He was sac - ri - ficed.
Joy and hope re - stor - ing When earth's com - forts leave.
At this foun - tain drink - ing, Heav - en's strength I share.
Springs di - vine are flow - ing, Mer - cy to pro - vide.
Safe from things dis - tress - ing, Peace I there em - brace.
Words copyright 1950 by Covenant Press.

516 Strait Is the Gate to All That Come

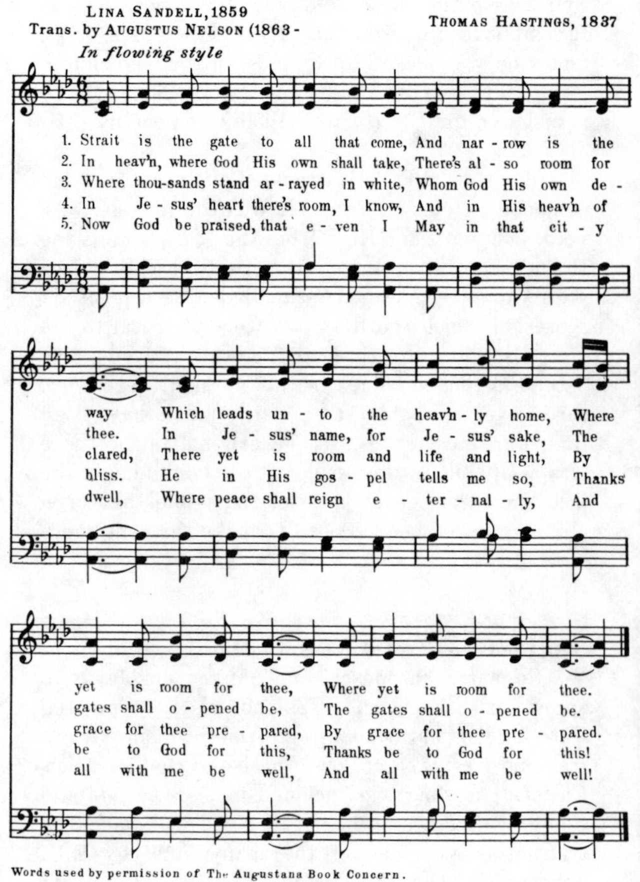
Ortonville
C.M.
Lina Sandell, 1859
Trans. by Augustus Nelson (1863-
Thomas Hastings, 1837
In flowing style
1. Strait is the gate to all that come, And nar - row is the way Which leads un - to the heav'n - ly home, Where yet is room for thee, Where yet is room for thee.
2. In heav'n, where God His own shall take, There's al - so room for thee. In Je - sus' name, for Je - sus' sake, The gates shall o - pened be, The gates shall o - pened be.
3. Where thou - sands stand ar - rayed in white, Whom God His own de - clared, There yet is room and life and light, By grace for thee pre - pared, By grace for thee pre - pared.
4. In Je - sus' heart there's room, I know, And in His heav'n of bliss. He in His gos - pel tells me so, Thanks be to God for this, Thanks be to God for this!
5. Now God be praised, that e - ven I May in that cit - y dwell, Where peace shall reign e - ter - nal - ly, And all with me be well, And all with me be well!
Words used by permission of The Augustana Book Concern.

Strait Is the Gate to All Who Come

Lina Sandell opens this song of invitation and heaven with the words of Jesus as recorded in Matthew 7:14, "Den port är trång, den väg är smal." It was first published in the 1859 edition of Wadstrom's *Andeliga Sånger*. As was true of so many of the Sandell songs, this one was included in many of the free church collections in Sweden and America as well as in the early Augustana songbooks. Augustus Nelson is responsible for the English version, which was first published in the Augustana *Hymnal*, 1925. The Covenant's use of the song in English has been restricted to *The Hymnal* (1950).

ORTONVILLE was written by Thomas Hastings for the hymn "Majestic Sweetness Sits Enthroned" and first appeared in his *The Manhattan Collection* (New York, 1937).

Tell Me, Who Are These

This is one of the several songs in our hymnody that have had interesting and circuitous pilgrimages. The original hymn was the creation of an Ohio professor, Tullius C. O'Kane. His All Saints' Day song, based on Revelation 7, was entitled "Who, Who Are These beside the Chilly Wave?" The song was in *Sankey's Sacred Songs*, 1874, and was translated into Swedish by Erik Nyström for his *Sånger till Lammets lof*, 1875. "Vilka äro dessa, som vid flodens strand" appeared later in several of the songbooks in Sweden and in most of the early Swedish hymnals in this country. The English version in *The Hymnal* (1950) is a translation by Signhild Gustafson of the Swedish text.

Following is the first stanza and chorus of the original text:

Who, who are these beside the chilly wave,
Just on the borders of the silent grave,
Shouting Jesus' power to save,
"Washed in the blood of the Lamb"?

"Sweeping through the gates" of the New Jerusalem,
"Washed in the blood of the Lamb."

The tune, which was named after the Swedish opening line, VILKA ÄRO DESSA, was composed by O'Kane for the original English text.

517 Tell Me, Who Are These

Vilka äro dessa

11. 10. 7. 7. with refrain

Original English version, TULLIUS C. O'KANE (1830-1912)
Trans. (into Swedish) by ERIK NYSTRÖM, 1875
Trans. (from Swedish) by SIGNHILD V. GUSTAFSON, 1947

TULLIUS C. O'KANE (1830-1912)

Jubilantly

1. Tell me, who are these that, on the bless-ed strand, Raised from the dark-ness, now in splen-dor stand, Prais-ing God with palms in hand, Washed in the blood of the Lamb?
2. These are they who, glad-ly, in the strength of youth, Fol-lowed their Mas-ter in the path of truth, And with grace and pow'r went forth, Washed in the blood of the Lamb.
3. These are they who, liv-ing in the world's dis-tress, Found in the Sav-ior peace and hap-pi-ness, Ev-er did His name pro-fess, Washed in the blood of the Lamb.
4. These are they who faced the flame and fier-y sword, Serv-ing in bat-tles for their King and Lord, Now re-ceiv-ing their re-ward, Washed in the blood of the Lamb.
5. Gath-ered are they now up-on the bliss-ful shore, Free from the sor-row and the cross they bore, Prais-ing God for-ev-er-more, Washed in the blood of the Lamb.

REFRAIN

Ju-bi-lant-ly sing-ing, through the gates they go, Washed in the blood of the Lamb. Washed in the blood of the Lamb!

622 Thanks to God for My Redeemer
August Ludvig Storm, 1862-1914
Tr. Carl E. Backstrom, 1901-
TACK O GUD 8.7.8.7.D.
J. A. Hultman, 1861-1942
1 Thanks to God for my Re-deem-er, Thanks for all thou dost pro-vide!
2 Thanks for prayers that thou hast an-swered, Thanks for what thou dost de-ny!
3 Thanks for ros-es by the way-side, Thanks for thorns their stems con-tain!
Tack, O Gud, för vad du va-rit, Tack för allt, vad du be-skär!
Thanks for times now but a mem-'ry, Thanks for Je-sus by my side!
Thanks for storms that I have weath-ered, Thanks for all thou dost sup-ply!
Thanks for home and thanks for fire-side, Thanks for hope, that sweet re-frain!
Tack för ti-der-na, som fa-rit, Tack för stun-den, som nu är!
Thanks for pleas-ant, balm-y spring-time, Thanks for dark and drear-y fall!
Thanks for pain and thanks for pleas-ure, Thanks for com-fort in de-spair!
Thanks for joy and thanks for sor-row, Thanks for heav'n-ly peace with thee!
Tack för lju-sa var-ma vå-ror, Tack för mörk och ku-len höst!
Thanks for tears by now for-got-ten, Thanks for peace with-in my soul!
Thanks for grace that none can meas-ure, Thanks for love be-yond com-pare!
Thanks for hope in the to-mor-row, Thanks thru all e-ter-ni-ty!
Tack för re-dan glöm-da tå-rar, Tack för fri-den i mitt bröst! A-men.

The Highest Joy That Can Be Known 283
Nils Frykman, 1842-1911
Tr. Signe L. Bennett, 1900-
Tr. Andrew T. Frykman, 1875-1943
HIGHEST JOY 8.6.8.6.8.6.
Amanda S. Waesterberg, 1842-1918
1 The high-est joy that can be known By those who heav'n-ward wend— It is the Word of Life to own, And God to have as friend; It is the Word of Life to own, And God to have as friend.
2 The Word doth give me wealth un-told, All good it has in store; My deep-est sor-rows yield their hold To joys for-ev-er-more; My deep-est sor-rows yield their hold To joys for-ev-er-more.
3 How oft-en when in deep de-spair My soul has been re-stored; And when the tempt-er would en-snare 'Twould strength to stand af-ford; And when the tempt-er would en-snare 'Twould strength to stand af-ford.
4 It tells me of a love di-vine, How Je-sus' blood was shed; Each day this joy-ous song is mine As paths of grace I tread; Each day this joy-ous song is mine As paths of grace I tread.
5 When stars a-bove shall shine no more, God's Word is still my light; When pleas-ures of this world are o'er, My joys will reach their height; When pleas-ures of this world are o'er, My joys will reach their height.

THANKSGIVING

HOLY SCRIPTURES

Thanks to God for My Redeemer

There are very few songs of Swedish heritage that have been more popular than "Tack, O Gud, för vad du (som) varit." The lyrics were written by August Ludvig Storm, a Salvation Army officer, and first published in *Stridsropet* (The War Cry), December 5, 1891. Each line of the four stanzas begins with the word "thanks" and states one thing for which the author expresses gratitude to God. But in the words of Oscar Lövgren, "There are no cheap commodities in the thirty-two thanks found in the song." Storm thanks God for "dark and dreary fall" as well as for "pleasant, balmy springtime"; for "pain" as well as "pleasure"; for "thorns" as well as "roses." Although this was written before a severe back ailment left him painfully crippled, Storm could write a poem just a year before his death in which he thanked God for the years of calm and quiet and the years of pain.

The song appeared in the Salvation Army songbook with a Welsh tune. The text was published in *Hemlandsklockan* (Minneapolis, 1900) with a note that it should be sung to a tune by August Elfåker. It was not until J.A. Hultman published it with his own tune in *Solskenssånger*, 1910, that the song really took hold, and after that it was included in free church hymnals here and in Sweden. Carl E. Backstrom was responsible for the three-stanza version in our 1931 hymnal. Although he omitted stanza three, he did incorporate some of its ideas.

As already noted, the music was composed by J.A. Hultman. TACK O GUD is one of his best tunes and is fitting for the text.

The Highest Joy That Can Be Known

"Den högsta lycka på vår jord" was one of the last of the Frykman songs written before his move to America. Although it was first published in *Pilgrimstoner* (Stockholm, 1886), it did not come into use in Sweden. In fact, its use has been restricted almost exclusively to the Covenant in America. The English translation in *The Covenant Hymnal* (1931) was the work of Signe Bennett and Andrew Frykman.

HIGHEST JOY was composed by Amanda S. Waesterberg. Evidently it was written for this particular text; it is not a common metrical system.

The Hour in Dark Gethsemane

This is another of the songs that have undergone several translations. It was originally written in English by Edward Payson Hammond—"My Jesus, I Would Ne'er Forget That Hour I Spent with Thee." It was printed in his *Gems of Praise* with a note stating that it was a visit to Gethsemane in 1866 that inspired the song. A Norwegian translation appeared in *Hjemlandstoner*, 1895. The version in *Sions Basun*, "En timme i Getsemane," is by Albert Johanson. Our English version is a translation from the Norwegian made in 1931 by T.O. Burntvedt. It appeared in the *Concordia Hymnal.*

IN DARK GETHSEMANE was composed by Asa Hull, a musician in Boston and later New York. He published a hymnal in 1859 entitled *Gospel Praise Book.*

152 The Hour in Dark Gethsemane

In dark Gethsemane (Hull)
C. M. with refrain

From the Norwegian
Trans. by T. O. Burntvedt, 1931

Asa Hull, 1869

With quiet reverence

1. The hour in dark Geth-sem-a-ne I nev-er shall for-get, When Christ a-lone the bat-tle fought, In grief and blood-y sweat.
2. When I a-mong thy sol-emn trees, In spir-it gazed a-round; I saw the bur-den of my sin On Him with judg-ment bound.
3. I saw Him tempt-ed to de-spair, By an-guish, grief, bent low; The depth of pain He suf-fered there No man can ful-ly know.
4. If ev-er, Lord, my love to Thee Should cold and fruit-less be, O show me in Geth-sem-a-ne Thy suf-f'ring there for me.

Refrain

Geth-sem-a-ne, Geth-sem-a-ne, I must re-mem-ber thee, Where God's e-ter-nal Son I saw In pray'r on bend-ed knee.

Words used by permission of T.O. Burntvedt.

608 There Are Treasures for Children in Heaven
From the Swedish
Tr. Ernest Edwin Ryden, 1886-
TREASURES 12.9.12.9. with Refrain
Source unknown
1 There are treas-ures for chil-dren in heav-en a-bove, For the
2 They shall join in the an-thems of glo-ry and praise, They shall
chil-dren who trust in their Lord; They shall dwell in the light of his
sing with the an-gels so fair; And no sor-row or sigh-ing shall
fa-vor and love, They shall praise him with joy-ous ac-cord.
hush their sweet lays, When they meet their Re-deem-er up there.
REFRAIN
There are treas-ures in heav'n, there are treas-ures in heav'n, There are
treas-ures for chil-dren in heav'n; In the man-sions so bright, where the
LIFE EVERLASTING
Words used by permission of Fortress Press.

There Are Treasures for Children in Heaven

"Det blir något i himlen för barnen att få" first appeared in Sweden in the Methodist *Sånger for söndagsskolan,* Part 1, 1869. Lövgren thinks it is a translation from English, since many of the songs in the collection were from that source. And still the files of the yet-to-be-published *Dictionary of American Hymnology* show only the E.E. Ryden version. Hultman included the song (Swedish) in the second part of *Cymbalen,* 1888, and it also appeared in *Hemlandssånger,* 1892. Its first printing in a Covenant hymnal was in *De Ungas Sångbok,* where it is credited to Lina Sandell. There is a remote possibility that she was the translator. E.E. Ryden's version first appeared in Augustana's *The Junior Hymnal,* 1928, and then in our 1931 songbook.

In Sweden the text has usually been associated with the tune we call ELFÅKER (see *The Covenant Hymnal,* [*1973*] No. 307). This is probably based on an old folk melody from Värmland. The tune NÅGOT FÖR BARNEN or TREASURES is of unknown origin. Perhaps it was the melody associated with the original text.

Thou Tender, Gracious Father

"Du ömma fadershjärta" (actually, Tender Father's Heart) appeared in *Barnens Tidning,* No. 3, 1859, at the conclusion of an article about "bird talk." Lina Sandell had in mind Matthew 23:37 or Luke 13:34, where Jesus used the metaphor of a hen's gathering of her chicks under her wings. In fact, the original title of the poem used the metaphor, but it was changed upon publication in *Pilgrims-Sånger,* 1859. The song has been quite widely used in free church congregations in Sweden and America. It also was included in early Augustana collections. It was translated by Carl O. Dahlen for the Swedish Baptists' first English hymnal, *The New Hymnal,* 1925. In 1931 the hymn appeared in *The Covenant Hymnal.*

FAR OFF LANDS was used with the text when the hymn was first published in *Pilgrims-Sånger.* For a further note on the tune, see "Mine Eyes Look toward the Mountains."

Thou Tender, Gracious Father
97
Lina Sandell, 1832-1903
Tr. Carl O. Dahlen, 1867-1938
FAR-OFF LANDS 7.6.7.6.D.
From the Bohemian Brethren
1 Thou ten - der, gra - cious Fa - ther, Who watch - es o - ver me,
2 With rai - ment, food and shel - ter, What - e'er my needs im - ply,
3 In child - like, true o - be - dience Help me to do the right;
4 Thy heart is all com - pas - sion, With love it o - ver - flows;
How shall I ev - er praise thee, How love and hon - or thee?
For soul and bod - y ev - er, Do thou in grace sup - ply.
May pre - cious be thy stat - utes, Thy yoke be pleas - ant, light!
What - e'er of ill be - tide me, Thou know - est, and my woes.
Thou guid - est me with cau - tion From ev - 'ry se - cret snare,
O Lord, I soon would per - ish If aught thou should ex - clude;
And when some hard - ship threat - ens, A dan - ger fright - ens me,
Thou dost not sleep nor slum - ber By night nor thru the days;
And 'neath thy wings a ref - uge I find in my de - spair.
O could I love thee bet - ter And prove my grat - i - tude.
May thou in all my tri - als My pres - ent help - er be.
Thine arms, al - might - y Fa - ther, En - fold all time and space. A - men.
Words used by permission of Harvest Publications.
GOD'S LOVE AND FATHERHOOD
371
Through the Night of Doubt and Sorrow
Bernhardt S. Ingemann, 1789-1862
Tr. Sabine Baring-Gould, 1834-1924
LAMMETS FOLK 8.7.8.7.D.
Attr. to Anders Carl Rutström, 1721-1772
"Sions Nya Sånger," 1854
1 Through the night of doubt and sor - row On - ward goes the
2 One the light of God's own pres - ence O'er his ran - somed
3 One the strain that lips of thou - sands Lift as from the
4 On - ward, there - fore, pil - grim broth - ers, On - ward, with the
pil - grim band, Sing - ing songs of ex - pec - ta - tion,
peo - ple shed, Chas - ing far the gloom and ter - ror,
heart of one; One the con - flict, one the per - il,
cross our aid; Bear its shame and fight its bat - tle,
March - ing to the prom - ised land. Clear be - fore us
Bright - 'ning all the path we tread; One the ob - ject
One the march in God be - gun; One the glad - ness
Till we rest be - neath its shade. Soon shall come the
through the dark - ness Gleams and burns the guid - ing light; Broth - er
of our jour - ney, One the faith which nev - er tires, One the
of re - joic - ing On the far e - ter - nal shore, Where the
great a - wak - ing, Soon the rend - ing of the tomb, Then the
clasps the hand of broth - er, Step - ping fear - less through the night.
ear - nest look - ing for - ward, One the hope our God in - spires.
one Al - might - y Fath - er Reigns in love for - ev - er - more.
scat - t'ring of all shad - ows And the end of toil and gloom.
Words copyright by J. Curwen and Sons, Ltd.
Used by permission of G. Schirmer, Inc.
LOYALTY AND COURAGE
Alternate tune: AUSTRIAN HYMN, No. 25

Through the Night of Doubt and Sorrow

"Igjennem nat og traengsel" is one of two lyrics by which Bernhardt S. Ingemann is especially remembered as a hymn writer. The other is "Dejlig är jorden" (Fair Is Creation), which was written to be sung to the tune CRUSADER'S HYMN. Both of the hymns are pilgrim songs. "Through the Night . . ." was written in 1825 and published in 1855 in the Church of Denmark hymnal, of which Ingemann was the editor. The translator, Sabine Baring-Gould, was an English clergyman and the most prolific of all British authors. Besides his many principal works, one of which was the fifteen-volume *Lives of the Saints*, he published two volumes of original hymns and translated a number from the Danish. The English version of the song first appeared in *The People's Hymnal* in England, 1867. Later it appeared in several American hymnals.

The hymn has had several musical settings, one of which is HARWELL by Lowell Mason. This was the tune used in *The Hymnal* (1950). The melody in our present hymnal is LAMMETS FOLK, for which see "Chosen Seed and Zion's Children."

Thy Holy Wings, Dear Savior
45
Lina Sandell, 1832-1903
Tr. Ernest Edwin Ryden, 1886-
HOLY WINGS 7.6.7.6.D.
Swedish Folk Melody
Harm. by Mark S. Dickey, 1885-1961
1 Thy ho - ly wings, dear Sav - ior, Spread gen - tly o - ver me;
2 Thy par - don, Sav - ior, grant me, And cleanse me in thy blood;
And thru the long night watch - es, I'll rest se - cure in thee.
Give me a will - ing spir - it, A heart both clean and good.
What - ev - er may be - tide me, Be thou my hid - ing place,
O take in - to thy keep - ing Thy chil - dren, great and small,
And let me live and la - bor Each day, Lord, by thy grace.
And, while we sweet - ly slum - ber, En - fold us, one and all. A - men.

Words used by permission of Ernest Edwin Ryden.
Harm. used by permission of William K. Provine, music executor of the estate of Mark S. Dickey.

EVENING

Thy Holy Wings, Dear Savior

No doubt the metaphor in "Bred dina vida vingar" is from Deuteronomy 32:11: "As an eagle stirs up its nest, that flutters over its young, spreading out its wings . . ." and Psalm 36:7: ". . . the children of men take refuge in the shadow of thy wings." In a letter to a friend, Lina Sandell began with the words, "In God's cottage, August 30, 1860." At the conclusion she wrote: "And now—Thy holy wings, dear Savior, Spread gently over me." Then followed the remainder of stanza one. The second line read, "and let your little chicken hide in you" instead of the final version, "and let me calmly rest. . . ." The complete work did not appear until five years later when it was published in *Korsblomman* for the year 1866 under the title "Children's Evening Prayer." It became that in many Swedish homes. In the series *När vi var unga*, (When We Were Young), Volume III, Esther Malmström of the Salvation Army wrote: "Mother taught us at night to fold our hands and pray to the children's Friend: 'Thy holy wings. . . .' " But the song from the beginning was Lina Sandell's deep heartfelt prayer, for her letter and diary entries from this period emphasized her deep need of God's grace, forgiveness, and guidance.

Although it appeared in *Sionstoner*, 1889, as a hymn, it did not catch on for several years. It was published in the hymnal of the Swedish Covenant in 1920 and in the 1937 edition of the *Psalmbok*. Several of the early Augustana hymnals included it, but its use in Covenant churches did not begin until its publication in *De Ungas Sångbok* in 1914. The excellent translation in *The Hymnal* (1950) was by E.E. Ryden.

HOLY WINGS is believed to be a folk melody from Skåne. It was the setting for the hymn in *Sionstoner*, 1889.

Time Is As Swift As a Vanishing Dream

"Tiden försvinner så snabbt som en dröm" was published unsigned in *Lilla Sändebudet*, November 2, 1874. It has been assumed that the author was Carl A. Stenholm, since he was the editor of the paper at that time. The song was not widely used in Sweden, perhaps because there were so many with the same theme, e.g., "Time Hastens," "Time Flies," "Time Unceasingly Hastens On," and "Time Is So Short." In America the song appeared in many of the early privately-published hymnals and in *Hemlandssånger*. Covenanters were introduced to the song through *Cymbalen*, *Sionsharpan*, and *Sions Basun*. The translation by E.G. Johnson was first published in North Park College's *Pegasus*.

The tune, TIDEN FÖRSVINNER, is a Swedish folk melody of unknown origin. It seems to have been used with this text first in America. Several publications have slight variations in the melody line, and in at least two printings there are six beats to the measure rather than four.

551 Time Is as Swift as a Vanishing Dream

Tiden försvinner
10. 7. 10. 7.

C. A. Stenholm, 1874
Trans. by E. Gustav Johnson, 1946

Swedish folk melody

Buoyantly

1. Time is as swift as a van - ish - ing dream, Year af - ter year rolls a - way. Life rush - es on like a fast flow - ing stream, Short are the hours of its day.
2. Nev - er re - turn - ing are days that are gone, Sure - ly that fact is de - creed, But how we use them will ev - er be known, God is re - cord - ing each deed.
3. In - to this world we are born but to die, Small is our meas - ure of years. Flick - er - ing flames are the days pass - ing by, Quick - ly the light dis - ap - pears.
4. Par - ents and chil - dren are part - ed by death, Youth is not spared by the foe. Man in his prime comes to naught in a breath; When we are called we must go.
5. Flee from the world, all its e - vil dis - dain, Kneel at the feet of the Lord, Seek His for - give - ness, sal - va - tion ob - tain, God will His bless - ing af - ford.

Trust in the Savior, O Precious Soul

The text "Håll dig vid klippan, dyrköpta själ" was inspired by a story Otto Ottander had read in *Söndagsskolklockan*, 1877. It was from an American newspaper account of a girl and her younger brother. They were caught in a narrow railroad tunnel through a mountain just as two trains were about to meet. The girl hastily guided her brother to an indentation in the rocky wall, and while rushing to another, cried out, "Håll dig vid klippan!" (keep close to the rock). The trains rushed by, and the children were unharmed. Ottander used the story in a longer dissertation in his own newspaper, *Östra Smålands Missionsblad*. In the previous issue he had published the text of the song. A.G. Lindqvist revised it for the Swedish Covenant hymnal of 1894. He substituted the word "Jesus" for "klippan," and it was his version that was accepted among the free churches in Sweden. The original text was used in the Swedish free church songbooks in the United States. Eldon Palmquist translated the hymn for the 1950 hymnal.

The tune, EKSTRÖM, is named for the composer. It was first published in *Föreningen*, 1860, a periodical for schoolteachers and church musicians. There it was the setting for his own text, "Klockorna klämta, hör deras ljud (The Bells Are Tolling, Hear Their Sound).

402 Trust in the Savior, O Precious Soul

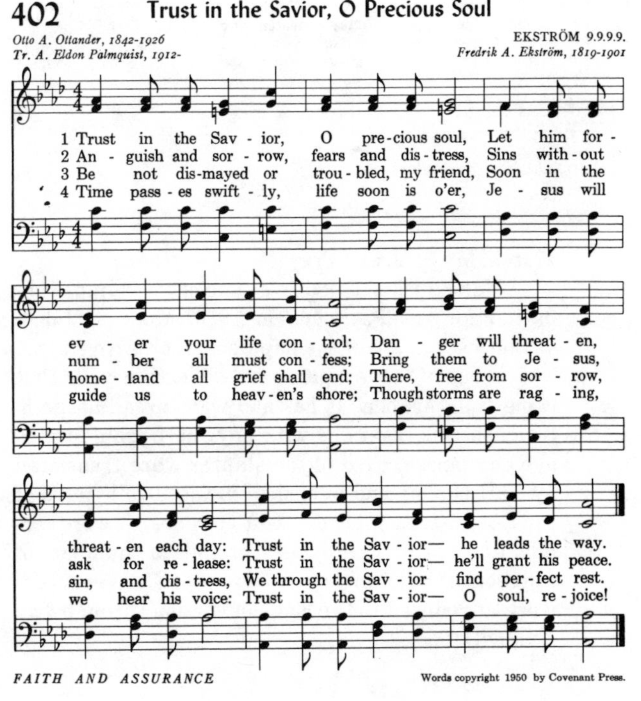
Otto A. Ottander, 1842-1926
Tr. A. Eldon Palmquist, 1912-
EKSTRÖM 9.9.9.9.
Fredrik A. Ekström, 1819-1901
1 Trust in the Sav - ior, O pre - cious soul, Let him for - ev - er your life con - trol; Dan - ger will threat - en, threat - en each day: Trust in the Sav - ior— he leads the way.
2 An - guish and sor - row, fears and dis - tress, Sins with - out num - ber all must con - fess; Bring them to Je - sus, ask for re - lease: Trust in the Sav - ior— he'll grant his peace.
3 Be not dis-mayed or trou - bled, my friend, Soon in the home - land all grief shall end; There, free from sor - row, sin, and dis - tress, We through the Sav - ior find per - fect rest.
4 Time pass - es swift - ly, life soon is o'er, Je - sus will guide us to heav - en's shore; Though storms are rag - ing, we hear his voice: Trust in the Sav - ior— O soul, re - joice!
FAITH AND ASSURANCE
Words copyright 1950 by Covenant Press.

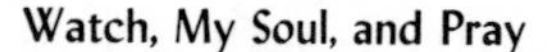

Watch, My Soul, and Pray 445

Johann Olof Wallin, 1779-1839
Tr. Carl Doving, 1867-1937

SEELENBRÄUTIGAM 5.5.8.8.5.5.
Adam Drese, 1620-1701

1 Watch, my soul, and pray, Arm for life's af - fray!
2 Watch and pray, my soul, Flesh and blood con - trol!
3 See the good - ly land On the heav'n - ly strand!
4 Through thy pil - grim - age Guard thy her - i - tage!
5 Watch and fight and pray Through this mor - tal day!
When the dan - ger least thou fear - est,
When the world, in tempt - ing sto - ry,
See God's peo - ple, thith - er tend - ing,
Pray and fight, on Christ re - ly - ing,
Soon thy Ca - naan thou at - tain - est,
Watch, the tempt - er's snares are near - est;
Tells of pleas - ure, wealth, and glo - ry,
Through the sea and des - ert wend - ing;
Live to him, thy - self de - ny - ing;
Soon the crown and palm thou gain - est,
Such is e'er his way: Watch, my soul, and pray.
Be not led a - stray: Watch, my soul, and pray.
Led by Josh - ua's hand: Seek the good - ly land.
On - ward to the goal: Win the crown, my soul.
Peace is won for aye: Watch, my soul, and pray.

Words used by permission of Fortress Press.

INNER LIFE

346 We May Trust in Every Way

O jag litar
7. 7. 7. 7. with refrain

FANNY CROSBY (1820-1915) Original English version
Adapted by E. GUSTAV JOHNSON, 1947
from an anonymous Swedish translation

WILLIAM H. DOANE (1832-1915)

With quiet assurance

1. We may trust in ev - 'ry way In the Sav - ior's prom-ise high.
2. When our days are cheer-ful, glad, What a joy the Lord to praise;
3. May we pa - tient - ly en - dure As we on His name de-pend,

As with con - trite heart we pray On His grace we can re - ly.
Great-er when the days are sad Is to know His ten - der grace.
Know-ing that we are se - cure When we trust Him to the end.
REFRAIN
I am trust-ing, sim-ply trust-ing In His mer - cy day by day;

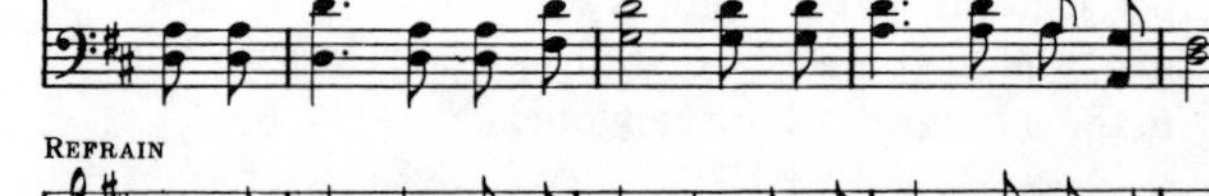
Prone am I to go a - stray, On - ly Je - sus is my stay.

Words copyright, 1950, by The Covenant Book Concern.

Watch, My Soul, and Pray

"Vaka, själ, och bed" was one of the hymns submitted for the *Psalmbok* in 1816. Most of Johan Wallin's songs are of the impersonal, objective type. This is one of the few personal, subjective lyrics that came from his pen. It has had widespread usage in Swedish congregations with anywhere from four to eleven stanzas. Five of the stanzas were translated by Carl Doving and published in the 1925 hymnal of the Augustana Church. Our forebears were acquainted with the hymn through a number of songbooks, including *Sions Basun*, and Covenanters were introduced to the English version through *The Hymnal* (1950).

SEELENBRÄUTIGAM was composed by Adam Drese, a German composer, and was written for his own hymn, "Seelenbräutigam, Jesu, Gotteslamm." It was first published in *Hasselesches Gesangbuch*, 1695, but used in manuscript form as early as 1690. It is a simply constructed tune, well-suited to the text. It is usually used as a setting for "Jesus, Still Lead On" by Zinzendorf.

We May Trust in Every Way

Here is another hymn that has been translated twice before coming to us in its present form. "O hur ljuft att lita på" (actually, O How Sweet to Have Confidence In) is a Swedish version of a song by Fanny Crosby. The song has not been known in Sweden, so evidently the whole process has taken place here, and most likely within the Covenant, since, as far as I can determine, the song has appeared in Swedish only in *Sionsharpan* and *Sions Basun.* E.G. Johnson translated the anonymous version for use in *The Hymnal* (1950), and the song was improved in the process. Fanny Crosby's original first stanza and chorus read as follows:

Simply trusting all the way,
Taking Jesus at his word;
Simply trusting, when I pray,
Ev'ry promise of my Lord.

Simply trusting, simply trusting,
Trusting Jesus, that is all.
At the cross of Christ I fall,
Simply trusting, that is all.

O JAG LITAR takes its name from the opening words of the Swedish version. It was composed by William Doane for Fanny Crosby's text. The two hymnists collaborated on many songs, of which there are five in each of our last two hymnals.

We Wait for a Great and Glorious Day

Many of the songs that have struck a responsive chord among Covenant people have been those concerned with the second coming of Christ. The best loved of these has been "Snart randas en dag" by A.L. Skoog. It was first published in his *Söndagsskolvännen* in 1890 and then in his *Lilla Basunen* the same year. Soon it appeared in most Swedish free church hymnals in the United States and later in several in Sweden. It was translated by the author and included in *Mission Hymns.* A portion of the text is inscribed on the monument over Skoog's grave.

Since this is his most popular hymn, it is fitting that the tune should be called SKOOG. In order to simplify the rhythm in the refrain, the six-beat measure was continued (instead of a nine-beat), and the long holds were decreased from five to two beats.

230 We Wait for a Great and Glorious Day
A. L. Skoog, 1856-1934
SKOOG 10.7.10.7. with Refrain
A. L. Skoog, 1856-1934
1 We wait for a great and glo - ri - ous day, As many - y as love the Lord, When shad-ows shall flee, and clouds pass a - way, And weep - ing no more be heard.
2 In glo - ry and pow'r our King shall ap - pear And call to him - self his own; No dis - tance nor death shall part them as here, Nor sin with its pains be known.
3 For cross - es we've borne then crowns will be giv'n, For tem - pests e - ter - nal calm; For path - way of thorns rich man - sions in heav'n, For war - fare the vic - tor's palm.
4 We know not the day, we know not the hour When sounds the last trump so clear; But loud rings a cry from truth's loft - y tow'r, "The day of the Lord is near."
Snart ran - das en dag så här - lig och stor För al - la, som äls - ka Gud; Dess sol ald - rig skyms av skug - gor - nas flor, Och ald - rig hörs kla - gans ljud.
REFRAIN (after last stanza only)
O won - der - ful day that soon may be here!
O här - li - ga dag som ran - das för mig!
O beau - ti - ful hope the pil - grim to cheer!
O här - li - ga mål på pil - gri - mens stig!
Thy com - ing we hail in tune - ful ac - cord,
Min läng - tan och blick allt mer till dig drag,
Thou glo - ri - ous day of Christ, our Lord.
Du här - li - ga Je - su Kri - sti dag!
COMING IN GLORY
Harm. copyright 1973 by Covenant Press.

55 What Joy There Is in Coming
Johan Ludvig Runeberg, 1804-1877
Tr. A. Samuel Wallgren, 1885-1940
SANCTUARY 7.6.7.6.D.
Johan Isidor Dannström, 1812-1897
1 What joy there is in com - ing To God's own courts so fair,
2 How beau - ti - ful the un - ion Of souls re-deemed and free,
3 Come, see the Lord's sal - va - tion And taste his love sin - cere;
4 May ne'er my foot-steps fal - ter Tow'rd night a - way from day;
Where faith - ful souls are bloom - ing Like lil - ies in his care!
Who hold with God com - mun - ion In faith and pu - ri - ty!
Come, pray with-out ces - sa - tion, Watch with his peo - ple here.
My light shines from God's al - tar—My sun I'll seek al - way.
They raise their cha-lic - es ten - der For heav'n's re-fresh - ing dew,
While songs of praise are fill - ing Their sa - cred place of rest,
Out - side, the world makes mer - ry, Un - hap - py 'mid its toys,
Here in his pres - ence glo - rious It is so good to be—
'Mid bless - ings God doth ren - der They life and strength re - new.
Who then can be un - will - ing To join their cir - cle blest?
But in God's sanc - tu - a - ry The soul finds heav'n - ly joys.
Let here my soul vic - to - rious Its tab - er - na - cle see.
OPENING

What Joy There Is in Coming

Perhaps "Hur ljuft det är att komma" is Sweden's greatest hymn about worship. Gösta Hagelin, in *De som skrev våra psalmer*, Volume I, says that more than any other of his hymns, this characterizes Johan Runeberg's faith and philosophy of life. He writes, "The world for him is a wonderful garden. It is always God's world, God's creation. And like St. Francis he feels a kinship with all the earth's flora and fauna." So in the sanctuary the worshipers are "like lilies in his care." This is a metaphor that Runeberg liked to use. In one of his children's poems he wrote:

A little flower in thy garden fair
My life to thee has been given.

Although Runeberg lived in Finland, he wrote in Swedish, and the hymn was published in the Swedish hymnal of the Finnish church in 1886. The song had been written in 1857 and appeared that year in a sixty-six page collection of proposed songs for the hymnal of which Runeberg was an editorial committee member. In 1881, the hymn was included with a collection of six Runeberg texts and I. Dannström tunes. But it was not until after the turn of the century that it was included in the free church hymnals in Sweden, and not until 1937 in the *Psalmbok*. In America, *Sions Basun* was one of the few songbooks in which it was published. The English version by A. Samuel Wallgren was introduced in the "brown hymnal" in 1931.

Although various musical settings have been used with the text, SANCTUARY (originally, HUR LJUFT DET ÄR ATT KOMMA) has been the most frequent. It was composed by Johan I. Dannström and published in his *Sex andeliga sånger* in 1881.

When All the World Is Sleeping

Lina Sandell's delightful evening song "När hela jorden sover" has not been widely used. It was first published in *Stockholms söndagsskolföreningens sångbok* in 1888 and in several editions of *Sionstoner* thereafter. J.A. Hultman introduced it in this country with his tune in *Sånger för söndagsskolan* (Worcester, Massachusetts, 1907) and later, in Part One of *Solskenssånger*, 1913. This arrangement was published in the Swedish Covenant's *Sånger och Psalmer*, 1951. Karl Olsson translated the song for the North Park College choir in 1968.

The hymnal commission named the tune NOCTURN. It was composed by Hultman for the Sandell text and has always been associated with it.

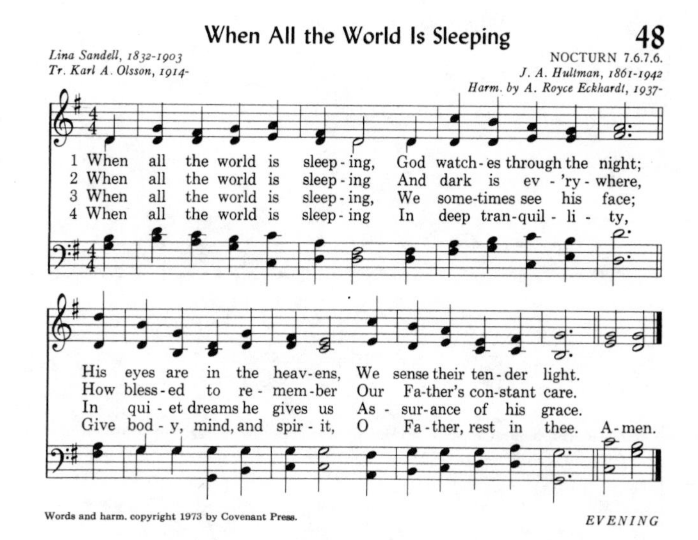
When All the World Is Sleeping
48
Lina Sandell, 1832-1903
Tr. Karl A. Olsson, 1914-
NOCTURN 7.6.7.6.
J. A. Hultman, 1861-1942
Harm. by A. Royce Eckhardt, 1937-
1 When all the world is sleep-ing, God watch-es through the night;
2 When all the world is sleep-ing And dark is ev-'ry-where,
3 When all the world is sleep-ing, We some-times see his face;
4 When all the world is sleep-ing In deep tran-quil-li-ty,
His eyes are in the heav-ens, We sense their ten-der light.
How bless-ed to re-mem-ber Our Fa-ther's con-stant care.
In qui-et dreams he gives us As-sur-ance of his grace.
Give bod-y, mind, and spir-it, O Fa-ther, rest in thee. A-men.
Words and harm. copyright 1973 by Covenant Press.
EVENING

When Christmas Morn Is Breaking

Although Abel Burckhart was believed to be a German writer (known only through his Christmas carol), the first apparent publication of "När juldags morgon glimmer" was in a Swedish periodical, *Andelig Örtagård för Barn.* The editor was G. Berggren, a school teacher in Kalmar. On the basis of its appearance in Betty Ehrenborg-Posse's *Andeliga Sånger för Barn,* the song often has been attributed to her. In fact, some hymnologists feel that it was her original composition. At first it was largely restricted to collections of children's songs, but later it was included in most hymnals in Sweden. Here in America it appeared in the early Swedish hymnals. The translation by Claude W. Foss was first published in Augustana's English hymnal, 1901. It came into Covenant use in a different version through *Mission Hymns* and again in *The Hymnal* (1950). Our present hymnal printed the same first stanza, but stanzas two and three are from the Foss version. As far as I can determine, the carol does not appear in any of the other current denominational hymnals in the United States except the Lutheran *Service Book and Hymnal.* It is included in a few special Christmas collections.

CHRISTMAS DAWN is a German folk melody known as early as 1819 with the text "Wir hatten erbaut."

When Christmas Morn Is Breaking
146
Attr. to Abel Burckhardt, 19th century
Arr. by Elizabeth Ehrenborg-Posse, 1818-1880
Tr. Claude William Foss, 1855-1935, Sts. 2,3
CHRISTMAS DAWN 7.6.7.6.
German Folk Melody, 1819
1 When Christ-mas morn is break-ing, The man-ger I would seek,
2 How kind, O lov-ing Sav-ior, To come from heav'n a-bove!
3 We need thee, bless-ed Je-sus, Our dear-est friend thou art!
Where God, his throne for-sak-ing, Is rest-ing low and meek;
From sin and e-vil save us, And keep us in thy love;
For-bid that we by sin-ning Should grieve thy lov-ing heart;
Where God, his throne for-sak-ing, Is rest-ing low and meek.
From sin and e-vil save us, And keep us in thy love.
For-bid that we by sin-ning Should grieve thy lov-ing heart. A-men.
BIRTH

 When My Lord Is Dear to Me

Nils Frykman, 1842-1911
Tr. Lennart E. Anderson, 1911-
PENNOCK 7.7.7.7. with Refrain
Nils Frykman, 1842-1911
1 When my Lord is dear to me, Joy is mine, wher-e'er I be,
2 When his peace a-bides with me, Joy is mine e-ter-nal-ly,
3 Peace, con-tent-ment, joy are mine, What a her-it-age di-vine!
4 Kept thru faith in Christ a-bove, Shel-tered in his arms of love,
Wheth-er dark and drear the way, Or, like E-den, fair as day.
When the sun shines fair and bright, When it shad-ows in-to night.
With that pearl su-preme-ly rare, Earth-ly gold can-not com-pare.
In what-ev-er may be-fall, He is now my all in all!
REFRAIN
Hal-le-lu-jah! Hal-le-lu-jah! Je-sus is my friend!
He is faith-ful to de-fend His re-deemed un-to the end.
JOY
Words copyright 1950 by Covenant Press.

When Lights Are Lit on the Christmas Tree

See "How Glad I Am Each Christmas Eve."

When My Lord Is Dear to Me

During the two years that Nils Frykman was pastor of the Tabernacle Covenant Church in Chicago he wrote no hymns. But soon after taking over the Salem circuit in Minnesota, he picked up his lyre again, and many songs came from his pen in that period. He was on the editorial committee for *Sionsharpan* and it was in that volume that "När min Gud jag håller kär" was first published. It was translated by Lennart Anderson for the 1950 hymnal.

The tune by Frykman is named PENNOCK after the town near which the Salem Covenant Church is located.

HEAVEN AND HOMELAND

521 When Toil Is Done, a Sabbath Rest Is Waiting

Sabbatsvila
11. 10. 11. 10.
J. FREDRIK LUNDGREN, 1884 alt.
Trans. by E. LINCOLN PEARSON, 1946
J. A. HULTMAN (1861-1942)
Meditatively
1. When toil is done, a Sab-bath rest is wait-ing
2. No griefs shall mar the bliss of that re-u-nion,
3. A throng shall come from ev-ery tribe and na-tion
4. When that e-ter-nal Sab-bath morn is break-ing
For God's own chil-dren in His man-sions fair;
For God Him-self shall wipe all tears a-way,
To stand in awe be-fore the throne of God;
That now in faith we see through earth's dim haze,
A Sab-bath day, a glo-rious con-gre-gat-ing
And in the glo-ry of that high com-mun-ion
And with their song of grate-ful a-dor-a-tion
O bless-ed Sav-ior, speed my soul in mak-ing
Of souls re-deemed, e-ter-nal rest to share.
No trace shall be of heart-aches or dis-may.
The Sav-ior's name in joy for-ev-er laud.
Its jour-ney home to join that song of praise.
Words copyright, 1950, by The Covenant Book Concern.
Music used by permission of Mrs. J. A. Hultman.

When Toil Is Done, a Sabbath Rest Is Waiting

Fredrik Lundgren's inspiration for "Det står Guds folk en sabbatsvila åter" came from Hebrews 4:9: "So then, there remains a sabbath rest for the people of God." Also there are pictures from Revelation 7. The hymn was first published in *Pilgrimstoner,* 1884, and later in several of the Swedish free church collections. J.A. Hultman introduced it to the Covenant with his musical setting in *Sions Basun,* and it was included in the 1950 hymnal in a translation by E. Lincoln Pearson.

In Sweden, several different tunes have been used with the text, including one by Frykman. But in the United States only Hultman's SABBATSVILA has been used.

Wheresoe'er I Roam

Friendship with Jesus was a recurring theme in the writings of Carl Olof Rosenius; "Var jag går" is a good example. In the original version there were five stanzas, three of which were a reworking of a song from the Herrnhut *Samling av äldre och nyare andeliga sånger och werser,* 1806. In stanza three of our version we recognize the Herrnhut emphasis upon the wounds and blood of Christ. The song was based upon the confrontation between Jesus and Thomas after the resurrection. The last phrase is the outcry of Thomas, "My Lord and God." The text was printed in *Pietisten* in 1847 and with music in Ahnfelt's *Andeliga Sånger* in 1868. It soon became a favorite of the "läsare" in Sweden and later of Swedish free church people everywhere. It was included in the first English hymnal of the Augustana Lutheran Church in 1901. The translator was Victor O. Peterson. This version was introduced to the Covenant church through *Mission Hymns.*

VAR JAG GÅR is a tune of unknown origin. It has often been identified as Danish, but careful research in Denmark shows that there is no basis for the supposition.

398
Wheresoe'er I Roam
Carl Olof Rosenius, 1816-1868
Tr. Victor O. Peterson, 1864-1929
VAR JAG GÅR 10.9.10.9.10.9.10.7.
Ahnfelt's "Sånger," 1868
1 Where - so - e'er I roam, thru val - leys drear - y, O - ver
2 All my needs e - ter - nal - ly sup - ply - ing, All in
3 Pierc - ed heart, with love o'er - flow - ing, guide me, Help me
moun - tains, or in path - less wood, Ev - er with me is a
all to me that Friend shall be; Ev - 'ry - thing for which my
through life's des - ert find my way; Let my faith, no mat - ter
Friend to cheer me, Warn - ing, com - fort - ing as none else could.
heart is sigh - ing He per - ceives, and helps me lov - ing - ly.
what be - tide me, Find as - sur - ance in thy wounds for aye.
'Tis the Shep - herd, who once dy - ing, bleed - ing, Still through
Though I oft - en feel for - sak - en, lone - ly, He is
To thy bos - om— for this life is fleet - ing— Take me,
all e - ter - ni - ty shall live; As he leads his flock, pro -
ev - er near, for he did say: "I am with you al - way,"
wash my gar - ments in thy blood; And a - ris - ing may I,
tect - ing, feed - ing, He the ten - d'rest care doth give.
and this on - ly Gives me cour - age on my way.
at thy meet - ing, Cry with joy, "My Lord and God!" A - men.
FAITH AND ASSURANCE
Words used by permission of Fortress Press.

415 Why Should I Be Anxious?
Nils Frykman, 1842-1911
Tr. Aaron Markuson, 1910-
SUNNE 11.8.11.8.
Source unknown
1 Why should I be anx - ious? I have such a friend,
2 Though I am un-worth - y he chose e - ven me,
3 His mer - cy, I know, is suf - fi - cient for me,
4 Each day he is near me, he walks by my side,
5 The pow - er of hell holds no ter - ror for me,
6 Thus on - ward I go to that won - der - ful land,
Who bears in his heart all my woe;
By grace in his king - dom to dwell;
And there - in my soul finds its peace;
His strength nev - er fails, as does mine;
My strong - hold is Is - ra - el's God;
That beau - ti - ful home of the blest;
This friend is the Sav - ior, on him I de - pend—
That grace so a - bun - dant my ref - uge will be—
He chas - tens with love, ev - er pa - tient is he—
In glo - ry with him I at last shall a - bide—
In tri - al and sor - row my ref - uge is he—
Though storms rage in fu - ry, I'm safe in his hand—
His love is e - ter - nal, I know.
Thy good - ness, O God, I would tell.
My joys through his bless - ing in - crease.
For that is his prom - ise di - vine.
O Sav - ior, thy mer - cy I laud!
I'll en - ter the ha - ven of rest.
COMFORT AND PEACE
Words copyright 1950 by Covenant Press.

Why Should I Be Anxious?

Nils Frykman told this story about the origin of "Ack, varföre gråta?" (literally, Why Should I Cry?):

> *It was a Saturday afternoon. I was on my way to a school house where I was to preach that evening. On the way I became so overwhelmed by despair, both over my own and other people's sins, that I threw myself to the ground and cried like a spanked child. Oh, how I prayed, and how the tears flowed! I can't remember ever having cried like that. Yet I knew through it all I was a child of God, saved by grace. And without a doubt, it was this assurance that made the tears flow so easily and so heavily. After I had wept out my burden, I resumed the journey with a light heart and light steps. And then it was easy to write and sing.*

When he reached his destination, the song had been born. It was published in *Hemlandssånger*, 1879, and later in most of the free church collections in Sweden. Free church people in America came to know the song through *Sionsharpan* and *Sions Basun*. Aaron Markuson is responsible for the English version which first appeared in *The Hymnal* (1950).

The tune used in Sweden is the work of Theodor Söderberg. The source of SUNNE (originally, MEN VARFÖRE GRÅTA) is unknown. Since it has been associated with the Frykman text, it was named after the town in which he lived when the song was written.

With God and His Friendship

"Med Gud och hans vänskap" is another Carl Rosenius text which stresses friendship with God. However, here it is not "I" and God but "we" and God. He and his brothers and sisters are a "host," a band of "pilgrims," who, like Israel of old, are marching to the promised land under the guidance of God. A leading Swedish hymnologist, E. Liedgren, in a Stockholm newspaper article, called the hymn "Middle Sweden's revival Marseillaise." The song, especially the last stanza, brought comfort to our emigrant forebears who were pilgrims in a strange land. The text was first published in *Pietisten* No. 1, 1851, and with music in Ahnfelt's *Andeliga Sånger* later the same year. Soon it was included in almost every Swedish hymnbook on both sides of the Atlantic. Ernst Olson's translation, beginning "With God and his mercy," was published in the Augustana *Hymnal*, 1901. Another version by C.R. Osbeck appeared in the Swedish Baptists' *The New Hymnal*, 1925. It was this translation that was used in *The Covenant Hymnal* (1930). The 1950 hymnal printed the last three stanzas of Olson's version under the title "The Sign of the Cross." The current hymnal presents a combination of the two.

The tune, AHNFELT, was composed for the text. It was also used with a text written several years later by Mrs. Ahnfelt—"Ack saliga stunder," a song popular among our forebears.

488 With God and His Friendship
Carl Olof Rosenius, 1816-1868
Tr. C. R. Osbeck, Sts. 1, 2
Ernst W. Olson, 1870-1958, Sts. 3, 4, 5
AHNFELT 11.11.11.6.6.11.
Oscar Ahnfelt, 1813-1882
Harm. by James P. Davies, 1913-
1 With God and his friend - ship, his Spir - it and Word,
2 In per - il - ous times, thru the gloom of the night,
3 The sign of the cross we tri - um - phant - ly bear,
4 The pil - lar that guides us through per - il and strife,
5 O Shep - herd, a - bide with us, care for us still,
With breth - ren par - tak - ing the bread of our Lord,
A host march - es on through the dark - ness to light;
Though none of our kin - dred that em - blem may wear;
The rock that is cleft, giv - ing wa - ters of life,
And feed us and lead us, and teach us thy will;
With cour - age and joy we will meet com - ing days:
These pil - grims, ob - scured, are dis - owned by the world:
We joy - ful - ly fol - low the cham - pions of right,
Is Christ and his cross: By his Spir - it and word
And when in thy heav - en - ly fold we shall be,
The Shep - herd is with us, The Shep - herd is with us,
But owned by the Mas - ter, But owned by the Mas - ter,
Who march on to glo - ry, Who march on to glo - ry,
The heart he re - fresh - es, The heart he re - fresh - es,
Our thanks and our prais - es, Our thanks and our prais - es,
To lead us, pro - tect us and teach us his ways.
They march on to glo - ry with ban - ners un - furled.
Who march on to glo - ry with weap - ons of might.
The heart he re - fresh - es— our Sav - ior and Lord.
Our thanks and our prais - es we'll ren - der to thee. A - men.
UNITY AND FELLOWSHIP
Words used by permission of Harvest Publications and Fortress Press.
Harm. copyright 1973 by Covenant Press.

91 With My Deepest Feeling

Fram en suck sig smyger
6. 5. 6. 5. 6. 5.

C.W. BÖTTIGER, 1830
Trans. by E. GUSTAV JOHNSON, 1947

Anonymous

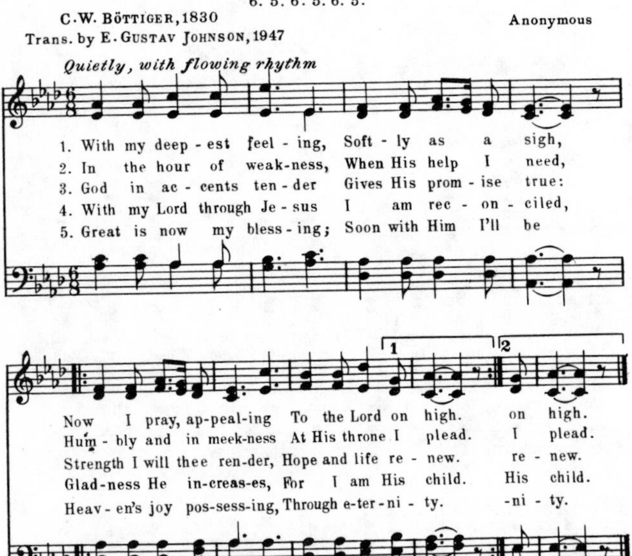
Quietly, with flowing rhythm
1. With my deep - est feel - ing, Soft - ly as a sigh,
2. In the hour of weak-ness, When His help I need,
3. God in ac - cents ten - der Gives His prom - ise true:
4. With my Lord through Je - sus I am rec - on - ciled,
5. Great is now my bless - ing; Soon with Him I'll be
1
2
Now I pray, ap-peal-ing To the Lord on high. on high.
Hum - bly and in meek-ness At His throne I plead. I plead.
Strength I will thee ren-der, Hope and life re - new. re - new.
Glad-ness He in-creas-es, For I am His child. His child.
Heav - en's joy pos-sess-ing, Through e-ter-ni - ty. -ni - ty.

With My Deepest Feeling

In 1830, Carl Wilhelm Böttiger published his first collection of poetry, *Ungdomsminnen från sångens stunder.* Under the title "Bönestunden" (The Hour of Prayer) was the text that became the basis for "Fram en suck sig smyger" (actually, A Sigh Steals Forth). The song went through several revisions and was published in *Pilgrims-Sånger*, 1859. There were several more alterations in subsequent editions. Later the song was included in most of the free church hymnals in Sweden and America, as well as in the Lutheran *Hemlandssånger*. In 1947, E.G. Johnson translated the hymn for use in *The Hymnal* (1950).

The tune, FRAM EN SUCK SIG SMYGER, was published in the 1860 music edition of *Pilgrims-Sånger*, but it is believed that it stems from the 1830s.

Biographies

AHNFELT, OSCAR (b. Gullarp, Skåne, Sweden, May 21, 1813; d. Karlshamn, October 22, 1882) was born in a minister's family. Although the parish was near an area strongly influenced by Herrnhut piety, Jonas Ahnfelt had no sympathy for Moravians or pietists. The atmosphere of the home was cultured, and eminent people were frequent guests. The young Ahnfelt grew up with good music and literature. He received most of his elementary education from his older brothers, and in 1829 he enrolled at Lund University. His intention was to become a minister in the church of Sweden, but he lost interest in the study of theology.

For several years he tried tutoring, but in 1840 moved to Stockholm to undertake music studies. There he came in contact with the Rosenian revival and entered a period of spiritual crisis. He found peace after hearing a sermon on the resurrection preached on Easter Sunday, 1841, by Carl Rosenius. Soon he became active in the conventicle movement, playing his ten-stringed guitar and singing, earning him the name "spiritual troubadour." Urged by Rosenius, he began witnessing and preaching, making his ministry increasingly effective. His travels took him to all parts of Sweden as well as to Denmark and Norway. Because of the Conventicles Edict, Ahnfelt frequently was harassed by the police, was often summoned for court appearances, and on several occasions paid fines. At one time the authorities petitioned Karl XV to put an end to his preaching and singing. The king refused to act without hearing the "spiritual troubadour," and Ahnfelt put on a command performance at the royal palace. He sang a song that his friend, Lina Sandell, had written for the occasion:

Who is it that knocks upon your heart's door
in peaceful eve?
Who is it that brings to the wounded and sore
the balm that can heal and relieve?
Your heart is still restless, it finds no peace
in earth's pleasures;
Your soul is still yearning, it seeks release
to rise to the heavenly treasures.

The king listened with tearful eyes. He grasped Ahnfelt's hand and exclaimed, "You may sing as much as you desire in both of my kingdoms." Ahnfelt was involved in a court case when the Edict was repealed in 1858.

Ahnfelt's singing and preaching were significant in the revival movement, but of even greater importance was his contribution to the hymnody of the period. Several writers, including Lina Sandell and Carl Rosenius, were writing verses that reflected the spiritual climate of the time, and Ahnfelt gave himself to setting many of these to music. He was not financially able to publish the songs, but he received help from Jenny Lind, the "Swedish nightingale," who also was a pietist. The first collection of twelve songs appeared in 1850 with the title "Spiritual Songs with Accompaniment for Piano or Guitar"—usually referred to as Ahnfelt's *Andeliga Sånger*. This was followed by eleven editions appearing at intervals until 1877, when a total of two hundred songs was included. None of the texts were by Ahnfelt, but of the 143 tunes almost half of them were his originals.

Composer:
AHNFELT (ACK, SALIGA STUNDER) 488 (246)*
BLOTT EN DAG 381 (325)
GUDS GODHET 90 (77)
GLÄDJE (HOS GUD ÄR IDEL GLÄDJE) 605 (510), 614 (526)
O SALLA LUND (337)

**The numerals following the hymn titles and tune names refer to the hymn numbers in* The Covenant Hymnal *(1973) and those within parentheses to* The Hymnal *(1950).*

ANDERSON, JOSEPH EMANUEL (b. Haxtun, Colorado, December 20, 1890; d. San Francisco, California, August 23, 1954) spent his early childhood in Nebraska. In 1905, the O.P. Anderson family moved to Hilmar, California, where Joseph attended high school. After studies at the University of California he took a course at Heald's Business College and then remained there as an instructor. He spent two and a half years in the military service during World War I and then returned to teach at the business college, where he remained until illness forced him to resign. He was an active member of the Covenant church in San Francisco, serving as secretary, choir member, and trustee.

Translator:

Christ the Lord Is Risen! (164)

Hide Not Thy Face, O My Savior 235 (507)

ANDERSON, LENNART E. (b. Milaca, Minnesota, March 9, 1911) grew up in the area around and north of Milaca. He studied at the University of Minnesota and has pursued a career in public accounting. The family makes its home in Willmar, Minnesota, where Mr. Anderson has been active in the Covenant church, serving in various capacities, including chairman. He is also an active member of the Gideons. Growing up in an emigrant home, he was bilingual and took an interest in languages and translating. In recalling his experience in translating "När min Gud jag håller kär," he said it "came . . . rather quickly."

Translator:

When My Lord Is Dear to Me 425 (377)

ARRHENIUS, JAKOB (b. Linköping, Sweden, October 31, 1642; d. April 13, 1725), after studies in his home town and at Uppsala, joined the staff at the university—first as a member of the administration and later as a professor of history. He was credited with organizing the records and financial affairs of the school. Arrhenius is remembered especially for his contribution to the hymnody of the Swedish Church. Several of his lyrics were included in Jesper Swedberg's edition of the *Psalmbok* in 1694. Some were translations and psalm paraphrases, but there were original texts as well. His songs, especially the so-called "Jesus hymns," showed his friendship with pietism. In fact, he sounded a new note in Swedish hymnody.

Author:

Jesus, Lord and Precious Savior 433 (386)

Attributed author:

Mine Eyes Look toward the Mountains (83)

ASCHAN, PETER JONSSON (b. 1726; d. 1813) has been difficult to identify. Karin Dövring, in her work *Striden kring Sions sånger* (The Dispute about the Songs of Zion), is certain that he is the Aschan who was the principal of the school in Växjö in southern Sweden. He was active in Moravian circles in the area and wrote some poetry with Moravian emphases. The song that has been identified with him in our hymnal was signed "P. J.A."

Author:

O Let Your Soul Now Be Filled with Gladness 423

ÅSTRÖM, JOHAN (b. Gävle, Sweden, November 30, 1767; d. February 29, 1844) was the son of an organ-blower. When the boy was thirteen, his father died, but the mother was determined that her intellectually curious son should have the opportunity to study. His early education was received under the tutelage of his mother as she worked at her spinning wheel. He attended the university at Uppsala and was ordained in 1793. The following year he received his master of philosophy degree and for two years was chaplain of the mental hospital in Uppsala. After a pastorate in the German church in Norrköping, he was made rector of the archbishopric in Tuna and Stavby in 1805 and in Sigtuna and Altuna in 1821. He was honored with the degree of doctor of theology in 1809.

Åström's theological training and insight, combined with a deep personal piety, led Wallin to seek his assistance with the *Psalmbok* during the years from 1816 to 1818. The 1819 edition included eleven original texts by Åström and many translations. Five of his original hymns are still often used in Sweden.

Reviser:

In Heaven Above 604 (509)

BACKSTROM, CARL ERNEST (b. Stockholm, Sweden, May 2, 1901) came to Brooklyn, New York, with his parents in 1907. There the Backstroms became active in the Swedish Pilgrim Church (Covenant), where Carl was confirmed and converted. After graduation from Commercial High School, he worked four years at the Chase National Bank. He took evening courses at the American Institute of Banking, from which he graduated in 1922. While attending the University of Pennsylvania, the sudden death of his pastor caused him to think about studying for the ministry. After a period of indecision he began studies at North Park Theological Seminary and graduated in 1926.

While pursuing graduate studies at the University of Chicago, Backstrom accepted a call to the Covenant church in Lincoln, Nebraska. He was ordained in 1928. From 1934 to 1936 he served the Covenant church at Lanyon, Iowa, and following that became pastor of the Youngstown, Ohio, congregation, where he remained for eleven years. In 1948 he transferred his membership to the Presbyterian church. He is now retired and lives in Chautauqua, New York.

In the volume *Three Covenant Presidents* (1945), Backstrom was the author of the biographical sketch of Carl August Bjork. He also wrote several series of articles in the *Covenant Weekly*, one of which dealt with the history of the Covenant.

Translator:

Heavenly Father, Hear My Supplication 344 (79)

Thanks to God for My Redeemer 622 (543)

BENNETT, SIGNE L. (b. Chicago, Illinois, November 22, 1900), the daughter of Swedish emigrants, attended the business school and academy at North Park. Later she took evening classes at Moody Bible Institute. For many years she was in the employ of the government, working in various capacities. Since 1920 she has been an active member of the North Park Covenant Church in Chicago.

Translator:

The Highest Joy That Can Be Known 283 (220)

BERGGREEN, ANDREAS PETER (b. Copenhagen, Denmark, March 2, 1801; d. Copenhagen, November 9, 1880) set out on a career in law, but also pursued private studies in music. Gradually he grew more interested in music and made it his life's work. In 1838, he became organist at Trinity Church in Copenhagen and later teacher of music in the Metropolitan School. In 1859, Berggreen became involved in the music program of the public schools in Denmark. He was the editor of a periodical called *Musikalisk Tidene*, and from 1842 to 1871 published eleven volumes of *Folksange og Melodier*, containing about two thousand songs. His greatest contribution to church music was the editing of the Danish chorale book in 1853.

Composer:

DANA (AMEN, JESUS HAN SKAL RAADE) 66 (273), 342 (50)

BLOMQVIST, JOEL (b. Stockholm, November 15, 1840; d. Kullarstad, October 30, 1930) was the son of a tailor who was active in free church circles in Stockholm. After a meager elementary education, Joel went to trade school and became a skillful upholsterer. At the age of nineteen he joined the firm of Carl Widman in Uppsala. It was in "Widman's Hall" that a conventicle met regularly. Here Blomqvist had a significant spiritual experience, and besides serving as organist and song leader of the group, he became busy on Sundays as a traveling preacher. At the meetings he sang his own songs as well as those of others and accompanied himself on a portable organ. This launched his career as a hymnwriter and composer.

In 1874, he accepted the call of the Uppsala City Mission to serve as a colporteur. His salary was only 800 crowns per year, but he was able to supplement this through the sale of his songbooks. It was no easy task, however, to support his large family; though several had died young, eleven children had been born to the Blomqvists. After about four years of the itinerant life, he settled with his family in Gavle, where he resumed his former occupation, but he continued to preach and sing. Later the family moved to Uppsala and then to Stockholm. The declining years were spent with a daughter in Skovde and a State Church preacher son in Östergötland.

Blomqvist wrote about 400 song texts and almost as many melodies. His first collection, *Kanaan*, was published in 1867 and included thirty songs. This was followed in 1869 by *Pilgrimen* and three parts of a melody edition for *Sions Nya Sånger* during the years 1873 to 1875. Then came his most important works: *Sabbatsklockan* and *Fridstoner*, 1877 to 1882. Later he published several minor collections. During the years 1884 to 1886 he edited a music periodical entitled *Fridsrösten*.

Although many of Blomqvist's hymns never "made it" and many "have had their day," there remains a useful remnant. *Sånger och Psalmer* includes twelve of his texts and four melodies. His works are representative of the revival period. The tunes are quite simple and rhythmic, much like Swedish folk music; the texts are uncomplicated and direct. Many are prayers typical of a time of revival. Theology does not play an important part, but his later works reflect his acceptance of the Waldenströmian view of the atonement. The introduction of Sankey's songs in Sweden was an influence in his writing as were the earlier pietistic and Herrnhut revival songs.

Author:

Heavenly Father, Hear My Supplication 344 (79)
Heavenly Spirit, Gentle Spirit 269 (202)
Praise the Lord, All Praise and Blessing 81 (70)
Sabbath Day of Rest and Cheer 33 (20)

Composer:

BLOMQVIST (DET ÄR ETT FAST ORD) 491 (211)
HEAVENLY DOVE (HIMLADUVA) 269 (202)
LOVEN HERREN 81 (70)
SABBATSDAG 33 (20), 276 (535), 621 (545)

BOBERG, CARL GUSTAF (b. Mönsterås, Sweden, August 16, 1859; d. Kalmar, January 7, 1940) was the son of a shipyard carpenter. His mother was a thoughtful and sensitive person. After trying the life of a sailor for several years, Carl attended the craft school at Nybro, and for a while taught crafts in Mönsterås. At the age of nineteen he had a conversion experience and began to preach the Gospel. After two years in the Bible school at Kristinehamn, he accepted a pastorate in his home town. In 1890, he was called to become the editor of *Sanningsvittnet*, the organ of Evangeliska Fosterlandsstiftelsen. He soon became its owner and remained as editor until 1916. Under his leadership the periodical became an increasingly important arm of the evangelical movement. From 1912 to 1931 he was a member of the Swedish parliament. Boberg was a popular speaker and an appreciated writer. He published several collections of poetry and a number of important hymns. He was a valued member of the committees responsible for the compilation of the first two hymnals of the Swedish Covenant. Lövgren describes Boberg's songs as "clear in thought, simple in composition, as well as romantic in feeling." In smooth flowing lines and easy rhymes he touches on many themes, but the grace of God is his favorite message. Quite a number of his songs are still being sung in Sweden (*Sånger och Psalmer* includes twenty-nine), but only three have been translated.

Author:

Jesus, Jesus, Name Most Precious 252
My Soul Now Magnifies the Lord 421 (375)
O Mighty God 19 (9)

BRIEM, VALDIMAR (b. Grund, Iceland, February 1, 1848; d. Stori-Napur, May 3, 1930) received his theological training at the Theological Seminary in Reykjavik. He was ordained in 1873 and seven years later became the pastor of the Stori-Napur parish, where he served for thirty-eight years. He became vice-bishop of the Skalholt diocese in 1909 and held this position until his death.

Briem was one of Iceland's greatest hymn writers. His works are noted for their poetic beauty and deep feeling. He contributed 102 original hymns and thirty-nine translations to the Icelandic hymnal of 1886, and the latest songbook of the Icelandic church still includes a number of his lyrics.

Author:

How Marvelous God's Greatness 79

BRORSON, HANS ADOLPH (b. Randerup, Denmark, June 20, 1694; d. June 3, 1764), one of Denmark's greatest hymn writers, was the son of a pastor. In spite of a poor economic status and the death of the father when Hans was only ten, he and his three brothers were able to study for the ministry. They attended the cathedral school at Ribe and then studied at the university in Copenhagen. While he was still pursuing theological studies and tutoring his uncle's children, Hans came in contact with the pietistic revival and underwent a spiritual awakening in his own life. His first pastorate was in Randerup, where he began writing hymns.

In 1729, Brorson was called to become a member of the pastoral staff at Tönder. Here he worked with Johan Herman Schraeder, a German pastor, pietist, and hymnist. The church had a mixed congregation of Danes and Germans. Brorson preached in Danish, but the singing was in German. As a result, in 1731 he wrote a number of Danish Christmas hymns which gave him the name "Poet of Christmas." The story is told that the Danish king, Christian VI, once asked Brorson if he was the author of "Awake, All Things That God Has Made." When the poet modestly said that he was, the king promised him a bishopric. In 1747, he became bishop of the Ribe diocese. When Eric Pontoppidan was appointed to revise "Kingo's hymnal," which had been the hymnal of Norway and Denmark for forty years, he received valuable assistance from Brorson, from whose pen much of the new material came.

He published several collections of hymns, all of which were later included in a single volume which passed through six editions before his death. The death of his wife, poor health, and other troubles darkened Brorson's declining years. He continued to write beautiful poetry, but his thoughts turned more and more toward heaven and the after life. A year after his death seventy of the hymns he had written in the last year of his life were published by his son as *Hans Adolph Brorson's Swan-Song.* "A celestial radiance is reflected in the hymns," wrote E.E. Ryden about the collection.

Author:

Behold a Host Arrayed in White 601 (504)

BRUN, JOHAN NORDAHL (b. Byneset, Norway, March 21, 1745; d. July 25, 1816) was the son of a farmer, and very early he assisted in the work around the farm. From his pious mother he received a great appreciation for the Bible, which he read through twice before the age of eleven. After attending Latin school and the university at Trondhjem he studied theology in Copenhagen. Then followed three years in Trondhjem as a tutor, preacher, and writer. In 1771, he returned to Copenhagen as the private secretary of Bishop Gunnerius. While there he wrote the drama *Zarine,* which created quite a sensation in the Danish capital. Beginning in 1772 Brun served as assistant pastor of a church in his home parish of Byneset and two years later became pastor of a church in Bergen. In 1804, he was elevated to the bishopric of the Bergen diocese.

Brun was a powerful preacher and a defender of the faith against the rationalism of the period. He had exceptional literary gifts and wrote a good number of hymns. In 1786, he published a collection of sixty-five original songs entitled *Evangeliske Sange.* Four of his hymns were included in *Den Evangelisk-Christelig Psalmebog,* a hymnal he had banned from his diocese because of its rationalistic tendencies. Only a few of his songs have been translated into English.

Author:

In Heaven All Is Gladness 605 (510)

BURCKHARDT, ABEL was probably a German writer known only through a Christmas song.

Author:

When Christmas Morn Is Breaking 146 (116)

BURNTVEDT, THORVALD OLSEN (b. Kragero, Norway, May 29, 1888; d. May 12, 1960) came to the United States in 1903. He received his education at the Northwestern Conservatory of Music in Minneapolis, Augsburg College and Seminary, New York Biblical Seminary, and the University of Minnesota. He was ordained in the Norwegian Lutheran Church in 1915 and served churches in Tacoma, Washington; Brooklyn, New York; and Minneapolis. Burntvedt was a lecturer at the Lutheran Bible Institute and Augsburg Seminary.

From 1930 to 1959 he was the president of the Lutheran Free Church. In 1946, he was decorated by the king of Norway with the Royal Order of St. Olaf. He was given an honorary doctorate degree by St. Olaf College. Burntvedt wrote several religious booklets and periodical articles and was co-editor of an unofficial hymnal bearing the name *Concordia*.

Translator:
The Hour in Dark Gethsemane (152)

CARLSON, NATHANIEL (b. Gothenberg, Sweden, April 17, 1879; d. Minneapolis, August 2, 1957) studied at the Free Church Bible School in Chicago and the Northwest Bible College at Storm Lake, Iowa. He was a pastor in the Evangelical Free Church. For several years he was the editor of *Chicagobladet*. Carlson translated many songs from the Swedish, wrote several original texts, and composed a number of tunes. His songs were published in his *Songs of Trust and Triumph*, which came out in three editions between 1929 and 1932.

Translator:
Consecrated to Thy Service (259)

DAHLEN, CARL O. (b. Jämtland, Sweden, November 21, 1867; d. Joliet, Illinois, July 21, 1938) emigrated to the United States as a young man and settled in Moline, Illinois. He was converted and baptized in 1887 and almost immediately began to preach. From 1892 to 1895 he was a student at the Baptist seminary, and again in the fall of 1899. He also studied at Moody Bible Institute. He served Swedish Baptist churches in the following locations: Dalbo, Minnesota; Ishpeming, Michigan; Brockton, Massachusetts; Worthington, Fergus Falls, and Milaca, Minnesota; Roseland, Chicago, and Joliet, Illinois.

Dahlen was friendly and optimistic, a good poet and singer. He published a collection of verse entitled *Solljus och sång* (Sunshine and Song) and a songbook, *Toner*, with arrangements for choir, men's voices, and duets. In his later years he translated from Swedish song literature.

Translator:
Thou, Tender, Gracious Father 97 (90)

DANNSTRÖM, JOHAN ISADOR (b. Stockholm, December 14, 1812; d. October 17, 1897) inherited his love for music from his mother. At the age of fourteen he became a student in the Academy of Music. It was his father's wish that he enter the business world, and at seventeen he accepted a position in the office of a merchant. Four years later he resumed his music studies, and during the years 1837 to 1841 he toured Germany, France, and Italy, studying and giving lectures and concerts. Upon his return to Stockholm, he tried the theater, but soon settled down to teaching music. In 1856, he opened a piano shop.

Composer:
SANCTUARY (HUR LJUFT DET ÄR ATT KOMMA 55 (27)

DOVING, CARL (b. Norddalen, Norway, March 21, 1867; d. October 2, 1937) received private instruction from Bishop Astrup, missionary to South Africa. He came to the United States at the age of twenty-three. He attended Luther College in Decorah, Iowa, where he earned an A.B. degree in 1903, and Luther Seminary in St. Paul. Doving served Norwegian Lutheran congregations in Red Wing and Montevideo, Minnesota, and Brooklyn, New York. He could converse in at least six different languages. In his hospital visits as a city missionary in Chicago, he spoke with many different patients in their native tongues. He was a member of the committee appointed by three Norwegian synods to prepare an English hymnal. The volume was published in 1913 as the *Lutheran Hymnary*. It included thirty-two of Doving's translations of German and Scandinavian hymns.

Translator:
Behold a Host Arrayed in White 601 (504)
Built on the Rock 472 (412)
Watch, My Soul, and Pray 445 (408)

EKSTRÖM, FREDRIK AUGUST (b. Stockholm, January 5, 1819; d. May 24, 1901), after attending elementary school, studied art and for a while worked as a bookkeeper. After further studies he became a teacher and organist in Floda, Södermanland. In 1844, he moved to Dalkarlsberg, where he taught school and served as a chaplain to miners. After three years he transferred to Gunnilsbo in Västmanland to teach school and play the organ. Ekström also had some ability as a composer.

He left his career as a teacher in 1861 to become the postmaster at Stjärnvik and then in Öregrund in 1881, which position he held until retirement.

Composer:

EKSTRÖM 402 (342)

ERICKSON, JOHN IRVING (b. Stambaugh, Michigan, July 19, 1914) attended the public schools in his home town and was a member of the Covenant church there. He graduated from the general music course at Moody Bible Institute in 1935 and attended North Park College and Theological Seminary between 1935 and 1941. Later he earned the following degrees: A.B. from Wheaton College in 1945, M.A. from the University of Chicago in 1956, and M.L.S. from Rosary College in 1963. He served Covenant churches in Seattle (internship) and Wiley Heights, Washington, and Glen Ellyn, Illinois. From 1947 to 1961 he was chaplain of North Park College and Theological Seminary, and from 1961 to 1972, chaplain and director of the library in the seminary. In 1941, he married Myrtle Hulting, and two daughters were born to the couple.

Erickson was chairman of the Covenant Hymnal Commission from 1967 to 1973, is secretary of the Committee for the Revision of the Book of Worship (1973 to the present), and is chairman of the Commission on Church Music and Worship (1975 to the present).

Co-translator:

Now Shine a Thousand Candles Bright 145

FALCK, FREDRIKA, ELEANORA (b. Södermanland, Sweden, November 9, 1719; d. December 3, 1749) was the daughter of Count D.R. Nieroth, an army officer. She married Jonas Falck, rector of the Vallerstad congregation in the diocese of Linköping. Nothing more is known about her life except that she wrote the hymn "My Crucified Savior," which witnesses to a deep inner religion influenced by Herrnhutism. She died when she was but thirty.

Author:

My Crucified Savior 195 (150)

FOSS, CLAUDE WILLIAM (b. Geneva, Illinois, August 28, 1855; d. Rock Island, Illinois, February 8, 1935), the son of Swedish immigrants, graduated from Augustana College in 1883. The same year he began teaching history at the college, a position which he retained for fifty years. From 1888 to 1901 he also served as vice-president. Foss was a prolific writer, his greatest contribution being in the area of translating. His foremost work was *Masterpieces of Swedish Literature*. He served on the committees that produced the English Augustana hymnals of 1901 and 1925. A number of the translations from the Swedish in both volumes were done by Foss.

Translator:

Chosen Seed and Zion's Children 473 (414)
My Crucified Savior 195 (150)
When Christmas Morn Is Breaking, Sts. 2 and 3 146

FRANZEN, FRANS MICHAEL (b. Uleåborg, Finland, February 9, 1772; d. Härnosänd, Sweden, August 14, 1847), although born in Finland, was of Swedish lineage. When Sweden lost Finland to Russia, he left his post as professor in the University of Åbo to become the pastor of Kumla parish in Sweden. Since his native language was Swedish and all of his poetry had been written in that language, the change was not difficult in one respect. But the life in the rural parish was quite a contrast to life in the academic community. It was at this time, however, that some of his finest hymns were written. In 1825, he was called to the pastorate of St. Clara Church in Stockholm and was named secretary of the Swedish Academy. As a preacher he was warmly evangelical and boldly berated the coldness and sinfulness of his congregation. At the age of sixty-two he was appointed Bishop of Härnosänd, where he served faithfully until his death.

Franzén started writing verse at an early age, and while he was still in Finland, his works were being read on both sides of the Gulf of Bothnia. He proved to be a valuable assistant to Wallin in the compilation of the 1819 *Psalmbok*. It contained no less than twenty-nine of his original lyrics. The 1937 edition retained twenty-three of them. Concerning his hymns, one of his biographers has written that "they bear the imprint of tender sensitivity, good form, and gentle intimacy. This has caused his hymns to be loved not the least among people of revival."

Author:

Prepare the Way, O Zion 119 (107)

FROSTENSON, ANDERS (b. Loshult, Malmöhus län, Sweden, April 23, 1906) studied at Lund, where he received his theology degree and was ordained in 1932. The following year he became curate in the Gustaf Vasa Church in Stockholm and later was the associate pastor there. In 1948, he was appointed rector at Lovo. He has published several collections of poetry and has written many hymns, as well as songs for children. Nine of his hymns were included in the 1937 *Psalmbok*. Since the organization of the Hymnological Institute in the late 1950s, Frostenson has been a leading figure in the attempt to revise the hymnody of the Swedish Church. Several new collections have been produced, including a supplement to the *Psalmbok* called *71 Psalmer och Visor*. Many of the texts and revisions are the work of Frostenson. His themes are many, and his lyrics have depth and power.

Author:
Jesus of Nazareth Passes By 163

FRYKMAN, ANDREW T. (b. Sunne, Värmland, Sweden, August 8, 1875; d. Rockford, Illinois, November 7, 1943) was the son of Nils and Betty Frykman. Andrew grew up in Minnesota where his father was the pastor of the Salem circuit of Covenant churches in Kandiyohi County. After attending North Park College and Theological Seminary, he served the church in Helena, Montana. While there he earned his A.B. degree at Montana Wesleyan University. From 1901 to 1904 he was president of Northwestern College in Minneapolis. In 1902, Frykman married Ruth E. Skogsbergh, the daughter of the "Swedish Moody." Then followed pastorates in Superior, Wisconsin; First Covenant, Jamestown, New York; Wausa, Nebraska; and First Covenant, Rockford, Illinois. In Rockford Frykman built and operated that city's first radio station.

From 1934 to 1943 Frykman was director of evangelism for the Covenant. He retired in the spring of 1943 and served the congregation at Conover, Wisconsin, a few months before his death.

Translator:
List to the Gospel Resounding 293 (231)
Our Mighty God Works Mighty Wonders 72 (66)
Reviser:
The Highest Joy That Can Be Known 283 (220)

FRYKMAN, CARL M. (b. Sunne, Sweden, August 17, 1880; d. Minneapolis, Minnesota, August 7, 1931) was the son of hymnist Nils Frykman. He came to the United States with his parents, five brothers, and two sisters in 1888. He grew up near Pennock, Kandiyohi County, Minnesota. Carl was an electrician by trade, and with his youngest brother, Victor, operated the Frykman Electric Company in Minneapolis. He was an active member of the Swedish Tabernacle Church (now First Covenant).

Composer:
HEAVENLY VOICE (JESUS DIG KALLAR) 293 (231)

FRYKMAN, GUSTAF (b. Norrköping, Sweden, March 21, 1873; d. Minneapolis, Minnesota, February 15, 1953), a son of Nils Frykman, studied at Carleton College and the University of Minnesota. For some time he was the editor of Minneapolis *Veckobladet*, a Swedish language newspaper reporting noteworthy happenings among the Mission Friends. At the same time he served on the charter commission for the city of Minneapolis. For several years Frykman worked in the treasury department of the city. At one time he was the manager of a bank in Bock, Minnesota. In the 1930s he accepted a position with the Northern States Power Company, where he remained until retirement. He was an active member of the Elim Covenant Church.

Translator:
I Have a Future All Sublime, sts. 2-5 609 (512)

FRYKMAN, NILS (b. Sunne, Värmland, Sweden, October 20, 1842; d. Minneapolis, March 30, 1911) was born Larson, but when he enrolled in normal school, he took the name Frykman after his native Fryksdalen. Although he was born of humble parents and was left fatherless at an early age, he was able to enroll at the teachers' college in Karlstad. He graduated in 1868 and began his career as a schoolteacher, first at Grums and then at Norrköping. He married Betty Jonsson in 1869, a union that proved to be a happy one. Ten children were born to the couple. In 1875, he returned to Sunne, the parish which had experienced revival in the 1850s and 1860s and again soon after his return. Frykman became active in the meetings, teaching school during the days and preaching evenings and Sundays.

Up until this time he had written no hymns, but now they came freely and frequently. He kept pencil and paper near at all times so that he could jot down the songs as they came. They were mainly songs of praise and gladness from a heart filled with the joy of salvation. For many of his lyrics he composed happy rhythmic tunes. He introduced them in the cottage meetings, and as a rule they were first printed in *Sanningsvittnet* or collections of songs published by that periodical.

Partly because of his acceptance of the views of Waldenstrom and partly because of his participation in communion outside of the state church, tension arose between Frykman and the school board. The matter became so serious that only an appeal to the king saved him from dismissal. New difficulties arose when he had one of his children baptized by a free church pastor rather than by a priest of the established church. The case followed the same course as previously, and Frykman resigned rather than bear continued harassment. For the next few years he served as an itinerant preacher. Through the efforts of August Skogsbergh, he was called to the pastorate of the Tabernacle Church in Chicago and began his work there in 1888. He remained in Chicago only two years and on December 20, 1889, arrived at Salem, Minnesota, where he served a circuit of five churches. The eighteen years spent there were happy and productive ones. The work prospered, souls were won for the Kingdom, and the inspiration to write hymns revived. At the age of sixty-five he resigned from the pastorate and moved to Minneapolis.

The Covenant Annual Meeting of 1906 decided to publish a hymnal, and Frykman was selected to serve as chairman of the committee. The first official hymnal of the Covenant, *Sions Basun*, was published in 1908. No less that 123 of the 731 hymns were written by Frykman. Because of his experience, ability, and wisdom, Frykman served in various other capacities in the Covenant and the Northwest Mission Association (now the Northwest Conference). He was vice-chairman of the denomination for a number of years, chairman of the ministerial board, and chairman of the Northwest Ministerial Association. During his declining years he continued to preach occasionally and lecture on the theme "The History of My Songs," which later was published.

About 2,000 people attended Frykman's funeral service in the Swedish Tabernacle (now First Covenant Church) in Minneapolis. He was laid to rest in Lakewood Cemetery, where in 1928 the Covenant erected a monument. Below his name is inscribed the first stanza of "I Have a Future All Sublime."

Author:
God, My God in Heaven Above 90 (77)
How Beautiful, Serene, and Grand (508)
How Wonderful It Is 520 (433)
I Have a Friend Who Loveth Me 416 (370)
I Have a Future All Sublime 609 (512)
I Sing with Joy and Gladness 418 (355)
Joy Bells Are Ringing 143 (114)
List to the Gospel Resounding 293 (231)
Our Mighty God Works Mighty Wonders 72 (66)
The Highest Joy That Can Be Known 283 (220)
When My Lord Is Dear to Me 425 (377)
Why Should I Be Anxious? 415 (366)
Composer:
FRYKMAN (JAG HAR EN VÄN) 416 (370)
GEMENSKAP (DET ÄR EN HÄRLIG TING) 520 (433)
JOYFUL PILGRIM (NU ÄR JAG NÖJD) 418 (355)
MIN FRAMTIDSDAG 609 (512)
PENNOCK (NÄR MIN GUD JAG HÅLLER KÄR) 425 (377)

GRIEG, HAGERUP EDVARD (b. Bergen, Norway, June 15, 1843; d. September 4, 1907) was the son of the British consul in Bergen. When he was fifteen, the young Grieg entered the Leipzig Conservatory and graduated with honors in 1862. He visited Rome in 1865 and there wrote his first orchestral work, "In Autumn," which won him the prize of the Stockholm Academy of Music. He established himself as a piano teacher in Christiania (Oslo) and founded a music society there. He was also appointed conductor of the philharmonic society.

Grieg was active in Norway and Denmark as a composer, teacher, and conductor, and had great influence upon the music of the Scandinavian countries. He composed piano and orchestra music, the best known being *Concerto in A Minor* and the music to Ibsen's *Peer Gynt*. He also wrote about 150 songs. He has sometimes been called the "Chopin of the

North," because he did for Norway what Chopin did for Poland and there are similarities in their melody and harmony effects. Grieg drew many of his themes from Norwegian folk stories and national airs.

Composer:
BEHOLD A HOST 601 (504)

GRUNDTVIG, NIKOLAI FREDERIK SEVERIN (b. Udby, Denmark, September 8, 1783; d. September 2, 1872) was the last of the great triumvirate of Danish hymn writers. Kingo, the "Poet of Easter," Brorson, the "Poet of Christmas," and Grundtvig, the "Poet of Whitsuntide," made up this noble group. Grundtvig's father was a Lutheran pastor who remained faithful to evangelical Christianity in a time when rationalism was making inroads in the church. The young Grundtvig's first contact with the "new theology" at the University of Copenhagen caused him to lose all interest in religion. But it was not long before his eyes were opened to the spiritual poverty of the people, and he became violently opposed to the new teaching. While teaching in a school for boys, he received a request from his father to become his assistant in the parish of Udby. He applied for ordination and preached a trial sermon before the church officials. In the sermon he spoke out boldly against the rationalistic hypocrisy of the clergy, and this marked the beginning of a long and bitter struggle with the church authorities.

In 1811, he was duly ordained and a few days later, installed at Udby. But for many years he was a pastor without a parish and was in constant theological controversy. Nevertheless, his preaching was heard by many, and he helped to infuse new spiritual life into the Danish church. He was successful also in bringing about reforms in the school system. His leadership in education spread throughout the Scandinavian countries, and he has rightly been called "the father of the public school in Scandinavia." The nation gradually recognized his worth, and in 1839 he was fully reinstated and appointed pastor in Vartov. At the celebration of his golden jubilee as pastor in 1861, the king bestowed on him the title of bishop. E. E. Ryden has characterized Grundtvig as the sage of Denmark "who always will be remembered as the greatest historian, educator, religious philosopher, hymn writer, and folk leader the nation has produced."

Grundtvig's greatest hymns deal with the church and the sacraments. As the "Poet of Whitsuntide" he wrote hymns of the Spirit. After his death his poems and hymns were published in five volumes, entitled *Hymns and Spiritual Songs.* Although at one time his songs were banned from the Danish hymnal, there are more of his hymns in the present edition than of any other author.

Author:
Bright and Glorious Is the Sky 155
Built on the Rock 472 (412)

GUSTAFSON, EMIL (b. Kräklinge, Närke, Sweden, July 12, 1862; d. May 5, 1900) grew up in a rural home. While still young he had an unusual understanding of the Christian faith. In adolescence there was a period of rebellion, but he had an experience of renewal at the age of sixteen. Gustafson entered agricultural school, but poor health caused the termination of his studies. Gradually his health began to return, though never in full measure, and he gave himself to writing and evangelistic work. But he still was often plagued with sickness, and he became quite withdrawn and introspective. This is reflected in his songs and writings, which are concerned with the inner spiritual life and the consecration of the whole person. Gustafson published three song collections: *Betlehemsjärnan* (The Star of Bethlehem), *Hjärtesånger* (Songs of the Heart), and *Förbundssånger* (Songs of Covenant). Several of the musical settings were composed by him.

Author:
Consecrated to Thy Service (259)
Composer:
AVSKILD FÖR MIN HERRES RÄKNING (259)

GUSTAFSON, SIGNHILD V. (b. Boston, Massachusetts, December 15, 1894; d. Fort Lauderdale, Florida, March 22, 1967) was the daughter of immigrants who helped found the Covenant Congregational Church in Boston. Her father, Alfred Gustafson, wrote poetry and hymns, several of which were included in *Svenska Söndagsskolans Sångbok.* He was also the editor of the Swedish language newspaper, *Svea,* published in Worcester, Massachusetts. Signhild, the fourth of eight children, graduated cum laude from Radcliffe College in 1915 and taught languages for forty years at Classical High School in Springfield, Massachusetts. One summer she taught Swedish at North Park College and Theological Seminary. She studied a year (1922-23) at Uppsala University under a grant from the American Scandinavian Foundation. Miss Gustafson translated several books from Swedish, as well as many articles published in the *Scandinavian American Review.* After retirement from public school teaching she tutored pupils at the MacDuffie School for Girls for many years.

Translator:
Tell Me, Who Are These (517)

HAGFORS, ERNEST AUGUST (b. 1827; d. 1913) was a composer and music instructor in Finland's oldest teachers' college at Jyväskylä. He published a song collection and chorale book.

Composer:
PILGRIM SONG 462

HANSEN, FRED C.M. (b. Vejle, Denmark, June 25, 1888; d. Blair, Nebraska, April 4, 1965) immigrated with his parents to America in 1890. He was educated at Dana College, the University of Nebraska, and Trinity Seminary and was ordained in the United Evangelical Lutheran Church in 1914. Hansen served pastorates in Davenport and Audubon, Iowa; Milwaukee, Wisconsin; Council Bluffs, Iowa; and Golgotha Church, Chicago, Illinois. He held many church positions and served on all the hymnal commissions of his church. He represented his church on the commission that produced the *Service Book and Hymnal,* translating and revising several of the hymns.

Reviser:
Built on the Rock 472 (412)

HARRIS, THORO (b. Washington, D.C., March 31, 1873; d. Eureka Springs, Arkansas, March 27, 1955) was a gospel song writer, composer, and translator. He published several songbooks that were used mostly in several southern states. A number of his texts, translations, and musical arrangements appeared in Nathaniel Carlson's *Songs of Trust and Triumph* No. 3. He was the author and composer of the song "All That Thrills My Soul Is Jesus," perhaps his best known work.

Translator:
All That Our Savior Hath Spoken (320)

HEDBORN, SAMUEL JOHAN (b. Heda, Sweden, October 14, 1783; d. Åskeryd, December 26, 1849) was another of Wallin's contemporaries. He was born into the home of a poor Swedish sailor. In spite of many difficulties but with the help of friends, who recognized his talents, he was able to secure a basic education and begin studies for the ministry. The following years were characterized by indecision and depression. His taste of university life aroused a desire for an academic career, but this was out of his reach. He wrote to a friend that it was with "dark forebodings, a burdened mind, and empty pockets" that he resumed the path to ordination. To become a minister was, in his words, "to enter the mystic night to preach to others about light and hope without possessing them myself." And yet it was during these years, 1810 to 1814, that he wrote all of his hymns.

They witness to a personal experience of both distress and grace, and this is what gives them such deep intimacy and power. His hymns bear a strong resemblance to those of the early pietists and Herrnhuters. Hedborn improved gradually, finished his theological studies, and received his ordination. From 1820 until his death he was the pastor of the parish of Åskeryd and Bredestad. In 1812, Hedborn published a collection of hymns and a second volume the following year. It is said that the Christo-centric note in his lyrics influenced Wallin's theological views. Ten of his hymns were included in the *Psalmbok* of 1819 and the edition of 1937.

Author:
Holy Majesty, before Thee 5 (4)

HERZOG, JOHANN FRIEDRICH (b. Dresden, Germany, June 6, 1647; d. March 21, 1699) studied law at the University of Wittenberg. For several years he was the tutor of General von Arnim's son. He returned to Dresden where he practiced law until his death. It seems that, so far as hymn writing is concerned, he is known for one text only.

Author:

Again a Day Has from Us Gone 40 (31)

HOPPE, ANNA (b. Milwaukee, Wisconsin, 1889; d. Milwaukee, August 2, 1941) began writing verse while still a child. She did not attend school beyond the eighth grade. When employed as a stenographer in various business offices, she spent her spare time writing hymns and sacred poetry. "Many of my hymns," she said, "have been written on my way to and from church, and to and from work." She used the lunch hour to type them and keep up her correspondence. Some of her work was published in the *Northwest Lutheran,* official organ of the Wisconsin Synod, of which she was a member. Her lyrics attracted the attention of Dr. Adolf Hult, a professor at Augustana Seminary. He influenced her to write a series of hymns for the church year. These were published by Augustana in 1928 as *Songs of the Church Year.* Her most outstanding recognition came when twenty-three of her hymns were included in the Augustana *Hymnal,* 1925. Her songs are characterized by a deep certainty of faith and fervency of spirit.

Translator:

O Precious Thought! Some Day the Mist Shall Vanish (337)

HULTMAN, JOHN ALFRED (b. Hjärtlanda, Småland, Sweden, July 6, 1861; d. Glendale, California, August 7, 1942), the second of the triumvirate of Covenant Swedish-American hymnists, was born on a small farm. Very early in life he evidenced an interest in music, and on occasional visits to the parish church at Hultsjö, the boy enjoyed listening to the organ. The family immigrated to America in 1869 and settled on a farm near Essex, Iowa. Here the young emigrant and his brother worked as cowboys, singing gospel songs as they went about their duties. After much saving and sacrifice, Alfred was able to purchase an organ and his music education began. After his conversion, he was invited by the Rev. A. Hallner to teach school and direct the church choir in Fridhem, Nebraska. Later he succeeded Hallner as pastor of the church. In 1879, he represented that church at the conference of the Mission Synod in Chicago. He decided to remain in Chicago, so he resigned from his church and for two years studied at the Chicago Atheneum.

While in Chicago he served as choir director in the church which later became the Douglas Park Covenant Church. He also preached and sang in the Evanston church. After two years of study in Chicago Hultman became an itinerant preacher-singer. His travels brought him to Omaha, Nebraska, in the summer of 1881, where he helped organize a congregation and served as pastor for fourteen years. Before leaving Chicago, he had met Carolina Palmer, who became his wife and co-laborer in the church. Three daughters (one died as a child) and one son were born to the couple. Under Hultman's ministry the church in Omaha became one of the leading Covenant churches in the west. When the Evangelical Mission Covenant Church was organized in 1885, Hultman was one of the charter members. In 1889, he was given a three-month leave of absence from his church in order to accompany P.P. Waldenström on a preaching tour of the United States. Hultman's singing was a great addition to the services.

In 1896 and 1897, he was on the staff of the music school at North Park College, but he declined the offer of the position as director. Throughout his life, however, he maintained a warm interest in the school. He was ordained in May, 1900, and accepted a call to the pastorate of the Salem Square Church in Worcester, Massachusetts. The church provided an assistant so that he was given more time for concert tours. After six years he resigned as pastor in order to give more time to concerts and his music business. His son Paul, now an accomplished pianist, often accompanied him.

The family moved to Sweden in 1909, and during the next four years Hultman gave hundreds of concerts. From this time he became known as "The Sunshine Singer," partly because of his songs and partly because of his personality. Upon returning to Worcester, the father and son opened the Hultman Conservatory of Music, which later was moved to Chicago. The Hultmans returned to Sweden in 1919, where Mrs. Hultman died. From now on he spent most of his time in the land of his birth, returning to

America to rest and give concerts. When he was seventy-five, he had crossed the Atlantic twenty-seven times. On one of his visits to the United States he married Margaret Jansson, who proved to be a most compatible companion.

In the earlier days of his concert activities in Sweden, Hultman had been criticized often in the press for his repertoire, his informality, and his manner of singing. At times he was refused entrance into certain churches. But wherever he went, the churches and auditoriums were packed and his critics soon ceased their attacks. Many institutions, causes, and individuals were given material aid through his concerts. He usually gave a third of the proceeds to the church he was visiting and a third to some good cause, and with the third he kept, he was unusually generous. Foreign missions, sick preachers and missionaries, soldiers' and sailors' missions, church building programs, organ funds, and many other causes were given assistance. North Park's Caroline Hall was made possible partly through proceeds from Hultman concerts. At the age of eighty-one "The Sunshine Singer" was still active. In fact, he died as he had lived—while singing a concert.

But Hultman was more than a singer; he was also a writer, composer, and publisher of hymns. His first collection, *Cymbalen*, came out in 1885. Ten years later, in partnership with A.L. Skoog, he published *Jubelklangen*, which was used widely in several Swedish denominations. While in Sweden he began the publication of *Solskenssånger*, which appeared in a series of pamphlets and later bound in one volume. Several other smaller collections were published from time to time. He helped to compile *Sions Basun*, the first official hymnal of the Covenant. Several of his texts and fifteen tunes were included.

Author:
I Sing of the Savior (374)
Composer:
DET BRISTER EN STRÄNG (511)
NOCTURN 48
O NU VILL JAG SJUNGA (374)
SABBATSVILA (521)
STILLA STUNDER 302 (245)
TACK O GUD (12), 622 (543)

INGEMANN, BERNHARDT SEVERIN (b. Thorkildstrup, Island of Falster, Denmark, May 28, 1789; d. Sorø, February 24, 1862) was the son of a Lutheran pastor. After the father died in 1800, the large family moved to Slagelse, an old city on the island of Sjaelland. There the young Ingemann attended Latin school, and in 1806, entered the University of Copenhagen. He published his first collection of poems in 1811 and his famous epic, *The Black Knights*, three years later. From 1822 to 1862 he was professor of Danish language and literature at the Academy of Sorø. Ingemann's first collection of hymns appeared in 1822—*Morgonsalmer*. This was followed by *Höimessesalmer* (High-Mass Hymns) in 1825 and enlarged in 1843.

By this time Ingemann had attracted attention as a hymn writer, and he was commissioned to prepare a new hymnal for the Church of Denmark. This volume, which was completed in 1855, included some of his hymns and was the first official songbook to print some works of Grundtvig. The latest edition of the Danish hymnal has twenty-nine Ingemann texts.

Author:
Through the Night of Doubt and
Sorrow 371 (317)

JESPERSON, JOHN (b. Dalum, Västergötland, Sweden, October 14, 1858; d. Orlando, Florida, May 25, 1943) emigrated to America with his parents in 1873. The family settled in Rockford, Illinois, where the young Jesperson was confirmed and received his secondary education. He attended Augustana College and Seminary, graduating and being ordained in 1885. For four years he served the Messiah Lutheran church in Burlington, Iowa. From 1889 to 1903 he was the business manager of Augustana College and Seminary. The next four years he was pastor of Salem Lutheran Church in Spokane, Washington.

Jesperson was called by the Columbia Conference in 1907 to establish Coeur d'Alene College in Idaho, where he served as president and treasurer for seven years. In 1914, he was called to the post of superintendent of the Augustana Inner Mission in Chicago, a position he retained until his retirement in 1939. In 1922, he received an honorary doctorate from his alma mater.

Translator:
I Have a Friend, So Patient, Kind,
Forbearing (380)

JOHNSON, E. GUSTAV (b. Väse, Värmland, Sweden, May 21, 1893; d. Miami, Florida, November 13, 1974) was ten years of age when his family moved to Hartford, Connecticut, where he received his elementary education and took up the printer's trade. When he was already a mature man of thirty, Johnson came to North Park and earned diplomas in the academy, college, and theological seminary. He studied further at the University of Chicago, where he received a Ph.B. degree, and at Duke University, where he earned an M.A. degree.

In 1931, Mr. Johnson began a teaching ministry at North Park College which lasted thirty years. He taught English language and literature in both the academy and college and Swedish in the college and served for many years as faculty adviser for student publications. His friendliness and concern for individual students earned him the title "Mr. North Park." He took a special interest in the off-campus students, especially members of minority groups, and no one knows how many were given financial assistance through his generosity. His teaching career ended in 1959, but he stayed on the campus as Covenant archivist.

Johnson held membership in many learned societies: Modern Language Association, American Dialect Society, Society for the Advancement of Scandinavian Study (president, 1946 to 1947), Swedish Cultural Society of America (1946 to 1952), and Swedish Pioneer Historical Society (a founder and board member, 1948 to 1974). His literary efforts have been noteworthy. He contributed to many periodicals and for many years served as editor of the *Swedish Pioneer Historical Quarterly.* He was one of the editors of the three-volume *The Swedish Element in America* (1933). For his continuing interest in Swedish culture and its promotion in the United States he was knighted by the king of Sweden in 1951 with the Royal Order of Vasa. In 1968, North Park College presented him with the honorary degree, Doctor of Humane Letters.

Conversant with both the Swedish and English languages, Johnson developed a creative technique in translating. He translated several books, including *Travel Memories from America, 1876,* by C.J. Nyvall, and *A Swedish-American Preacher's Story* by Erik Wallgren. His greatest contribution, though, was his translation of Swedish hymns. As a valued member of the Covenant Music Commission, 1944 to 1951, he translated twenty-three songs for *The Hymnal* (1950). He was able to incorporate the content and spirit of the original text without destroying the meter. In *By One Spirit* Karl Olsson observed that "few translators have succeeded so well as he in suggesting the mood of the originals." Johnson's declining years were spent at Covenant Palms in Miami, Florida.

Translator:

A Quivering Chord Is Broken (511)
Are You Dismayed, Lonely, Afraid 83 (73)
For God So Loved All the World (75)
Give, O Lord, unto Thy Servant 408 (354)
God, My God, in Heaven Above 90 (77)
How Beautiful, Serene, and Grand (508)
How Wonderful It Is 520 (433)
I Sing of the Savior (374)
I Sing with Joy and Gladness 418 (355)
In Tenderness, Jesus, Enfold Me (394)
In Thy Temple Courts, O Father 54
Jesus, in Stillness, Longing I Wait 327 (261)
Joy Bells Are Ringing 143 (114)
O Mighty God, When I Behold the Wonder 19 (9)
O Savior, Thou Who for Us Died 461 (293)
O Zion, Acclaim Your Redeemer 118 (106)
Praise the Lord with Joyful Song 73 (67)
Savior, in Thy Love Abiding 399 (341)
Sing the Glad Carol of Jesus, Our Lord 255 (197)
Springs of Grace Are Streaming 510 (434)
Time Is As Swift As a Vanishing Dream (551)
We May Trust in Every Way (346)
With My Deepest Feeling (91)

Reviser:

In the Silent Midnight Watches (228)

JOHNSON, OBED (b. Lanyon, Iowa, May 5, 1881; d. Minneapolis, Minnesota, October 12, 1970) graduated from Carleton College in 1906 and Oberlin Theological Seminary in 1909. The next fifteen years were spent in China as a teacher and missionary. When he returned to the United States, he lectured at the University of California and took further studies there, earning a Ph.D. degree in 1925. From 1927 to 1929 he taught Chinese language and history at Leland Stanford University and then moved to Indiana where he served as chaplain and professor of philosophy and religion at Wabash College. After fifteen years in this position he became professor of philosophy and sociology at North Park College. After his retirement in 1951, the Johnsons remained in the North Park community for several years and then moved to Minneapolis. Johnson is remembered by many as a cheerful friend, an erudite conversationalist, and an inveterate storyteller.

Translator:
As Pilgrims in This World (502)
My Soul Now Magnifies the Lord 421 (375)

KANTONEN-HALKOLA, AINO LILJA (b. Saarijärvi, Finland, September 6, 1901) came to America with her parents at the age of three. The family settled in Ashtabula, Ohio, where Aino received her elementary and high school education. She attended Suomi College in Hancock, Michigan. She married the Rev. Sakari Halkola in 1922 and served with him in pastorates at Seattle, Washington; Gardner, Massachusetts; Rudyard, Michigan; and Milwaukee, Wisconsin, before his death in 1960. She is known among Finnish Americans as a poet, speaker, and lecturer. Mrs. Halkola is the author of hundreds of religious poems, some of which were published in *Rukoursrunoja* (Prayer Poems). Her present home is in Milwaukee, Wisconsin. She is a sister to Professor Taito A. Kantonen at Hamma Divinity School, Springfield, Ohio.

Translator:
Lord, As a Pilgrim 462

KINGO, THOMAS HANSEN (b. Slangerup, Denmark, December 15, 1634; d. October 14, 1703), Denmark's first great hymnist, was the son of a linen weaver. After attending Latin school in his native city, he studied theology at the University of Copenhagen. He was ordained in 1661 and served a parish near Vedby before becoming the pastor in Slangerup in 1668. Here he began to attract attention as a poet. His first collection of religious poetry, which he dedicated to King Christian V, appeared in 1673 with the title *Aandelig Sjungekors forste* (Spiritual Songs, First Part). In the dedication he deplored the fact that the Danes had depended so heavily upon hymns of foreign origin. In 1677, he was elevated to the bishopric of Fyen. *Spiritual Songs, Second Part* appeared in 1681. Many of his texts were written to be sung to popular tunes. To justify this he wrote, "If a pleasing melody set to a song of Sodom delights your ear, how much more, if you are a child of God, should not that same melody delight your soul when sung to a song of Zion?" In 1679, Kingo was made a member of the nobility and in 1682 was made doctor of theology.

The following year he was appointed by the king to prepare a new hymnal which was to include some of Kingo's hymns. The first part appeared in 1689 and was called "The Winter Part" (Advent to Easter). About half of the 267 hymns were by Kingo. It was approved by the king, but it met with so much criticism that a new editor was appointed. The new volume, appearing four years later, did not contain a single Kingo song, and it was rejected. A commission was then chosen to direct the work, and an approved hymnbook was completed in 1699. Kingo had again come into favor—the new hymnal was based largely upon his work and included eighty-five of his hymns. It is usually referred to as "Kingo's Hymnal."

Because many of his hymns were written on the theme of the resurrection, Kingo has been called the "Poet of Eastertide." His lyrics never failed to make a strong personal appeal. Nicolai Grundtvig paid tribute to Kingo in these words: "He effected a combination of sublimity and simplicity, a union of splendor and fervent devotion, a powerful and musical play of words and imagery that reminds one of Shakespeare."

The day before he died, Kingo is said to have exclaimed, "Tomorrow, Lord, we shall hear glorious music." On the monument over his grave in Odense is the epitaph written by Grundtvig:

Thomas Kingo is the psalmist
Of the Danish temple choir.
That his people will remember
As long as songs their hearts inspire.

Author:
Dearest Jesus, Draw Thou Near Me
64 (45)

KNUDSEN, PEDER (b. Våga, Norway, 1819; d. December, 1863), the son of a parish singer, evidenced musical talent at an early age. He was accepted as a member of the Pre-military Musical Organization in Christiania (Oslo). Here he took lessons on various instruments, especially the violin, and received encouragement from Johann Behreus, a well-known musician. Through the latter's recommendation, Knudsen was appointed choral director in Holinestrand. Later he became civic music director at Kragerö and administrator of music in the schools. He organized the Midsummer Eve musical festivals. In 1859, he became organist at Ålesund.

Composer:
CHRISTMAS EVE 131 (528)

KÖHLER, EMMY CHRISTINA (b. Stockholm, Sweden, May 22, 1858; d. Sollentuna, February 2, 1925), the daughter of an accountant, became interested in music at an early age. She learned to play the piano and took harmony lessons from Emil Sjögren. Emmy served as a child governess in the home of a doctor and then in the Köhler family home in Ryssbylund, Småland. In 1891, she married the Köhler son, Sven, a deputy circuit judge. Later he became principal assistant secretary in the finance department of the government in Stockholm.

Mrs. Köhler began to write delightful lyric stories, which she often set to melodies for her own children. Later these appeared in the Christmas publications called *Jultomten* and *Julklappan.* In 1898, there appeared an anonymous collection initialed "E.K." with the title *Gunnar's and Inga's Fun Book*. The names were those of her children. She published *Berit's Songs* in 1901. Between 1903 and 1907 she worked for *Ny Illustrerad Tidning, Svensk Domtidning*, and *Idun*.

Her works were full of mother love and evidenced a deep interest in the world of children. For some time she worked as a teacher in a school for the mentally retarded. After her death a friend said, "When I think of Emmy, I have a living example of what it means to be in this world but not of it."

Author:
Now Shine a Thousand Candles Bright 145

Composer:
CHRISTMAS CANDLES 145

LAGERSTRÖM, SELMA, see **SUNDELIUS-LAGERSTRÖM.**

LAURINUS, LAURENTIUS LAURENTII (b. Söderköping, Sweden, 1573; d. November 29, 1655), after studies in Uppsala, earned his master's degree at Wittenberg in 1603. He became headmaster of a school in Söderköping, was ordained,and later was called to be parish priest in Häradshammar. The parish of Jonsberg was added to his pastorate, and he continued as pastor of these congregations for forty-six years. He was blind during the last part of his life.

Laurinus wrote scholarly books in Swedish, German, and Latin. In 1622, he published *Musica rudimenta,* the first Swedish textbook on singing. At the end of his *Haffenrefferi Compendium Locorum Theologicorum* he appended several songs which have been included in hymnals. The most popular of these was "I himmelen, I himmelen." In 1650, he put out his *Plausus Seuecicus*, a Swedish poem about the Thirty Years War.

Author:
In Heaven Above 604 (509)

LINDEMAN, LUDVIG MATTHIAS (b. Trondhjem, Norway, November 28, 1812; d. Oslo, May 23, 1887) received his first instruction from his father, who was the organist of Our Savior's Church in Christiania (Oslo). Ludvig started theological studies, but his interest in music led him in another direction. In 1839, he became the organist in Our Savior's Church. Here he enjoyed the friendship of Wilhelm Andreas Wexels, a pastor and great hymn writer.

Magnus Landstad's new *Salmebog* was adopted for use in the Church of Norway in 1869, and Lindeman began to prepare musical settings for the new hymns. His book was completed in 1872, and by 1877 it had been approved and ordered published under the title *Koralbog for den Norske Kirke*. Bishop Skaar, who was a member of the commission which approved the hymnal and the music edition, once wrote, "Landstad's hymns and Lindeman's tunes have given to church song a new life in our country." Lindeman collected more than a thousand Norwegian folk songs, the first issue of which was published in 1848. Later they appeared in three volumes entitled *Aeldre og*

Nyere Norske Fjeldmelodier (Older and Newer Norwegian Mountain Melodies). It was said at his funeral that "he taught the Norwegian people to sing."

Composer:
EASTER GLORY (FRED TIL BOD) 32, 34, 213 (160)
HOLY MOUNTAIN 188 (143)
KIRKEN (BUILT ON THE ROCK) 194, 472 (412)

LINDQVIST, ANDERS GUSTAF (b. Korsberga, Småland, Sweden, May 5, 1834; d. November 11, 1897) was born into the home of a saddle maker, who, with his wife, were members of the older pietistic movement. Anders went to school in Växjö, where he pursued studies in education and organ. In 1856, he took a position as teacher and organist in Linderås and sixteen years later at Nye. In 1863, through reading *Pietisten,* he experienced spiritual renewal and immediately began to preach in Linderås and the surrounding area. He resigned from his teaching position in 1889 and became the superintendent for the Jönköping district of the Swedish Covenant. By 1867, several of his poems appeared in *Jönköpings-Posten.* Later he wrote several hymns and did some composing.

Author:
God's Name Is a Refuge to Hide Me (324)

LUNDGREN, JONAS FREDRIK (b. Grythyttan, Sweden, November 18, 1847; d. January 1, 1915) became fatherless at an early age, and the young lad began to work in a blacksmith shop. He had a burning desire to study and at the age of twenty gained entrance to the elementary teachers' school in Uppsala. He graduated in 1869, and after serving a term as a substitute, he received a position in Stockholm. A year later he returned to Uppsala for further studies at the Fjellstedska school. This institution had been founded in 1854 by Dr. Peter Fjellstedt as a training school for colporteurs. The headmaster at this time, V. Norlén, earlier had been Lundgren's spiritual adviser. Lundgren pursued studies at Uppsala University and then became assistant principal in the school of elementary education in Stockholm. From 1891 to 1913 he was headmaster.

Lundgren was a talented writer, and he used his pen in the service of education and the Christian faith. He also was a much-appreciated speaker who convincingly proclaimed the gospel. During the year from 1882 to 1883 he wrote the Sunday school lessons published in *Sanningsvittnet.* From time to time he wrote hymns which also appeared in that periodical.

Author:
When Toil Is Done, a Sabbath Rest Is Waiting (521)

MACCALL, WILLIAM (b. Largs, Ayrshire, Scotland, February 25, 1812; d. Bexley Heath, England, November 19, 1888) received a master of arts degree from Glasgow University in 1833. He attended a theological academy in Geneva, Switzerland, with the intention of becoming a Presbyterian minister. He became instead a Unitarian and served churches at Bolton, Lancashire, and Crediton, Devonshire, between 1837 and 1846. He then moved to London, where he wrote for several periodicals. Maccall became an accomplished linguist and did a considerable amount of translating. Some of his translations from the Danish appeared in Gilbert Tait's *Hymns of Denmark.* Among his publications were *Russian Hymns,* 1879; *Christian Legends,* 1884; and *Hymns of Sweden Rendered into English.*

Tranlsator:
In Heaven Above 604 (509)

MALMIVAARA, WILHELMI (b. Finland, 1854; d. 1922) was a prominent Lutheran clergyman and for many years was a leader in the pietistic movement in Ostrobothnia, northern Finland, at the end of the nineteenth century. Malmivaara was a devoted pastor and a poet. He wrote a number of hymns, many of which reflected a strong Christian faith in the midst of struggle and adversity. He edited the new *Hymns of Zion* in 1893.

Author:
Lord, As a Pilgrim 462

MARKUSON, AARON (b. Rockford, Illinois, September 1, 1910) attended high school in Rockford and then enrolled at North Park College in 1931. The following year he returned to his native city to work and resumed his studies at North Park in 1934. He graduated from the seminary in 1937. Markuson's first pastorate was the Covenant church in Winnetka, Illinois, where he served until 1942. He married Margaret Gusafson in 1940, and a son and daughter were born to the couple. For nine years he was pastor of the Cambridge church in Massachusetts. In 1946, Markuson was elected to the Covenant Board of Youth Work and in 1951 was chosen Executive Secretary of Youth Work, a position which he held for eighteen years. He accepted a call to the pastorate of the Bethany Covenant Church in Minneapolis in 1970. He resigned in 1975, and the Markusons retired to Vashon Island in Puget Sound, Washington.

Translator:

Why Should I Be Anxious 415 (366)

NELSON, AUGUSTUS (b. Sweden, September 20, 1863; d. Mankato, Minnesota, June 18, 1949) emigrated to America in 1883 and worked for fifteen months on a farm in Minnesota. He graduated from Gustavus Adolphus College in 1890. After taking graduate work at Yale University, he attended Augustana Seminary and graduated and was ordained in 1898. He served Augustana Lutheran parishes in Escanaba, Michigan; Waukegan, Illinois; New Haven, Connecticut; Manistique and Thompson, Michigan; and Clear Lake and Gibbon, Minnesota. Nelson was on the board of Upsala College from 1904 to 1906. For nine years he was secretary of the Superior Conference of the Augustana Church. He was also on the board of education from 1922 to 1924.

Perhaps Nelson's greatest contribution was his translations. He had the ability to express in simple and poetic language the thought and spirit of the original Swedish hymns. Seven of his translations were included in the Augustana *Hymnal* (1925).

Translator:

Jesus, Lord and Precious Savior 433 (386)
Prepare the Way, O Zion 119 (107)

NILSSON, ANDERS (b. Östraby, Skåne, Sweden, November 10, 1894; d. October 22, 1912) studied handcraft until he followed his parents to America. Here he worked for several years in a factory and then enrolled in Augustana Seminary. Homesickness drew him back to Sweden, where he continued his theological studies at Lund University. At the same time he began to preach at Västra Skånes Missionsförening (West Skåne's Mission Society). When this group called him as their pastor in 1876, he left the university and gave his full time to the work of the pastorate.

At this time Nilsson began to write poems, which were published in *Skånes Missionsblad.* He wrote under the signature "-d-" (for Anders) or simply marked his writings with an asterisk. Between 1880 and 1891 his songs appeared in nine pamphlets. In 1893, they were included in a volume of 184 songs, most of which were Nilsson originals. The book was published under the title *Andeliga sånger samlade och utgivna av A. Nilsson.* His hymns were similar to those of the other pietists—subjective, intimate, and personal, with emphasis upon the faithfulness of God, friendship with Jesus, and the bliss of the life to come.

Author:

Christ the Lord Is Risen! (164)

NORDQVIST, GUSTAF LAZARUS (b. Stockholm, Sweden, February 12, 1886; d. Stockholm, January 28, 1949) studied music in Stockholm from 1901 to 1912: organ, piano, counterpoint, composition, and church music. In 1913, he went to Berlin to take further composition studies with Artur Willner. He became the organist in Adolf Fredrik Church in Stockholm in 1914 and from 1925 taught harmony at the Royal Academy, where he was made professor in 1944. Nordqvist composed a variety of musical scores: pieces for piano and organ, choir anthems and cantatas, songs for solo voices, a sonata for violin and piano, children's songs, and romances. From 1937 until his death religious themes were dominant in his composing. This reflected a deepening of his own spiritual life in his declining years.

Composer:

NORDQVIST 163

NYSTRÖM, JOHAN ERIK (b. Stockholm, Sweden, September 8, 1842; d. Algeria, July 3, 1907) was the son of parents who belonged to the George Scott-Carl Rosenius circle. In fact, Rosenius was godfather at the child's baptism. In 1851, the family moved to Gävle where Erik attended the public elementary school. He became a student at Uppsala University in 1859 and was a degree candidate in 1866. The following year he joined the Baptist church and the faculty at Bethel Seminary. While there he compiled a Bible concordance, which was published in 1868. After five years he resigned from the seminary and several months later left the Baptist church. He was at odds with their view of the Lord's Supper. In 1878, Nyström went to Beirut as a missionary under the Evangelical Alliance. Upon his return to Sweden he worked for a time in the Covenant Church, but went back to the Baptists in 1884. Soon he returned to the Covenant without actually joining one of the churches. He went to Algeria in 1887 as a missionary and remained there until his death.

Nyström's greatest contribution was translating hymns from English to Swedish—especially the Sankey songs. These were published in ten parts between 1875 and 1886 under the title *Sånger till Lammets lof.* Also noteworthy was his work on the first official hymnal of the Swedish Covenant, published in 1894. Many of his translations and several original lyrics were included. When this hymnal was revised in 1920, Nyström's name appeared with more than a hundred of the hymns.

Author:
O Zion Acclaim Your Redeemer! 118 (106)
Translator:
Tell Me, Who Are These (517)

NYVALL, DAVID (b. Värmland, Sweden, January 19, 1863; d. St Paul, Minnesota, February 6, 1946) was the son of Karl Johan Nyvall, colporteur and organizer in the movement out of which the Covenant church grew. David's early education consisted of tutoring in the home, high school at Västerås, and junior college at Gävle. He was a gifted youth—in his teens he was well-known as a preacher in revival circles in Värmland. In 1884, he completed premedical studies at Uppsala and the following year registered at the Carolinian Institute in Stockholm. He was forced to discontinue because of ill health. He visited America in 1886 and was invited to teach at Skogsbergh's school in Minneapolis. In 1888, he began to teach in the Swedish department of Chicago Theological Seminary, where our early pastors were trained. He assisted Skogsbergh in founding a school for the Covenant in Minneapolis in 1891, and Nyvall became acting president and teacher of theology. The school was moved to Chicago in 1894 and became known as North Park College and Theological Seminary. As president, Nyvall encountered much opposition and was called a heretic, and many churches were closed to him.

He resigned in 1905 and moved to McPherson, Kansas, where he founded Walden College. This was later sold to the Free Methodists. In 1908, he became the editor of *Veckobladet*, but he was not happy in this position. From 1910 to 1912 he was professor of Scandinavian languages at the University of Washington. All the while he had many friends who hoped and prayed for his return to North Park. This was accomplished in 1912 and he remained on as president until 1923, except for the period from 1920 to 1921. Nyvall continued at North Park as dean of the seminary until 1925 and as a teacher until 1941.

Nyvall was the author of several books, most of them available only in Swedish. He was very articulate in the English language, but wrote only one book in English—*The Swedish Covenanters* (1930). A volume of essays, *Beacon Lights*, was published to celebrate his seventieth birthday in 1933. It was translated by E. Gustav Johnson. Nyvall was on the editorial committee for *Sionsharpan* and contributed several texts and tunes.

Author:
In Thy Temple Courts, O Father 54

ÖLANDER, ANNA HELENA (b. Linköping, Sweden, December 15, 1861; d. Linköping, October 23, 1939) was the daughter of a schoolteacher. When Anna was ten years old, the family moved to Svanhals, where her father became the parish pastor. She began to write poetry and stories at a very early age. Her writings began to appear in *Svenska Posten* in 1890 and later in *Förbundets-tidningen* (Covenant Paper). Her first collection of poems, *I skymningsstunden* (In the Twilight Hour), was published in 1896. This was followed by three more volumes between 1906 and 1920. At the urging of Dr. Karl Fries, Miss Ölander wrote a number of original texts and translated several hymns for the first hymnal of KFUM, the Swedish YMCA. One can see a similarity between her hymns and those of Frances Havergal, several of which she had translated. Both writers were in the tradition of revival, renewal, and consecration. Miss Ölander's signature was "A-der."

Author:
A Quivering Chord Is Broken (511)
If I Gained the World 441 (397)

OLSON, ERNST WILLIAM (b. Skåne, Sweden, March 16, 1870; d. Chicago, Illinois, October 6, 1958) emigrated to the United States with his parents in 1875. The family settled near Wahoo, Nebraska, but later they moved to Texas. Olson graduated from Augustana College in 1891, and until 1906 he served as editor of Swedish language weeklies. From 1906 to 1911 he was office editor at the Engberg-Holmberg Publishing Company in Chicago. Later he accepted a similar position with the Augustana Book Concern, a position which he held until his retirement in 1949.

Olson became well known through his talents as a writer and poet, and he was given an honorary degree by his alma mater. He was a valued member of the editorial committee which compiled the Augustana *Hymnal* (1925). The volume included four of his original texts and twenty-eight translations of Swedish hymns. He was also a member of the *Service Book and Hymnal* committee. He died soon after the book was published in 1958.

Translator:
All Hail to Thee, O Blessed Morn 124 (110)
Children of the Heavenly Father 382 (323)
Jerusalem, Lift Up Thy Voice! 105 (101)
Now Hail We Our Redeemer 114
Praise the Lord, Each Tribe and Nation 56 (51)
The Sign of the Cross (246)
With God and His Friendship 488

OLSSON, KARL A. (b. Renton, Washington, June 10, 1913) spent his early years in southern Sweden and Sharon, Pennsylvania. He was educated at North Park College and Theological Seminary, the University of Minnesota, and the University of Chicago, where he received his Ph.D. in 1948. He was assistant pastor in the First Covenant Church, St. Paul, Minnesota, from 1933 to 1934; pastor at Stillwater, Minnesota from 1934 to 1935; and pastor of the Tabernacle Church in Chicago from 1935 to 1938. During World War II Olsson was a chaplain in the United States Army in Europe, and served a second term from 1950 to 1952. He married Dorothy Carlson of Iron Mountain, Michigan, and four children were born to the couple.

He taught humanities at the college of the University of Chicago and was assistant dean of students from 1946 to 1948. Olsson served on the faculty at North Park from 1938 to 1942, 1948 to 1950, and 1952 to 1959. He was then elected to the presidency of the school. Since 1970 he has been director of leadership training for Faith at Work, Inc., in Columbia, Maryland, where the Olssons have made their home.

Dr. Olsson has been a frequent contributor to various religious and denominational periodicals, besides writing his own column in *The Covenant Companion* since 1955. He is the author of several books, including *Passion, Seven Sins and Seven Virtues, By One Spirit*, and *A Family of Faith* (histories of the Covenant); and *The God Game* (a novel), *Come to the Party*, and *Find Yourself in the Bible.* Mr. Olsson has translated several Swedish hymns, most of them for use by the North Park College choir.

Translator:
Come, Let Us Praise Him 244
In the Springtime Fair 298
Jesus, Jesus, Name Most Precious 252
O Let Your Soul Now Be Filled with Gladness 423
When All the World Is Sleeping 48
Co-Translator:
Now Shine a Thousand Candles Bright 145

OLSSON, OLOF (b. Karlskoga, Värmland, Sweden, March 31, 1841; d. Rock Island, Illinois, May 12, 1900) was born in a devout Christian home. His mother was an ardent religious worker who was deeply committed to the pietistic movement. The boy attended the parish school and later studied music in the home of an organist in Västergötland. When he returned to his home a year later, he participated in the conventicles of the pietists. Through this activity he became acquainted with Karl Johan Nyvall, a friendship which lasted throughout his life. Olsson received his advanced education at Fjellstedt's Mission Institute, the Mission Institute in Leipzig, Germany, and Uppsala University. For several years he served various pastorates, participating wholeheartedly in the pietistic movement. He became a champion of the free-church cause although he never left the state church.

In 1869, he journeyed to America along with some friends and family. They were pioneers in the Smoky Valley in Kansas. A congregation was organized in Lindsborg with Olsson as pastor. In 1876, he became a professor at Augustana Theological Seminary in Rock Island, Illinois, and from 1891 until his death was the president of Augustana College and Seminary. In addition to his work as pastor, teacher, and administrator, he wrote a number of books and contributed regularly to the religious press and school publications. He translated several Swedish hymns and was one of the leaders in producing Augustana's first English hymnal in 1901.

Translator:

O Lamb of God, Most Holy 519 (435)

OSBECK, CARL RUDOLPH (b. Sunnerbo, Sweden, June 22, 1877; d. Oakland, California, February 8, 1963) came to America as a child. He attended public schools in Morris and Chicago, Illinois. He was converted in 1896 and baptized in the Moody Church by Dr. Robert A. Torrey in 1900. After attending Moody Bible Institute, he served for a time as a missionary of the American Sunday School Union. In 1901, he was ordained in the Swedish Baptist Church. While studying at Augustana in Rock Island, he served as supply pastor in Baptist churches in the vicinity. Then followed a time of ministry in Mead and Estina, Nebraska, where he also served as a Sunday school missionary. After travel and study in Europe in 1923, Osbeck became a conference missionary in New York. This was followed by pastorates in Trinity Baptist Church, New York City; Mead, Nebraska; and Willmar and Russell, Minnesota. Osbeck retired in Willmar and later moved to Oakland, California.

Translator:

With God and His Friendship, sts. 1 and 2 488

OTTANDER, OTTO ALFRED (b. Edshult, Småland, Sweden, October 6, 1842; d. June 30, 1926) studied for the ministry and was ordained in 1870. After serving as an assistant in Hässelby, Småland, and then in the St. Olai congregation in Norrköping, he became parish pastor in Östervåla. From 1905 on he was responsible for the supervision of several parishes in the north.

While he lived in Småland, Ottander for six years was chairman of the East Småland's Mission Society and edited its monthly paper. It was during these years that he wrote a number of songs which were published in several editions between 1877 and 1880 under the title *Sjunger Herranom alla land* (Sing unto the Lord, All You Lands). A final edition appeared in 1885 with the title *Korsblomman.* At this time Ottander was a typical pietist but later became more formal and "high-churchly." This proved injurious to many of his earlier relationships.

Author:

As Pilgrims in This World (502)

Trust in the Savior, O Precious Soul 402 (342)

PALMGREN, GERHARD W. (b. Alsheda, Sweden, December 18, 1880; d. Warren, Pennsylvania, June 5, 1959) was the son of pietistic parents who came to the United States in 1880. They settled in Pennsylvania, where the senior Palmgren resumed his occupation as a miner. When he was twelve, the young Palmgren was obliged to join his father in the work. The result was a rather sporadic secondary education. One of his earliest interests was the ministry. While still a young lad, he had read P. Waldenström's accounts of his travels and the book, *Herren är from.* At fifteen he knew the names of the almost three hundred pastors in the Covenant—and where they had their pastorates. Also he knew the numbers of at least 90 percent of the hymns in *Sionsharpan*.

Palmgren graduated from the Swedish department of Chicago Theological Seminary in 1905 and was ordained by the Eastern Missionary Association (now the East Coast Conference of the Covenant) the same year. In 1908, he married Esther Blomquist in Lynn, Massachusetts. The couple served parishes in Beverly and Quincy, Massachusetts; Hartford, Connecticut; Jamestown (Zion), New York; and New York City (Immanuel). After retirement Palmgren was interim pastor for a year in the Salem Square Church, Worcester, Massachusetts. He served in many conference and denominational positions, including that of vice-president of the Covenant.

Translator:
Again a Day Has from Us Gone 40 (31)
Heavenly Spirit, Gentle Spirit 269 (202)
Praise the Lord, All Praise and Blessing 81 (70)

PALMQUIST, AARON ELDON (b. St. Paul, Minnesota, March 29, 1912) was born into the home of a Covenant pastor whose name he bears. He graduated from Macalester College in St. Paul in 1934 and from North Park Theological Seminary in 1937 and was ordained in 1941. He married Helen Jones in 1938, and a son (also a Covenant pastor) and two daughters were born to the couple. Palmquist served the following Covenant churches: Odebolt, Iowa; Lockport, Illinois; Spokane, Washington; North Park, Chicago; Edina, Minnesota; and Hinsdale, Illinois. While serving the Edina church, he was acting president of Minnehaha Academy from 1959 to 1960. Since 1968 he has been the superintendent of the Central Conference. He has served on three denominational adminstrative boards—Christian Education, Publication, and Ministry (chairman, 1963 to 1967). He has also served on three commissions—Pastoral Relations, Educational Institutions, and Music. The Music Commission, which was appointed in 1944, produced *The Hymnal* (1950). The Palmquists reside in Northbrook, Illinois.

Translator:
Trust in the Savior, O Precious Soul 402 (342)

PALMQUIST, GUSTAF (b. Solberga, Småland, Sweden, May 26, 1812; d. Stockholm, September 18, 1867) first tried his hand at agriculture and carpentry. In 1835, he went to live with his brother in St. Mellösa, where he took pre-college studies. After further studies in Stockholm, he accepted a position as schoolteacher and organist in Gustavsberg and later in Stockholm. From 1851 to 1857 he was in the United States where he served Baptist churches in Rock Island and Chicago. Upon his return to Sweden, he conducted special Bible courses for the training of preachers. With his brother, Per, who was a public school teacher and publisher, he compiled a hymnal, *Pilgrims-Sånger*. The first part was published with 221 songs in 1859, and the second with eighty-eight songs in 1862. It was through this songbook that many English revival songs were introduced into Sweden. A number of them had been translated by Palmquist himself and some by Betty Ehrenborg-Posse. There were also some original texts by Palmquist. The hymnal proved to be very popular among free church people, especially the Baptists.

Author:
I Have a Friend, So Patient, Kind, Forbearing (380)

PALMQUIST, HERBERT EWALD (b. Minneapolis, Minnesota, July 9, 1896) is the son of the late veteran Covenant preacher, A.E. Palmquist, who for many years was the pastor of the First Covenant Church, St. Paul. Herbert attended Hamline University in that city and then went to the Covenant seminary at North Park. In 1920, he graduated from Wheaton College and was ordained the same year. In 1921, he married Florence Anderson; the couple have a son (also a pastor) and a daughter. Palmquist has served Covenant churches in Maplewood, Chicago; Spokane, Washington; First Covenant, St. Paul (assistant); and Redeemer (now Beverly), Chicago, where he remained for thirty years. While serving as an assistant to his father in St. Paul, he was also dean of the Bible Institute at Minnehaha Academy. After retiring from the pastorate, Palmquist served for several years as chaplain at Covenant Palms of Miami. More recently he and Dean Emeritus Eric Hawkinson have alternately served in this position.

Palmquist has served on many denominational boards and commissions, including the Executive Board (vice-president). In the 1920s, he wrote a series of Sunday school lesson helps in *The Covenant Companion.* Since 1955 he has written his own column in that periodical. He is the author of *Wait for Me,* a collection of informal essays, and *The Wit and Wisdom of Our Fathers.* He translated several sermons, lectures, and Bible discussions for publication in the "Covenant Heritage Series" under the title *The Word Is Near You.* The Palmquists make their home in Burlingame, California.

Translator:

Jesus Stands outside the Door 292

PEARSON, ERIC LINCOLN (b. Ashtabula, Ohio, January 17, 1917) attended North Park College and Seminary. He received his B.A. degree from St. Anselm's College, Manchester, New Hampshire, in 1945 and his M.S. in education at Northern Illinois University in 1967. He also studied at Tarkio College in Missouri. He was ordained in 1943. In 1945, he married Dorothy Carlson—the couple have four children. Pearson has served Covenant churches in Carlshend, Michigan; Port Allegany, Pennsylvania; Worcester (assistant at Salem Square), Massachusetts; Manchester, New Hampshire; Harris and Rush City, Minnesota; Shenandoah, Iowa; and Boulder Junction, Wisconsin. Since 1959 he has been teaching school in Rockford, Illinois, and serving as assistant pastor in the North Park Evangelical Covenant Church in that city.

Translator:

Great Hills May Tremble, sts. 1 and 4, 102 (93)

When Toil Is Done, a Sabbath Rest Is Waiting (521)

PETERSON, VICTOR O. (b. Stanton, Iowa, 1864; d. Huron, South Dakota, February 14, 1929) received his public school education in the city of his birth. After receiving his B.S. degree from Augustana College in 1889, he studied at Harvard University for a year and then returned to Augustana to complete his work for a master's degree. In 1890, he accepted a position as professor of physics and chemistry at his alma mater. He continued in this position for sixteen years. In 1906, he became one of the promoters of the Rock Island Tropical Plantation Company and managed a large rubber plantation in Mexico. Because of revolutions in that country he was forced to abandon the venture in 1913. For several years he lived in Rock Island, selling real estate and insurance. From 1920 to 1928, when illness forced him to retire, Peterson was head of the chemistry department at Huron College, Huron, South Dakota. He and his family were active members of the American Lutheran church of that city.

Translator:

O Bride of Christ, Rejoice 115 (104)

Wheresoe'er I Roam 398 (344)

PETHRUS, LEWI (b. Älvsborgs län, Sweden, March 11, 1884; d. 1974) studied at Bethel Seminary in Stockholm and took the pastorate of the Baptist church in Lidköping. In 1911, he was called to the Philadelphia congregation in Stockholm. Pethrus had been influenced by the Pentecostal movement which began to stir in Sweden in 1907, and his church was caught up in the movement as well. This caused a conflict between the congregation and the Baptist denomination, and in 1913 the church withdrew. The Philadephia church with its pastor became the leader of the Pentecostals in Sweden. The church set up its own publishing house and put out its own newspaper, *The Evangelical Herald.*

Pethrus and Paul Ongman published a hymnal, *Segertoner* (Strains of Victory), which became the official hymnal of the Pentecostals. The book included 230 translations of English songs and thirteen original hymns by Pethrus. He also contributed a few melodies. In 1945, he was instrumental in launching a newspaper, *Dagen,* of which he was editor-in-chief. Pethrus also was the author of several books.

Author:

All That Our Savior Hath Spoken (320)

Composer:

LÖFTENA KUNNA EJ SVIKA (320)

PETRI, OLAVUS (b. Örebro, Sweden, January 6, 1493; d. April 19, 1552) studied at Uppsala and then traveled to Wittenberg, where he continued his studies. There he came under the influence of Luther and the Reformation. He returned home in 1519 to become "The Luther of Sweden." He was a strong advocate of the Reformation and preached against the sale of indulgences, the worship of saints, and other abuses. Meanwhile, the Swedes had broken away from Danish rule, and Gustaf Vasa became king. He was sympathetic to the Reformation and gave Petri authority to preach to the populace in Stockholm in their native tongue. Through his preaching he won new friends to the cause. He was given ordination and later the pastorate of Storkyrkan, the cathedral church in Stockholm.

Petri was a great force in the transition from Catholicism to Lutheranism. Perhaps his greatest contribution was the translation of the New Testament. Also important was the first hymnal of the Swedish church. Petri translated some of the Latin hymns and several German hymns from Luther's collections. They appeared in four different editions between 1524 and 1536. The final volume contained forty-six hymns, eight of which were Petri originals. The collection was called *Swedish Hymns or Songs.* The 1937 edition of the *Psalmbok* credited nineteen of its hymns to Petri as author or translator.

Translator (to Swedish):
Now Hail We Our Redeemer 114

PILCHER, CHARLES VENN (b. Oxford, England, June 4, 1879; d. July 1960) was educated at Oxford, receiving his M.A. degree in 1905. He was ordained as an Anglican clergyman the following year. He moved to Canada, where he was a professor of theology at Wycliffe College, Toronto, from 1906 to 1936. He also taught Old Testament literature and New Testament language and literature. For some time he served as one of the pastors of St. James Cathedral. From 1936 to 1956 Pilcher was bishop coadjutor of Sydney, Australia.

He had an interest in the Church of Iceland and its hymns and translated many lyrics from *Passiusalmer* (Passion Hymns) by Hallgrimur Petursson (1614-1674), one of Iceland's great hymnists. These were published as *Icelandic Meditations of the Passion* (New York, 1923). Some of these and other translations were included in his *Icelandic Christian Classics* (Melbourne, 1950). The supplement to *The Book of Common Praise* of the Church of England in Australia contains a number of Pilcher's original hymns.

Translator:
How Marvelous God's Greatness 79

POSSE, CATHARINA ELIZABETH EHRENBORG (b. Råbäck, Kinekulle, Sweden, July 22, 1818; d. July 22, 1880), born Ehrenborg, began writing poetry at an early age. She inherited the gift from her mother, who helped and encouraged her daughter. From time to time they visited Uppsala where they heard famous lecturers like Geijer and Atterbom. Betty came into contact with the revival in Stockholm in 1851, and, at the suggestion of Matilda Foy, became active in Sunday school work. In 1852, she visited England for six months of study. When she returned to Sweden, she became the director of a teacher training school associated with the deaconess organization. When this closed, she began her own school. In 1856, she married J.A. Posse, the editor and publisher of a paper. Betty assisted her husband and continued to work on the paper after his death in 1865.

Mrs. Posse had a deep interest in the Christian education of children and was concerned that there be a good selection of children's hymns and songs in all the schools. In 1852, she translated several English songs, which appeared under the title *Spiritual Songs for Children.* Two more editions were published later. These included more translations as well as some of her originals. *Pilgrims-Sånger*, the hymnal produced by the Palmquist brothers, included some of Betty Ehrenborg's works.

Author:
For God So Loved All the World (75)

Adapter:
When Christmas Morn Is Breaking 146 (116)

RIDDERHOF, NICHOLAS LAMBERT (b. Dordrecht, Holland, March 2, 1869; d. Los Angeles, California, April 19, 1956) very early in life exhibited musical talent. At the age of eleven he was an organist and studied music and art. He was converted at the age of fourteen. In 1888, he immigrated to the United States, settling first in Kalamazoo, Michigan, and then in Chicago, Illinois, where he first worked as a painter and artist. There he met a young Swedish housemaid who promised to marry him if he would learn her language. This he did and soon began writing songs in Swedish.

In 1892, the couple moved to Minneapolis, where Ridderhof served as choir director and organist in the First Evangelical Free Church. He wrote many hymn texts and tunes and served as music editor for P. Benson's *Hemlands-Klockan* (1900), a hymnal widely used in the Free Church. Ridderhof also published other songs, classical music, and *Companion Studies* (for piano students).

The family moved to Los Angeles in 1903. There was no Free church there then, so they attended the Covenant church. Later Ridderhof was organist and choir director in the Swedish Baptist Church and then in the Free Church. In his fifties he attended the University of California in Los Angeles in order to obtain teaching credentials. Then he taught music in the public schools until the age of seventy and gave private lessons until he was eighty. Ridderhof served twelve years on the music staff of the Los Angeles YMCA and taught at the Conservatory of Music. He was assistant editor of *Christian Etude*, a hymn magazine.

Composer:
ACK, GÖM MIG (394)

ROSENIUS, CARL OLOF (b. Nysätra, Västerbotten, Sweden, February 3, 1816; d. February 24, 1868) was the son of a state church preacher with pietistic convictions. At the age of fifteen Carl began to participate in the conventicles. He was a mystic and spoke of a "voice" that warned and guided him. In later adolescence he had a period of doubt and agnosticism, but he wanted to believe in God and the Bible. Through reasoning he overcame his doubts about the existence of God, but he could not believe in the Bible as the Word of God. He sought the help of George Scott, an English Methodist minister, whose preaching in Stockholm was beginning a revival in the capital. Scott led Rosenius to a joyful faith so that he could say, "All is true, really true, divinely true, and everything is left which I have mourned as lost."

In 1840, on New Year's Day, he preached his first sermon. Rosenius joined Scott in his evangelistic ministry, the editing of *Missionstidning*, and the launching of *Pietisten* in 1842. This religious monthly was destined to play a major role in the revival and the free church movement. When Scott left Sweden that same year, Rosenius continued on as the editor and in this way became the main guiding figure in the revival until his untimely death in 1868. Although he greatly influenced the separatist movement, Rosenius remained Lutheran in theology, held the traditional view of the atonement, and remained a communicant in the state church. In order to stem the tide of separatism and keep the revival within the church, he, along with several others, organized the Evangeliska Fosterlandsstiftelsen (Evangelical National Foundation) in 1856.

In his activities as a lay preacher, Rosenius was often accompanied by the singer-hymnist Oscar Ahnfelt. The former wrote several lyrics which Ahnfelt set to music. Later most of them were published in the latter's *Andeliga Sånger*.

Author:
The Sign of the Cross (246)
Wheresoe'er I Roam 398 (344)
With God and His Friendship 488
Reviser:
I Have a Friend, So Patient, Kind, Forbearing (380)
Translator: (to Swedish):
O Precious Thought, Some Day the Mist Shall Vanish (337)

RUNEBERG, JOHAN LUDWIG (b. Jacobstad, Finland, February 5, 1804; d. Borgå, May 6, 1877), national poet of Finland, was educated at the University of Åbo. After its removal to Helsingfors in 1830, Runeberg became secretary to the council of the university. His verse romance of Finnish life, *The Grave of Perrho*, appeared in 1831. This received the small gold medal of the Swedish Academy. The same year he married Fredrika Tengström, the niece of the archbishop. In 1837, he accepted the chair of Latin at Borgå College and served as rector from 1847 to 1850. His two idylls, *The Elk-Hunters* and *Hanna*, had won for him a place second only to Tegner among the Swedish poets. One of his important later works was *FänrikStåls Sägner*, patriotic poems on the war of independence. He remained one of the most popular poets writing in Swedish, although he lived in Finland.

Runeberg often was critical of the established church and the clergy. On one occasion he encountered a pastor who proceeded to tell him how he treated parishioners who fell asleep while he preached. Runeberg said that it was natural for people, who had worked hard all week and probably walked far, to go to sleep in church. And he added this note of advice: "When you see your listeners begin to fall asleep, gradually lower your voice, and when all are sleeping, say the benediction and leave them in peace." But Runeberg was a deeply religious man, and this is reflected in his hymns, which have a warm devotional spirit. He was largely responsible for the Swedish hymnal of the Finnish Church published in 1857. It included fifty-seven of his texts and nine of his translations or revisions. The Finnish hymnal of 1938 still included twenty-three Runeberg hymns, and the Swedish hymnal of 1943 (used in Finland) had fifty.

Author:

What Joy There Is in Coming 55 (27)

RUTSTRÖM, ANDERS CARL (b. Rutvik, Sweden, November 30, 1721; d. October 27, 1772) was the most controversial figure among the Swedish hymnists. Some regarded him as an innocent martyr, and others looked upon him as a hateful hothead. After receiving his elementary education in Piteå and Härnosänd, he enrolled at Uppsala in 1742. In 1745, he was ordained and became assistant curate in Storkyrkan (the cathedral church) in Stockholm. Soon he was known as an outstanding evangelist, and he became active in Herrnhut circles. He was still quite immature, and it was difficult for him to retain his balance. One of his contemporaries said of him: "In disposition he is as hot as a live coal, and voluptuous, and his face shows it."

By 1748, the consistory had begun to issue complaints against him. At one time he was charged for his Calvinistic leanings, and at another, for his Herrnhutism. For his defense he appealed to the writings of Luther. When that would not work, he would apologize. Also he became involved in the crucial political struggles of the day, allying himself with one of the parties. This served him well so long as his party was in power. In 1756, he received the doctor of theology degree from the university in Greifswald, and two years later he was appointed pastor in the Hedvig Eleonora Church in Stockholm. His enemies gave him no peace there, and in 1765 his political party was no longer in power. He sought refuge in Denmark and Germany. After five years he returned, only to meet more persecution. He was arrested in August, 1772, and died in prison just as King Gustaf III's assurance of a lasting reparation reached him.

Today Rutström is remembered for his hymns. *Sions Nya Sånger,* often called "Rutström's Songbook," actually was not compiled by him. But there are more of his texts in it than of any other writer. It was compiled by his friends after his death, printed in Copenhagen, and smuggled into Sweden in 1778. This collection was widely used among the pietists for almost a century.

Author:

Chosen Seed and Zion's Children 473 (414)

O Savior, Thou Who for Us Died 461 (293)

Attributed Composer:

LAMMETS FOLK 54, 371, 473 (414)

RUTSTRÖM (MIN BLODIGE KONUNG) 195 (150), 301

RYDEN, ERNEST EDWIN (b. Kansas City, Missouri, September 12, 1886) was educated at Augustana College and Seminary. In 1914, he was ordained and served for some time as the pastor of Gloria Dei Church in St. Paul. For many years he was engaged in editorial work and writing. He was co-editor of the Augustana *Hymnal* (1925) and secretary of the joint commission which compiled the *Service Book and Hymnal*, 1945 to 1958. From 1936 to 1941 Ryden was the editor of the *Lutheran Companion.* He was the author of two excellent hymn histories—*The Story of Our Hymns* (1935) and *The Story of Christian Hymnody* (1958). For the *Encyclopedia of the Lutheran Church* (1964) he contributed the article "Lutheran Hymnbooks since the Reformation." He is the author and translator of many hymns.

In 1930, Ryden was honored by Augustana College with the D.D. degree. In recognition of his efforts to further Scandinavian hymnody in America the Swedish government bestowed on him the Royal Order of the North Star in 1949. For several years Dr. Ryden served as pastor of the Emmanuel Lutheran church in North Grosvenordale, Connecticut. He is still active in the field of hymnology, having recently co-authored a book entitled *American Hymns: New and Old.*

Author:
How Blessed Is This Place, O Lord 469 (556)
With Solemn Joy We Come, Dear Lord 524
Translator:
Day by Day Thy Mercies, Lord, Attend Me (325)
Lord, As a Pilgrim 462
There Are Treasures for Children in Heaven 608 (529)
Thy Holy Wings, Dear Savior 45 (42)

SANDBORG-WAESTERBERG, AMANDA (born Stockholm, Sweden, December 16, 1842; d. Bergvik, January 1, 1918) was the daughter of a church organist, under whom she first studied music. She took courses in composition and harmony at the Academy of Music. Later she studied to become a teacher and trained to be a telegrapher. Miss Sandborg worked as a governess for several years, and in 1876 she married L.M. Waesterberg, a merchant. They were members of the Bethesda Church in Stockholm. Besides assuming the duties of a housewife, Mrs. Waesterberg found time to give music lessons and compose melodies for hymns. She wrote many tunes for the lyrics of Carl Boberg, which usually were first published in *Sanningsvittnet.* Her signature was A.S-g.

Composer:
HIGHEST JOY (DEN HÖGSTA LYCKA) 283 (220)
JESU NAMN 252

SANDELL-BERG, KAROLINA WILHELMINA (b. Fröderyd, Småland, Sweden, October 3, 1832; d. Stockholm, July 26, 1903), better known as Lina Sandell, is one of Sweden's best known hymnists. She has sometimes been called "the Fanny Crosby of Sweden." Her father, Jonas Sandell, was the parish pastor at Fröderyd. He was sympathetic with the Moravian and pietistc emphasis upon the grace of God in Christ as against the church's stress upon ordinances, rites, and ritual, and he became an early leader in the renewal movement in southern Sweden. Lina inherited much of her religious outlook from her father, who also tutored her in a methodical plan of study. Her brother-in-law also served as her tutor, and under these two teachers she received a good liberal arts education as well as training in the interpretation of the Scriptures.

When she was twelve years of age, she had an experience that was to influence her whole life. Earlier she had been stricken with an illness that left her with a paralysis, and she was confined to her bed. The physicians considered her case hopeless, but the parents and Lina herself believed that God would restore her to health, so they continued to pray. One Sunday morning when everyone else was in church, she picked up her Bible and read the Gospel text for the day. It was the story of Jesus' raising the daughter of Jairus. She saw the similarities to her own situation and reasoned that if Christ could heal the little girl in the biblical account, he could heal her as well. So she prayed with all the fervor she had. Suddenly she was filled with a great joy that flooded her whole being, and she got up and dressed—and walked. The experience filled her with a profound sense of love and gratitude to God that no later troubles or sorrows could shake. She began to record her feelings, and at the age of sixteen published a little book of meditations and poems. As she grew older, she began to write more. One of her earliest hymns was "Tryggare kan ingen vara."

At the age of twenty-six she had another experience that greatly effected her life. She was accompanying her father on a visit to Gothenberg and part of the journey was a boat trip across Lake Vättern. Her father was standing by the railing when the boat gave a sudden lurch which threw him overboard into a watery grave. The tragedy brought her deep and extended grief, but it was immediately following this that she wrote some of her best hymns. Among them were "Great Hills May Tremble," "Thou Tender, Gracious Father," and "Jesus, in Stillness, Longing I Wait." For a while she lived in the household of her widowed brother-in-law in Jönköping. Here her social horizons were broadened, and she came to know and associate with several persons of eminence and great faith. Among these was the king's sister, Princess Eugenia.

After the death of her mother, Lina accepted a position on the editorial staff of the Evangelical National Foundation. Here she came to know Rosenius and often was a guest in the Rosenius home. He proved to be a great help in her spiritual pilgrimage. In a letter to a friend she wrote concerning Waldemar Rudin, another leader of the foundation: ". . . and when it comes to discussing some biblical passage or some other important subject, I always received some insight, something meaningful and instructive. But when it is a question of faith, of help in my sinfulness, then I must hear Rosenius."

In 1867, she married C.O. Berg, a wealthy businessman. Although the union brought her happiness, it brought problems as well. On October 4, 1868, she gave birth to a son, who was either stillborn or died in birth. Berg founded a sailors' mission, and his wife was a valued partner in the venture. When the Evangelical National Foundation planned a special mission project in East Africa, they wanted to send the Bergs. He was willing, but in spite of pressure put on Lina by P.P. Waldenström and others, she refused. She wrote: "To leave home, friends, relatives, work, in fact everything that has been dear to me—that is not easy." Some time later Berg was involved in an unfortunate project which depleted his resources and caused an unfair two-month imprisonment. Through it all Mrs. Berg was a great source of comfort to her husband. In spite of a frail body, Lina lived to be seventy-one years of age. At her funeral the choir sang "Tryggare kan ingen vara," and the congregation joined in spontaneously. In 1953, ten thousand people gathered in the parsonage yard at Fröderyd for the dedication of a bronze statue in her memory. The little cottage in which she lived for a time is now a museum. Each year on Transfiguration Sunday the people of the parish have a festive service in memory of Lina and her father.

Lina Sandell began writing very early in life, and the products of her pen make a list too long for inclusion here. She was involved in the publication of several periodicals and calendars. She edited the calendar *Korsblomman* for thirty-seven years. This was a yearly illustrated volume of stories, poems, biographies, and devotional readings. But her greatest contribution was her songs. One of her first tasks at the Foundation was to assist in the compilation of the group's first hymnal, *Sionstoner* (Strains of Zion). No less than 126 of the 550 texts were her originals or translations. The latest edition of this hymnal (1972) has seventy-six of her lyrics and five translations. There are fifty-five of her hymns in *Sånger och Psalmer* (hymnal of the Swedish Covenant). Her collected works came out in three parts between 1882 and 1892. They contained 650 poems and hymns. While her songs do not rise to the lofty expression of some of the noble hymns of Sweden, they have a strong spiritual appeal and find a warm response in the hearts of the people. Her most popular hymns are those which were written in the midst of her grief following the tragic death of her father.

Author:

Children of the Heavenly Father 382 (323)
Come, Let Us Praise Him 244
Day by Day and with Each Passing Moment 381 (325)
Give, O Lord, unto Thy Servant 408 (354)
Great Hills May Tremble, sts. 1 and 4, 102 (93)
Hide Not Thy Face, O My Savior 235 (507)
I with Thee Would Begin 353 (47)
In the Springtime Fair 298
Jesus, in Stillness, Longing I Wait 327 (261)
Now before Thee, Lord, We Gather 67 (49)
Straight Is the Gate to All That Come (516)
Thou Tender, Gracious Father 97 (90)
Thy Holy Wings, Dear Savior 45 (42)
When All the World Is Sleeping 48

SETH, J.E. (b. Småland, Sweden, April 26, 1865; d. Spokane, Washington, February 7, 1923) came to the United States in 1884. After attending school in Minneapolis, he studied in the Swedish department of Chicago Theological Seminary, graduating in 1892. He took further studies at Carleton College. Seth was ordained in the Evangelical Covenant Church and served churches in Escanaba, Michigan; Superior, Wisconsin; Duluth and Minneapolis (Tabernacle), Minnesota; Spokane, Washington; San Francisco, California; Moline, Illinois; and Minneapolis (Elim). During his later years he traveled in the interest of several different institutions: North Park College and Theological Seminary, the Home for the Aged in Buffalo, Minnesota, the Anti-Saloon League, and the Scandinavian Sailors' Home in Boston.

Author:
In Tenderness, Jesus, Enfold Me (394)

SJÖGREN, CARL ERIK (b. Hälleberga, Kronobergs län, Sweden, March 5, 1799; d. Strålsnäs in Åsbo, Östergötland, August 26, 1877) studied law and received certification from the mining company in Falu. In 1823, he went to Germany for further studies. The following year he was employed at the Sala mine, from which he retired in 1831. Sjögren had purchased an estate at Strålsnäs in Åsbo in 1830, and he lived there until his death. He was also a musician who composed several melodies that became popular in Sweden.

Composer:
STILLNESS (HERRE MIT HJÄRTA)
327 (261)

SKOOG, ANDREW L. (b. Gunnarskog, Värmland, Sweden, December 17, 1856; d. Minneapolis, October 30, 1934) was the second of the triumvirate of American hymnists born in Sweden. He was the son of pietistic parents. Bible and music were his favorite subjects in school. At the age of ten he was apprenticed to his father's trade of tailoring. When the boy was thirteen, the family emigrated to America and settled in St. Paul, Minnesota. Being the eldest of four brothers, Andrew was needed in his father's work and there was little time for formal education. His father bought him a melodeon, and a friend of the family gave him a course of twelve lessons. That was the extent of his formal music education. At the suggestion of his mother, the Rev. E. August Skogsbergh invited Andrew to play the organ at one of his evangelistic services. At the service he was converted, together with many others.

In 1879, he joined Skogsbergh in the South Side Tabernacle in Chicago as organist and choir director. It was at this time that he began to write hymns and compose music. In 1883, he married Augusta Delander, who sang soprano in his choir. When Skogsbergh accepted the pastorate of the Swedish Tabernacle in Minneapolis, he invited Skoog to be his minister of music, a position which he held until 1916. He also served as Sunday school superintendent in that church for thirty years. Skoog was sixty when he resigned as choirmaster of the Tabernacle. In 1919, he accepted a call as temporary choir director in the Bethany church, a "temporary" service which lasted six years. After his retirement, a number of celebrations were held in his honor, and his seventieth, seventy-fourth, and seventy-fifth birthdays were made occasions of festivity by concerts, banquets, and articles by journalistic friends. He died less than two months before his seventy-eighth birthday. In an obituary article his devoted friend Erik Dahlhielm related the following episode, which occured a few years before Skoog's death:

> *It was a dreary autumn Sunday. Mr. Skoog and his wife had accompanied us to Star Prairie, Wisconsin, where I used to preach on Sunday, and he volunteered to serve at the organ. After the opening hymns we read the Scriptures and prayed. Then I announced another hymn. But everything was quiet over at the organ. I glanced over to the corner, and there sat Mr. Skoog—fast asleep. . . . And now A. L. Skoog is dead! No, he has merely fallen asleep at the organ; he shall awaken one day to play the victorious song of the Lamb anew.*

A monument was erected over his grave and dedicated at the Annual Meeting of the Covenant held in Minneapolis, June 16 to 20, 1937. On the stone there is inscribed a portion of his best-loved hymn, "We Wait for a Great and Glorious Day."

Skoog's contributions to the music of the church came in different forms. As an editor, he helped provide hymnals for two generations. In collaboration with Skogsbergh *Evangelii Basun I* (Gospel Trumpet) was published in 1881 and *Evangelii Basun II* in 1883. The two were combined into one volume in 1894. *Lilla Basunen* appeared in 1890. In partnership with J.A. Hultman, *Jubelklangen* (Sound of Jubilation) was published in 1896. Skoog had a share in the preparation of the first three hymnals of the Covenant: *Sions Basun* (1908), *De Ungas Sångbok* (1914), and *Mission Hymns* (1921). As a writer, his main works were *Minnen* (Memoirs) and *Församlingskören* (The Church Choir). The former is an interesting account of his choir experiences, and the latter sets forth his principles regarding the purpose, responsibilities, and activites of the choir. In 1902, he wrote and published a small textbook of instructions for singers and choir directors entitled *Tonstudier*.

Besides the hymnals, Skoog's activities as a publisher were considerable. From 1892 to 1908 he put out a monthly choir journal called *Gittit*. This included his own anthems and some by other composers as well as helpful articles and editorials. Later the anthems were published in a series of ten bound volumes with the following titles: *Kristliga körsånger, Valda körsånger, Da Capo, Dal Segno, De Novo, Re Dita, Repris, Ancora, Septima,* and *Octava.* A large number of separate pieces, hundreds of items, were published between 1891 and 1925 by the Skoog Publishing Company. But A. L. Skoog is best remembered for his hymns, tunes as well as texts and translations. He was in the tradition of the pietists—especially Frykman. He wrote songs that were simple, rhythmic, joyous, and full of hope.

Author:
"Follow Me!" a Call So Tender 290 (223)
I Have a Friend Who Cares for Me (367)
I Think of That Star of Long Ago 159 (115)
Our Day of Joy Is Here Again 151 (123)
Praise the Lord with Joyful Sound 73 (67)
Sing the Glad Carol of Jesus 255 (197)
We Wait for a Great and Glorious Day 230 (181)

Translator:
Day by Day and with Each Passing Moment 381
I Have a Future All Sublime, st. 1, 609 (512)
Now before Thee, Lord, We Gather 67 (49)
O That Pearl of Great Price 294 (230)
Our Mighty God Works Mighty Wonders 72 (66)
Sabbath Day of Rest and Cheer 33 (20)

Composer:
BETLEHEMS STJÄRNA 159 (115)
GLAD CAROL (SÅNGEN OM JESUS) 255 (197)
HAN ÄR NÄR (367)
I DEN SENA MIDNATTSSTUNDEN (228)
JESUS LIVES (JESUS LEVER) 217 (161)
LOVEN GUD 73 (67)
PEARL OF GREAT PRICE (DEN KOSTLIGA PÄRLAN) 294 (230)
SKOOG (SNART RANDAS EN DAG) 230 (181)
TENDER CALL (LJUVA RÖST) 290 (223)
YULETIDE (NU GLÄDJENS TIMME) 151 (123)

SÖDERBERG, WILHELM THEODOR (b. Össebygarn, Uppland, Sweden, October 6, 1845; d. Karlshamn, November 1, 1922) was the son of a church organist. Beginning in 1861 he studied at the music conservatory in Stockholm. After serving as an organist in the capital city for several years, he moved to Karlshamn, where he taught music in the public schools until his retirement in 1912. He continued as an organist until his death. Although Söderberg was not involved in the revival movement, he composed many melodies for its songbooks, especially *Sånger till Lammets Lof* and *Hemlandstoner*.

Composer:
BEGYNNELSE (LÅT MIG BÖRJA MED DIG) 353 (47)
JULEN AR INNE 143 (114)

SOLBERG, CARL K. (b. Rushford, Minnesota, June 2, 1872; d. June 15, 1954) attended St. Olaf College and the seminary of the United Norwegian Lutheran Church. After ordination in 1900 he served churches in Vermillion and Yankton, South Dakota. From 1906 to 1911 he was pastor of Zion Evangelical Lutheran Church in Chicago, and from 1911 to 1918, Bethlehem in Minneapolis. Later he served in Madison, South Dakota, and at St. Paul's in Minneapolis. He was an evangelist for the Evangelical Lutheran Church from 1937 to 1945. Solberg was the author of several books and several hundred hymns in Norwegian and English.

Author:
Ride On, Ride On, O Savior-King 184 (141)
Translator:
Dearest Jesus, Draw Thou Near Me 64 (45)

STENHOLM, CARL AUGUST (b. Asarum, near Karlshamn, Sweden, November 21, 1843; d. February 22, 1884) studied for a time in his town's public schools and then became a bookbinder. During a residence in Örebro in 1870 he came in contact with the Methodist revival. He joined the Methodists and became an effective preacher. Stenholm was the pioneer of Methodism in Norrköping and later worked in Malmköping and Gothenberg. In 1874, he assumed the editorship of *Lilla Sändebudet,* the organ of the Methodist Church in Sweden. Two years later Stenholm journeyed to America and for a short while was a pastor in Galva, Illinois. He was not happy in this country, so he returned to Sweden the following year. For the remaining seven years of his short life he had pastoral appointments in Karlskrona, Uppsala, and Gävle. Although his poetic output was not great, he wrote several hymns that continue in use.

Author:
Springs of Grace Are Streaming 510 (434)
Time Is As Swift As a Vanishing Dream (551)

STORM, AUGUST LUDVIG (b. Motala, Sweden, October 23, 1862; d. Stockholm, July 1, 1914) spent most of his life in Stockholm. There he attended elementary school and then trade and agricultural schools. For a while he worked as an office clerk. He was a happy-go-lucky young man, and during his free hours he was intent upon having a good time. When the Salvation Army established its second corps in the city, Storm often attended the meetings. At first he went out of curiosity and to have something to do, but gradually he came under conviction. It was a difficult struggle, but one night he went directly from the theater to the mission and there knelt in penitence and gave his life to Christ.

He joined the corps soon after, and in 1892 he was made the finance secretary at the Army headquarters. Later he was promoted to the rank of lieutenant-colonel. In 1899, Storm had been stricken with a serious back disorder which left him crippled for life. He continued, however, to take care of his Army duties until his death. After his funeral the Swedish *War Cry* had this to say about him: "It was a delight to listen to his powerful, thoughtful, and well-articulated sermons. And the numerous verses that flowed from his pen are the best that have ever appeared in the Army's publications."

Author:
Thanks to God for My Redeemer 622 (543)

SUNDELIUS-LAGERSTRÖM, SELMA ANGELIKA OPHALIA (b. Nysund, Värmland, Sweden, November 26, 1859; d. Hjo, October 5, 1927) was the daughter of a clergyman. In 1862, the family moved to Lekvattnet, where Selma grew up. She began to write at an early age. Her father objected to her pietistic leanings and after confirmation sent her to live with an uncle in Dalsland. He had promised to make her like all the other young girls and take out of her all the "läsaregriller" (reader fancies—the adherents of the movement were called "lasare," or "readers"). But the plan backfired, and she became more grounded in the movement.

In 1886, Miss Sundelius married Johannes Lagerström, a teacher at the Swedish Covenant Bible School in Kristinehamn. They moved to Stockholm in 1890, where her husband continued his teaching. From the early 1890s on, both husband and wife began to break down emotionally. He was forced to resign from his teaching in 1894, and the couple gave themselves to writing. Lagerström died nine years later. His wife had already entered a mental hospital in Vadstena, where she stayed for twenty-five years. Three years before her death she was well enough to leave the hospital, and she went to live with a friend in Hjo.

Most of her hymns were written between 1880 and 1893. Several of them found wide usage and are still being sung. In 1896, she published a collection of poems entitled *Blommor i törnhäcken* (Flowers in the Thorn Hedge). The title is a good description of her life. She suffered much, but through God's grace she found roses among the thorns. Her hymns have the same imprint. Lövgren contrasted the songs of Nils Frykman and Selma Lagerström (both from Värmland) by saying that the former represented Christian joy, while the latter represented melancholy.

Author:
Are You Dismayed, Lonely, Afraid 83 (73)
Savior, in Thy Love Abiding 399 (341)

SVEEGGEN, PETER ANDREW (b. South Dakota, June 30, 1881; d. October 29, 1959) received his college education at the University of Minnesota, earning his M.A. degree in 1909. For four years he taught at his alma mater and then at the high school in Decorah, Iowa. Later he joined the faculty at Ellsworth College in Iowa Falls, Iowa. From 1919 to 1952 Sveeggen was head of the English department at Augsburg College in Minneapolis.

Translator:
How Glad I Am Each Christmas Eve 131

SWEDBERG, JESPER (b. near Falun, Sweden, August 8, 1653; d. Skara, July 26, 1735) was the first important hymnist in Sweden. The story of his life is a kind of "rags-to-riches" romance. He was a miner's son who became a friend of Swedish kings and a bishop of the church. He studied at the universities in Uppsala and Lund and was ordained a minister in 1683. His first assignment was as chaplain of the royal cavalry regiment in Stockholm. King Karl XI was impressed with the young clergyman, and soon he was elevated to court preacher. In 1692, he was appointed professor at Uppsala and then Rector Magnificus. Swedberg did much to develop discipline and improve moral conditions among teachers and students. He felt that personal faith and piety were more important than the mere possession of knowledge. He wrote, "There are many who possess only a faith of the head and not of the heart. . . ." He was critical of many practices of the pietists, but he was with them in the effort to bring about renewal in the church.

In 1691, Swedberg was commissioned to prepare a new hymnbook. With the help of talented poets and musicians he published a volume of 482 hymns in 1694. Immediately it met with opposition, his enemies charging that it contained "innumerable heresies." A revision, which omitted many of Swedberg's lyrics, was printed in 1696, and this remained in use until the 1819 *Psalmbok* took over. Although the rejection was humiliating to Swedberg, he lived to receive high honors from his country and church. In 1702, he was appointed bishop of Skara, a position he held until his death.

He was vindicated by later generations as well. Emil Liedgren (1879-1963), one of Sweden's greatest hymnologists, wrote, "The treatment given Swedberg's songbook is probably the greatest literary scandal in the history of our country." In spite of the rejection, the final version still had much of Swedberg's stamp upon it, so that a noted critic called it "the most precious heritage he left his native land." It is noteworthy that Swedberg's name appeared with thirty-three hymns in the *Psalmbok* (1937). The famous mystic and philosopher, Emmanuel Swedenborg, was a son of the famous hymnist.

Author:
O Lord, Give Heed unto Our Plea 68

WAESTERBERG, AMANDA S., see **SANDBORG-WAESTERBERG, AMANDA.**

WALLGREN, A. SAMUEL (b. Dalarna, Sweden, June 27, 1885; d. Chicago, Illinois, August 6, 1940) came to America as a child. He acquired his advanced education at North Park College and the University of Chicago, where he was awarded Phi Beta Kappa and earned his master's degree. In 1911, he married Ruth Svensen of Chicago; the couple had two children. From 1911 to 1940 Wallgren served North Park College as instructor in English, registrar, and dean. Among his contributions to the denomination was his involvement in the preparation of *The Covenant Hymnal* (1931). His translations faithfully transmitted the thought and mood of the original writers.

Karl Olsson's closing tribute to Dean Wallgren in *Our Covenant* (1940) is fitting here:

> *In the ultimate sense the Dean's contribution to the school was that of a warm-hearted Christian. It was appropriate that at the funeral service one of his students should sing his own translation of the Swedish hymn "Låt mig börja med dig" (I with Thee Would Begin). He began and ended his all too brief day with his Savior.*

Translator:
I with Thee Would Begin 353 (47)
If Asked Whereon I Rest My Claim 388 (331)
What Joy There Is in Coming 55 (27)

WALLIN, JOHAN OLOF (b. Stora Tuna, Dalarna, Sweden, October 15, 1779; d. Uppsala, June 30, 1839) was Sweden's greatest hymn-writer and the creator of a hymnal that, without revision, served the Church of Sweden for 118 years. When Longfellow translated Tegnér's poem "Children of the Lord's Supper," he spoke of Wallin in these lines: "And with one voice / Chimed in the congregation, and sang an anthem immortal / Of the sublime Wallin, of David's harp in the Northland."

In spite of poverty and poor health, Wallin had earned his Ph.D. at Uppsala at the age of twenty-four. Twice he won the chief prize for poetry at the university. He was ordained in 1806 and soon attracted attention by his ability as a preacher. In 1812, he became the pastor of the Adolf Fredrik Church in Stockholm, and four years later, dean of Västerås. He returned to Stockholm in 1818 to assume the pastorate of Storkyrkan. Six years later he was elevated to a bishopric and was made Archbishop of Sweden in 1837.

While he was still at the university, Wallin had begun to publish collections of old and new hymns. Some were translations of poetry from other languages. In 1811, the Swedish parliament appointed him as a member of a hymnbook commission. A first draft appeared in 1814, but it did not meet with approval. Wallin, whose genius had been made apparent, was given the responsibility for the completion of the task. By November, 1816, he had accomplished the mission. After a few minor changes were made, the book was officially authorized by King Karl XIV on January 29, 1819. Of the 500 hymns in the volume, 128 were Wallin originals and 164 were either revisions or translations done by him. When the *Psalmbok* was revised in 1937, more than one third of the 600 songs were either originals, translations, or revisions by Wallin. The hymnal was proof of the high standards he had imposed on himself. "A new hymn," he said, "aside from the spiritual considerations, which must never be compromised in any way, should be so correct, simple, and lyrical in form, and so free from inversions and other imperfections in style, that after a lapse of a hundred years, a father may be able to say to his son, 'Read the hymnal, my boy, and you will learn your mother tongue!' "

In his early years, Wallin had been influenced by Rationalism, and the hymns written during this period bore the marks of the "new theology." But as he became more immersed in his task, there was a deepening in his spiritual life, and his hymns took on a more evangelical cast. In an address he made in 1816 he came out against the "new theology" and declared his stand upon the confessions of the Lutheran church. Wallin was possessed of a strange personality. He was often melancholy in spirit. Someone said of him, "It was as if death's angel crossed the threshhold when he joined a group, so dark and gloomy he appeared." Few saw him smile. It seemed that he was never at home in this world. During the cholera epidemic in 1834, Wallin began an epic poem, "The Angel of Death," which was completed a few weeks before he died. Its tone was solemn and grave, but it expressed faith in the resurrection and life beyond death. Shortly before his own death on a Sunday morning, Wallin exclaimed, "My Lord, I am coming! My country, my king, my God!"

Author:
Again Thy Glorious Sun Doth Rise 39(22)
All Hail to Thee, O Blessed Morn 124 (110)
Jerusalem, Lift Up Thy Voice 105 (101)
O Bride of Christ, Rejoice 115 (104)
Watch, My Soul, and Pray 445 (408)

WENNERBERG, GUNNAR (b. Lidköping, Sweden, October 2, 1817; d. Läckö, August 24, 1901) was the son of a State Church pastor. He studied in Skara, and then enrolled in the University of Uppsala. There he began the study of classical languages and natural science and later, philosophy and esthetics. He became known and respected by his fellow students as a singer and composer. He published his first songs in 1846. The following year he put out the earliest numbers of *Gluntarna* (The Boys), thirty duets for baritone and bass. These continued to be issued from 1847 to 1850. In 1850, Wennerberg made a memorable tour of Sweden, singing and reciting in public concerts. He was made a member of the Swedish Academy in 1866 and was Minister of Education from 1870 to 1875 and again from 1888 to 1891. He was a member of the Swedish parliament until he was nearly eighty.

In the churches, Wennerberg is best known for his settings of the Psalms. These were arrangements for solo voice and choir appearing in ten parts between 1861 and 1869 under the title *Stycken ur Davids Psalmer*. The tune UPSALA, composed in 1850, is the setting to the text "Här är gudagott att vara" (It is divinely good to be here), which appeared in *Gluntarna*. HERRE UTRANSAKA MIG is the melody for Psalm 139 in the psalm collection. WENNERBERG is a short portion from the setting to Psalm 24.

Composer:
HERRE UTRANSAKA MIG (193)
UPSALA 291 (227), 319 (266)
WENNERBERG (189)

WEXELS, WILHELM ANDREAS (b. Copenhagen, Denmark, March 29, 1797; d. Oslo, Norway, May 14, 1866), after studies in Copenhagen and Christiania (Oslo), Norway, became catechist and later curate of Our Savior's Lutheran Church in Christiania. He held this position the remainder of his life. Wexels was a controversial figure. He preached against the inroads of rationalism, emphasizing the need of spiritual revival. This made him unpopular with the intelligentsia, but the pietists were displeased with him as well. After the death of his wife in 1830, Wexels turned his thoughts to life beyond the grave and came to accept the doctrine of Universalism. But he continued to proclaim the need to accept the grace of God in Christ—and the themes of resurrection and the life everlasting. Gradually his preaching attracted more listeners, and eventually he had as many friends as once he had enemies. Church historians claim that Wexels' ministry was a turning point in the Church of Norway.

Wexels also exerted a great influence through his hymn-writing. Although he failed in his attempt to give Norway an official hymnbook, many of his hymns survived, and in the words of Bishop Skaar, "will be sung in Norway as long as Christ is confessed."

Author:
O Precious Thought! Some Day the Mist
Shall Vanish (337)

WEXELSEN, MARIE (b. Östre Toten, Norway, September 20, 1832; d. Trondhjem, 1911) was the niece of Wilhelm Wexels, one of the great preachers and hymn-writers of Norway. Marie began to write at the age of twenty, and her hymns made her known throughout Norway.

Author:
How Glad I Am Each Christmas Eve 131

WIBERG, GLEN VERNON (b. Kansas City, Missouri, May 1, 1925) spent a year at Moody Bible Institute after graduation from high school. Following college studies at North Park and William Jewell, he pursued his theological education at North Park Theological Seminary and Yale Divinity School, where he earned an M.Div. degree in 1957. He took further studies at Union Theological Seminary in Richmond, Virginia, Union Seminary in New York City, and the University of Oslo, Norway. In 1949, he married Jane Mabes. Two daughters and a son were born to the couple. Wiberg was ordained to the Covenant ministry in 1953.

Wiberg has served Covenant churches in Oakland, California (intern); Haddam Neck, Connecticut; Princeton, Illinois; Youngstown, Ohio; and Chicago (North Park Covenant), where he has been since 1970. He also has served on the adjunct faculty at North Park Theological Seminary, teaching in the department of pastoral studies.

Translator:
Jesus of Nazareth Passes By 163

Bibliography

Handbooks

Companion to the Hymnal, a Handbook to the 1964 Methodist Hymnal. Nashville: Abingdon Press, 1970.

Hostetler, Lester, *Handbook to the Mennonite Hymnary*. Newton, Kansas: General Conference of the Mennonite Church of North America Board of Publications, 1949.

Liedgren, Emil. *Den Svenska Psalmboken.* Stockholm, 1967.

McCutchan, Robert Guy. *Our Hymnody: A Manual of the Methodist Hymnal.* Nashville: Abingdon-Cokesbury Press, 1937.

Reynolds, William Jensen. *Hymns of Our Faith.* Nashville: Broadman Press, 1967.

Ronander, Albert C., and Porter, Ethel K. *Guide to the Pilgrim Hymnal.* Philadelphia: United Church Press, 1966.

Seaman, William A. *Companion to the Hymnal of the Service Book and Hymnal.* The Commission on the Liturgy and Hymnal, 1976.

Wake, Arthur N. *Companion to Hymnbook for Christian Worship.* St. Louis: Bethany Press, 1970.

General and Hymnology

Arvaston, Allan. *Imatation och förnyelse.* Lund, Sweden: Berlinska Boktryckeriet, 1971.

Byström, Jakob. *Sånger och sångare.* 3 Vol. Stockholm: B.-M:s Bokförlag, 1936-1943.

Crowning a Century. Pennock, Minn.: Salem Mission Covenant Church, 1971.

Dahle, John. *The Library of Christian Hymns.* 3 Vol. (English translation by M.C. Johnshoy) Starbuck, Minn.: Luther Memorial Publishing Co., 1924.

Davies, James P. *Sing with Understanding.* Chicago: Covenant Press, 1966.

Erickson, J. Irving. "Covenant Hymnody and the Covenant Hymnal of 1973." *The Covenant Quarterly*, November, 1973.

Ericson, C. George. "Our Bilingual Hymns". *The Swedish Pioneer Historical Quarterly*, April, 1974.

Hagelin, Gösta. *De som skrev våra psalmer*. 2 Vol. Stockholm: Verbum, 1970.

_______. *Psalmboken berättar*. Stockholm: Lindblad, 1957.

Hawkinson, Eric G. *Images in Covenant Beginnings*. Chicago: Covenant Press, 1968.

Johnson, E. Gustav. *A.L. Skoog, Covenant Hymn-Writer and Composer*. Chicago: Covenant Historical Commission, 1937.

Johnson, Norman E. *A Study of the Hymnody of the Evangelical Covenant Church of America* (Master's Thesis, University of Southern California, 1958).

Lövgren, Oscar. *Den segrande sången*. Stockholm: Missionsförbundets förlag, 1967.

_______. *Joel Blomqvist*. Stockholm: Svenska Missionsförbundets förlag, 1941.

_______. *Läsarsång och folklig visa*. Stockholm: Gummessons, 1975.

_______. *Lina Sandell*. Stockholm: Gummessons, 1965.

_______. *Nils Frykman*, 3rd ed. Stockholm: Gummessons, 1972.

_______. *Oscar Ahnfelt* , Stockholm: Gummessons, 1966

_______. *Pennfäktare och predikare*. Stockholm: Missionsförbundets förlag, 1958.

_______. *Psalm- och sånglexicon*. Stockholm: Gummessons, 1964.

_______. *Psalmen vi sjunger*. Stockholm: Gummessons, 1959.

_______. *Så fick vi sånger*. Stockholm: Svenska Missionsförbundets förlag, 1949.

_______. *Solskenssångaren*. Stockholm: Gummessons, 1971.

_______. *Våra psalm- och sångdiktare*, 3 Vol. Stockholm: Svenska Missionsförbundets förlag, 1935-1939.

Miller, L. David. *Hymns, the Story of Christian Song*. Philadelphia:Lutheran Church Press, 1969.

När vi var unga, Vol. 4, Stockholm: Missionsförbundets Förlag, 1948.

Olson, Adolf and Virgil A. *Seventy-five Years*. Chicago: Conference Press, 1946.

Olsson, Karl A. *A Family of Faith*. Chicago: Covenant Press, 1975.

_______. *By One Spirit*. Chicago: Covenant Press, 1962.

Ryden, Ernest E. *The Story of Christian Hymnody*. Philadelphia: Fortress Press, 1959.

_______. *The Story of Our Hymns*. Rock Island, Illinois: Augustana Book Concern, 1935.

Selander, Sven-Åke. *Den nya sången*. Lund: CWK Gleerup, 1973.

Strom, Carl G., et al. *Frykman, Hultman, Skoog*. Chicago: Covenant Book Concern, 1943.

Sundgren, Nils. *Blott en dag*. Stockholm: Frikyrkliga Studieförbundet, 1974.

_______. *Det är solsken där borta på kullens topp.* Stockholm: Frikyrkliga Studieforbundet, 1974.

Svedlund, Karl-Erik. *De sågo himmelen öppen.* Stockholm: Normans förlag, 1966.

"The Development of Lutheran Hymnody in America" (Articles reprinted from the *Encycopedia of the Lutheran Church*). Minneapolis: Augsburg Publishing House, 1967.

The International Book of Christmas Carols. Englewood Cliffs, N.J.:Prentice-Hall, Inc., 1963.

Periodicals, Annuals, and Yearbooks

Baptist General Conference *Annual.* Board of Trustees, Baptist General Conference, 1963.

California. Turlock, California: Evangelical Mission Covenant Association of California, Feb. 15, 1923.

Covenant Yearbook. Chicago: The Evangelical Covenant Church of America. 1975.

Korsbaneret. Rock Island, Illinois: Augustana Book Concern, 1936.

North Park College News. Chicago: Students of North Park College, Oct. 25, 1944; Sept. 30, Nov. 4, 1959.

Our Covenant. Chicago: Covenant Book Concern, 1935, 1940, 1942, 1944, 1946, 1948, 1960.

The Covenant Companion. Chicago: The Evangelical Covenant Church of America, June 26, July 3, 1959; June 1, Aug. 15, Dec. 1, 1970; Jan. 1, 1975.

The Covenant Weekly. Chicago: The Evangelical Covenant Church of America, Nov. 13, 1934; Feb. 23, 1937; Aug. 13, 1940; Aug. 14, 1942; Nov. 12, 1943; Feb. 16, 1946; Oct. 12, 1956.

The Lutheran Companion. Rock Island Ill.: Augustana Lutheran Church, Feb. 23, March 9, 1929; Aug. 14, 21, 1941; Oct. 14, 1953; Oct. 22, 1958.

Underwood, Byron E. "How Great Thou Art", *The Hymn.* New York: Hymn Society of America, October, 1973 and January, 1974.

Who's Who in the Midwest. Chicago: The A. N. Marquis Co., 1949.

[illegible] 1960.
[illegible]
[illegible] Prentice-Hall, Inc., 1961.

Periodicals, Journals and Yearbooks

[illegible] Conference. Annual. Board of Trustees Report. [illegible] Conference, 1968.
[illegible] California: The [illegible] Mission Covenant Association [illegible]
[illegible] Chicago: The Evangelical Covenant Church of America, 1975.
[illegible]
[illegible] Chicago [illegible]
[illegible] Chicago [illegible] 1935, 1940, 1941, 1942 [illegible]
[illegible] Covenant Church [illegible]
[illegible]
[illegible]
[illegible] October 1978 and January 1979.
[illegible] Chicago: The [illegible] Company, 1930.

Index

This is a general index including authors, composers, translators, tune names, Scandinavian first lines, hymnal titles, and related items. The citing of page locations for names of persons and hymnals has been selective rather than exhaustive. There is a complete listing of each person's works after each biography. First lines are given within quotation marks, tune names are in caps, and titles are in italics.

HERRENS FRUKTAN
ÄR VISHETENS
BEGYNNELSE
PS 111:10